A LONG
TIME COMING

A LONG
TIME COMING

The story of Ngāi Tahu's treaty settlement
negotiations with the Crown

Martin Fisher

CANTERBURY UNIVERSITY PRESS

First published in 2020 by
CANTERBURY UNIVERSITY PRESS
University of Canterbury
Private Bag 4800, Christchurch
NEW ZEALAND
www.canterbury.ac.nz/engage/cup

ISBN 978-1-98-850311-0

A catalogue record for this book is available from the
National Library of New Zealand.

Maps: Sean Bragg
Front cover image: Sir Tipene O'Regan and Prime Minister Jim Bolger
at Takahanga Marae.
Back cover image: Pounamu hei tiki.
(Both images: Te Rūnanga o Ngāi Tahu Collection, Ngāi Tahu Archive)
Book design, layout and printing by: Caxton, Christchurch, New Zealand.
www.caxton.co.nz

Published with assistance from the Ngāi Tahu Research Centre

CONTENTS

ACKNOWLEDGEMENTS

A story that purports to tell the final chapter of a generations-long battle will, sadly, inevitably miss out the important contributions of the many whose names are not represented in the Treaty of Waitangi settlement negotiations themselves. It is important to acknowledge the hundreds, if not thousands, of people who provided helping hands, whether in the boardroom, the archives, the wharekai, on the road and at sea to arrive at the Ngāi Tahu settlement. Tēnā koutou mō tō koutou mahi.

This book grew out of a part of my PhD thesis and my supervisors provided invaluable support in getting it to that first stage. Thank you to Richard S. Hill, Cybèle Locke and James Belich, as well as my informal supervisor, Michael Allen.

Histories are only as good as their sources. I would like to thank the librarians and archivists of the Victoria University of Wellington library, Archives New Zealand (with the permission of Sir Douglas Graham), the Television New Zealand Archive, Ngā Taonga Sound and Vision, the Office of Treaty Settlements, the Macmillan Brown Library and Te Rūnanga o Ngāi Tahu archives for access to vital and often untouched sources. I would especially like to acknowledge Ngāi Tahu for allowing me to consult your taonga (treasures). Thank you especially to Takerei Norton, Helen Brown and Robyn Walsh at Te Rūnanga o Ngāi Tahu for commenting on drafts of the book and providing the amazing photographs from the Te Rūnanga o Ngāi Tahu private collection.

Catherine Montgomery and Katrina McCallum at Canterbury University Press were patient and diligent with the various drafts. Madeleine Collinge and Anna Rogers were helpful editors. Two friends, Peter Bakker and Andrew Collins, also read over late drafts. Thank you for your hard work on this important project.

I would also like to thank those who agreed to conduct informal interviews: Sir Douglas Graham, Sir Tipene O'Regan, Richard Meade, Anake Goodall, Sid Ashton, Te Maire Tau, Alex Frame, four Treaty of Waitangi Policy Unit officials, one Crown Law official and one Treasury official. Sir Tipene O'Regan was kind enough to also write a foreword for the book. I have greatly enjoyed any further discussions we have had when the opportunities arose.

My small whānau, consisting of my parents, my brother and my grandmother, have provided invaluable support over the years. Although we live far apart, spread across the globe, you all have always been there for me.

Te Maire Tau has honoured me with the wonderful opportunity to work with him at the Ngāi Tahu Research Centre at the University of Canterbury over the last six years. This book could not have been published without the Ngāi Tahu Research Centre and especially Te Maire's help and support. Thank you for making me think in ways I never thought possible.

FOREWORD

The title of this volume is more than apt. Ngāi Tahu are wont to assert that Te Kerēme, the Ngāi Tahu claim, is the longest running such Māori case against the Crown in New Zealand history. Our iwi account dates the claim from Matiaha Tiramorehu's letter of 1849 to the governor. He was complaining about the Crown's failure to honour the terms of the Kemp Purchase of 1848, just a year before. As a consequence, the 1998 Ngāi Tahu Settlement was hailed as the culmination of a seven-generation struggle.

While, in strictly legal terms, the rhetoric may be open to question, there is no doubt that the long-running, intergenerational claims of Ngāi Tahu against the Crown's failure to honour its contractual obligations have been more than sufficient to give Te Kerēme itself a measure of heritage status in its own right.

I have argued elsewhere that one of the central elements of Ngāi Tahu's post-colonial history has been that the claim itself has become a dominant element in our tribal culture and, indeed, in our identity. Beyond heritage and identity, though, and following the 1870s establishment of our regional multi-hapū rūnanga more effectively to pursue the claims, Te Kerēme became the political and social organisational basis of the Ngāi Tahu iwi. As such, it progressively extended beyond Matiaha's 1849 letter to include all the Ngāi Tahu purchase deeds from 1844 to the Rakiura Purchase of 1864, described by Paul Temm QC in his 1987 opening statement before the Waitangi Tribunal as the 'Nine Tall Trees – united by the common thread of mahinga kai'. In truth, Te Kerēme and its associated sense of grievance had become our unifying cultural centre.

The long history of the Ngāi Tahu grievance, which had thus given rise to its own institutional and cultural record, meant that our iwi was well placed to advance its historic cause as the New Zealand political ground began to shift during the early 1970s. We were much heartened by the Waitangi Tribunal proposals of the Kirk Labour government and developed extensive submissions on the initial legislation in 1975. Although disappointed by the limitations of that statute, Ngāi Tahu worked assiduously to advance the amendment in respect of historic claims finally achieved under the Lange Labour government in 1985. Although there was still a great amount of preparation to do prior to filing with the tribunal, Ngāi Tahu was better placed than most to take the lead in filing the first comprehensive historical claim (Wai 27) before the tribunal in 1986.

What makes this volume particularly compelling is the diversity of vantage points available to Martin Fisher from which he has been able to examine the processes combining to eventually produce the Ngāi Tahu Claims Settlement Act of 1998. His earlier doctoral thesis was essentially a comparative study of the Waikato–Tainui and Ngāi Tahu settlements – two very different processes surrounded by very different circumstances but comprising the two earliest examples of what have become known as 'historical claim settlements'. In producing that thesis he had access to both the Crown and the respective tribal resources. In the final stages of his PhD he worked for the Waitangi Tribunal as a research analyst but had also done research contracts for the Office of Treaty Settlements and for claimants through the Crown Forestry Rental Trust. As well, he had tutored history and politics courses at Victoria University, McGill University and the University of Otago. He has worked for the Ngāi Tahu Research Centre at the University of Canterbury since 2014. The sheer diversity of his experience and his breadth of understanding of his subject is unparalleled.

Whilst some may quibble with the odd conclusion and the acuity of the occasional observation, this work will stand as the definitive account of a significant phase in this nation's historical journey. That journey, towards the realisation of the treaty promise, has still some distance remaining as we wrestle with the place and standing of rangatiratanga in our future and the nature and status of customary rights in the context of our evolving demography. Thanks to Martin Fisher, the road we have thus far travelled is now much better illuminated.

Tipene O'Regan Kt
Former Chairman, Ngāi Tahu Negotiating Group
Former Chairman, Ngai Tahu Maori Trust Board

A NOTE ON MACRONS

Macrons to indicate the long vowel are now marked on Māori words and terms, tribal names and place names, but this is often not the case in historical material. Parliament only introduced mandatory use of macrons between the passage of the Te Runanga o Ngai Tahu Act and the Ngāi Tahu Claims Settlement Act. Macrons are included from the historical record only when they are used in the original source.

Introduction

The Ngāi Tahu settlement, like all other Treaty of Waitangi settlements, was a product of political compromise and expediency rather than measured justice. It was the result of 150 years of hard work and persistence, but for almost all Ngāi Tahu it could not be called fair.

The Ngāi Tahu claim, Te Kerēme, stretched over many decades and spanned two centuries from the first official land purchase in 1844 at Otago to the final hearing of the claim by the Waitangi Tribunal between 1987 and 1989. Generation after generation carried on the fight to obtain some measure of justice. What started as letters and protests eventually led to royal commissions of inquiry throughout the late 1800s and early 1900s. Very limited forms of redress were obtained in the 1940s, and some of the compensation was helpful, but it was in no way a capital base capable of rebuilding a tribe that was almost completely dispossessed of its land and assets.

The last phase of Te Kerēme, before its hearing by the Waitangi Tribunal, developed in parallel with the flowering of the Māori Renaissance of the post-war years. Protests accelerated around the country, as did political lobbying at a very high level. Labour governments seemed to offer some concrete measures to investigate and report on breaches of the Treaty of Waitangi. Ngāi Tahu members had political affiliations across the spectrum – Ben Couch was one example from National – but increasingly in the 1970s and 1980s the Ngāi Tahu claim was pushed through and had a generally more eager reception from Labour than from National administrations. The final hearing of the claim was certainly cathartic but then came the even harder part: how was the redress going to match the grievance and could it be matched at all?

The negotiations were led by two intelligent, hard-nosed and old-fashioned rangatira – Tipene O'Regan for Ngāi Tahu and Minister of Treaty Negotiations Douglas Graham for the Crown. The Ngāi Tahu negotiating team always had to answer to the communities back home and the diaspora scattered throughout Aotearoa New Zealand. Many strongly supported the team, but both low- and high-profile dissidents attacked them at hui, on the marae, in the media and in the courts and Parliament. The rest of Māoridom could also be contentious and critical, although there was support from some quarters. The Crown was led by Graham and his officials, but they had to answer to their own series of political masters – Cabinet and especially officials at the Treasury, the Crown Law Office and the Department of Conservation. Beyond the multiple personalities that made up the Crown, the general public – in the form of interested Pākehā, conservationists, farmers and others – had its own opinion on the justice of treaty settlements. Amid all these internal and external pressures, the two sides somehow managed to negotiate one of the country's longest legal documents.

Ngāi Tahu's claims were heard by the Waitangi Tribunal from 1987 to 1989 and their direct negotiations began soon after the release of the *Ngai Tahu Land Report* in early 1991. (The main 1991 report was published in two otherwise identical versions with differing titles: *The Ngai Tahu Report* and the *Ngai Tahu Land Report*. This book uses the *Ngai Tahu Land Report* throughout.) Their negotiations had two distinct phases, from 1991 to late 1994 when a breakdown cut off talks, and then from early 1996 to 1997. Ngāi Tahu and the Crown signed a heads of agreement on 5 October 1996 and a deed of settlement a year later, on 21 November 1997. Legislation formalising their settlement was passed on 1 October 1998.

This book explores how Ngāi Tahu sought to negotiate settlements to their historical grievances that would empower them socially and politically, as well as restoring a lost economic base.[1] However, the framework for settlement developed by the Crown did not meet these expectations. Although Māori themselves have been able to choose which body will represent them in negotiations, the Crown has determined how negotiations will take place and the boundaries within which Māori expectations could be fulfilled. The Treaty of Waitangi Policy Unit, which became the Office of Treaty Settlements in 1995, led the development of treaty settlement policy and spearheaded the direct negotiations, but the key institutions have been the Crown Law Office and Treasury. The first ensures that settlements have limited or controllable legal implications; the second that they are affordable in relation to other areas of government expenditure. The Crown has been involved in settlements in order to stabilise New Zealand's economic and political conditions, and in so doing has attempted to make settlements full and final. However, the boundaries placed on settlements have never acknowledged the full range of aspirations Māori have sought from treaty settlements, not only in fiscal terms (the amount of redress), but also in the way that their political authority (mana and rangatiratanga) might be recognised in the process.

This is partly because, during the negotiations, the Crown strove to maintain its sovereignty in the face of Ngāi Tahu demands to have their political authority – defined in treaty terms as rangatiratanga – recognised. How this played out is the major focus of this book. In many respects, the negotiating parties were often 'talking past each other', until eventually compromises resulted in a settlement.[2] Although the iwi may have perceived, perhaps correctly, that their compromises were far greater than those the Crown was willing to make, the number of concessions they achieved was also significant.

From the earliest point in the negotiations, Ngāi Tahu sought a legal personality as recognition of their rangatiratanga.[3] (A legal personality refers to a human or non-human entity that is treated as a person for specific legal purposes, such as sueing and being sued, owning property and entering into contracts.) This identity would replace the Ngai Tahu Maori Trust Board structure, which they viewed as impinging on their rangatiratanga because it was ultimately accountable to the minister of Māori affairs, rather than to Ngāi Tahu. After lengthy negotiations with the Crown Law Office and the Law Commission over the use of the term rangatiratanga, the Te Runanga o Ngai Tahu Bill was introduced to Parliament in 1993 and finally passed in 1996.

One writer has suggested that treaty settlement negotiations can have the effect of 'unsettling Māori communities', due to the prescriptive rules on mandate and representation applied by the Crown. Many treaty settlements negotiated in New Zealand have resulted in representation challenges in either the Waitangi Tribunal or the courts. Although the

Crown's focus on 'large natural groupings' allows for a quicker settlement process, it significantly constrains Māori groups that operate more at the whānau and hapū level.[4] During Ngāi Tahu's negotiations this policy had not been formally established, but the Crown was clear that it would negotiate only with the leaders of major iwi. Other claimants negotiated much more specific small-scale settlements during the early 1990s, but these were small and discrete claims.[5] In the case of Ngāi Tahu and Waikato–Tainui, iwi negotiators did not go through the formal mandating processes that exist today. The named claimant for Ngāi Tahu, Henare Rakiihia (Rik) Tau Snr, was intimately involved in the negotiation process. Throughout the negotiations Ngāi Tahu held hui-ā-iwi to confirm their negotiating status, but some within Ngāi Tahu wanted to negotiate settlements themselves. The political nature of treaty settlements ensured that the Crown and iwi-level leadership would dominate the process. Finally there was considerable support from many within Ngāi Tahu for the iwi-level approach advocated by the Crown because there were not really any other viable options.

The Crown's control of the negotiation process extended to the manner in which Crown land was protected from alienation, and the legal form in which it would be returned, but third parties also played a prominent role in deciding which specific lands were given back. Ngāi Tahu inserted the pursuit of rangatiratanga into the negotiations, especially in terms of the return of land. The Crown was hesitant about any discussion of sovereignty or autonomy since it was the sole and undisputed sovereign. The issue of compensation that had formed the initial framework for the Crown's thinking would become a point of contention. Throughout the negotiations there remained a disjunction between the Crown's view of the political nature of any negotiated solution, and the need for Ngāi Tahu to have some kind of structured system in which the extent of loss could be measured equally with the amount of compensation and apology provided. The Crown wanted full and final settlements; Ngāi Tahu were firm that this would not be the case with fiscally limited settlements. These opposing views underlay the lengthy negotiations between the Crown and Ngāi Tahu and the settlement itself was ultimately the product of consensus on them.

CHAPTER 1

The history of Te Kerēme: the Ngāi Tahu claim

Ngāi Tahu, who are spread across most of the South Island, from just south of Blenheim on the east coast, right down to Otago and Southland and up past the West Coast,[1] are recognised as consisting of three main lines of descent: the original inhabitants of the South Island – Waitaha; Ngāti Māmoe, who originated from the Ahuriri/ Hawke's Bay region and made their way south before Ngāi Tahu; and finally Ngāi Tahu itself, who migrated last. Ngāi Tahu has strong ancestral connections with Ngāti Porou from the East Coast of the North Island, as both stem from the ancestor Paikea. The connection is centred on Tahupōtiki, from whom Ngāi Tahu take their name, the younger brother of Porourangi, the eponymous ancestor of Ngāti Porou. As a result of internal struggles, in the later seventeenth century Ngāi Tahu moved south into the Te Whanganui-a-Tara/Wellington region. Two related iwi that had previously settled the area, Ngāti Ira and Ngāti Māmoe, eventually opposed Ngāi Tahu's presence and some Ngāi Tahu left the North Island for Te Waipounamu (the South Island), where they established themselves around the Tory Channel.[2]

A section of Ngāti Māmoe who had moved into the South Island before Ngāi Tahu allied themselves with the residents of the region – Ngāi Tara and Rangitāne. When hostilities broke out between Ngāi Tahu and Ngāi Tara, Ngāti Māmoe changed sides and formed an association with Ngāi Tahu. Together they attacked and defeated Rangitāne in Wairau and Ngāti Māmoe left the coastline north of the Clarence River to Ngāi Tahu. Eventually two key hapū of Ngāi Tahu, Ngāti Kurī and Ngāi Tūhaitara, established themselves around Kaikōura and then in the Canterbury/Banks Peninsula area. Before Ngāti Kurī and Ngāi Tūhaitara, another hapū, Ngāti Irakehu, joined Ngāti Māmoe in some areas, including Banks Peninsula and further south. Eventually Ngāi Tahu and Ngāti Māmoe clashed as the hapū of Ngāi Tahu pushed their boundaries southwards. By the late eighteenth century a truce between Ngāi Tahu and Ngāti Māmoe was cemented through two chiefly marriages and this connection remained strong well into the nineteenth century. The culture of the original Waitaha inhabitants was gradually subsumed into that of Ngāi Tahu, especially the many traditions associated with the great explorer Rākaihautū's names for and stories about the land. By the time the Treaty of Waitangi/te Tiriti o Waitangi was signed with the British Crown on 6 February 1840,[3] all the Ngāi Tahu South Island signatories were descendants of the union of Ngāi Tahu, Ngāti Māmoe and Waitaha.[4]

Hundreds of Māori leaders around New Zealand signed the treaty, which they viewed as a political compact that would enable the British to control their subjects living in New Zealand, and work with their treaty partner to govern, but that Māori would retain their independent sovereignty. The British believed they had acquired sovereignty. The treaty was a concise document consisting of only three articles and written in both English and Māori. The third article was fairly accurately translated, but the first two articles had significant differences and laid the basis for philosophical and practical disagreements between Māori and the Crown.[5] In Article 1 of the English version Māori leaders gave Queen Victoria 'all the rights and powers of sovereignty' over their lands. In the Māori version it gave the Queen 'te kawanatanga katoa' – the right to govern over their lands. In Article 2 of the English version Māori leaders and people were guaranteed 'exclusive and undisturbed possession of their lands and estates, forests, fisheries, and other properties', but in the Māori version they were guaranteed 'te tino rangatiratanga' – the unqualified exercise of chieftainship or self-determination over their lands, villages and all their treasures.[6] (The third article guaranteed to Māori all the rights and privileges of British subjects.)

The British Crown, and later the New Zealand government, claimed that the Treaty of Waitangi had established Crown sovereignty, while Māori claimed that they had merely granted the Crown the right to govern. Māori claimed that the second article had guaranteed them their continuing rangatiratanga or self-determination. The Crown claimed undisputed sovereignty as a result of the first article. From 1840 to 1865 the Crown controlled the market for Māori land through a pre-emption policy set out in Article 2 of the Treaty of Waitangi. Under this, only the Crown could purchase Māori lands, although exceptions were provided to private purchasers such as the New Zealand Company and the Canterbury Association. All Ngāi Tahu's lands were purchased under Crown pre-emption.[7]

Ngāi Tahu's grievances against the Crown stretched back to the 1840s. Members of the iwi had been involved in whaling and sealing enterprises with Pākehā in the early nineteenth century and they believed that their land sales to the Crown and European settlers would guarantee their own usage rights to the resources in the region and strengthen robust political, economic and social relationships with newcomers. But this is not what happened. Between 1844 and 1864 Ngāi Tahu 'sold' 34.5 million acres (1,375,930 hectares) of land over 10 separate purchases, known as the Ngāi Tahu Deeds. The area sold in the less densely populated South Island was enormous compared with the land sales in the North Island. The iwi claimed that it should have received at least a tenth of each purchase as reserves, continued access to mahinga kai or food-gathering places and that schools and hospitals would be built for them. None of these undertakings was honoured.

In 1844, the New Zealand Company bought what was originally believed to be about 400,000 acres (161,875 hectares) of land at Otago, in the vicinity of Dunedin, for £2,400. The area, when surveyed, turned out to be approximately 534,000 acres (216,000 hectares). Ngāi Tahu were left 9600 acres (3885 hectares) as reserves. A promised reserve at Princes Street in Dunedin became the subject of extended petitioning in the second half of the nineteenth century and the case for tenths was built on the specific New Zealand Company basis of the purchase. The company had reserved tenths in its other settlements – Wellington, Nelson and New Plymouth – but it never established its settlement at

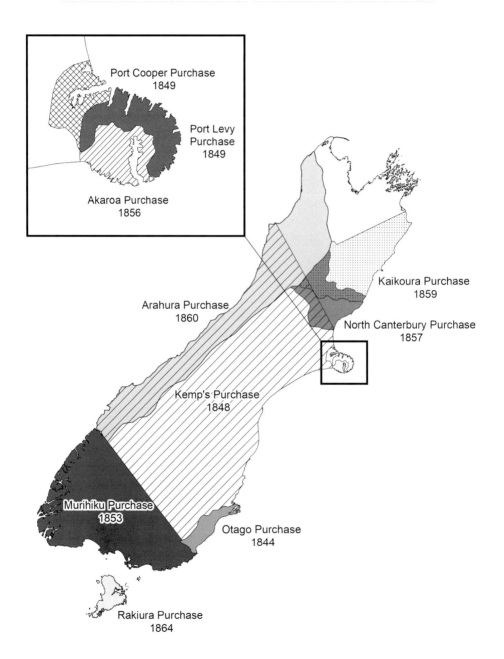

Port Cooper Purchase
1849

Port Levy
Purchase
1849

Akaroa Purchase
1856

Arahura Purchase
1860

Kaikoura Purchase
1859

North Canterbury Purchase
1857

Kemp's Purchase
1848

Murihiku Purchase
1853

Otago Purchase
1844

Rakiura Purchase
1864

The Ngai Tahu Deeds
There was considerable crossover: Kemp's Purchase overlapped with the Kaikoura,
North Canterbury and Arahura purchases; the North Canterbury Purchase also
overlapped with the Kaikoura Purchase.

The Otago Purchase and the minimal reserves granted at the Otago Heads and the Taieri rivermouth.

Dunedin, which was swiftly settled by Scottish migrants from the Otago Settlers Association.[8]

Four years later, in 1848, came the infamous Kemp's Deed. Henry Tacy Kemp, acting in the role of Crown land purchasing officer, bought over 20 million acres (more than 8 million hectares) of land stretching from northern Otago through the Main Divide and up towards northern Canterbury for £2,000. The following year Kemp was replaced by Walter Mantell, who was sent to implement the paltry Ngāi Tahu reserves. The iwi were left just 6359 acres (2573 hectares) spread across the massive purchase area. Ngāi Tahu initially demanded millions of pounds for the enormous block, but were pressured to sell at an incredibly low price. They were compelled to sell lands in the Canterbury region because their nemesis, Te Rauparaha of Ngāti Toa, had already mischievously 'sold' to the Crown lands along the north-eastern coast of the South Island around Kaikōura and down to Kaiapoi, claiming them as his own despite having no valid claim to them. Governor George Grey had naively taken Te Rauparaha at his word. As a result of this fraudulent sale, settlers began to move into the region and establish

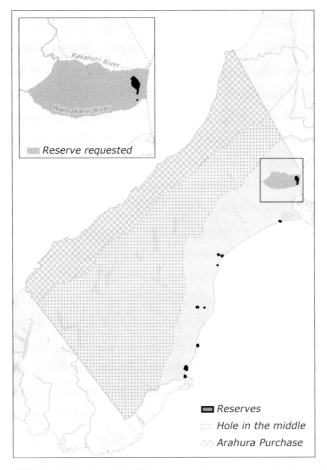

With Kemp's Purchase, Ngāi Tahu requested a large reserve in the north of the block between the Waimakariri and Rakahuri (Ashley) rivers. The iwi claimed not to have sold the Main Divide, also known as the 'hole in the middle'. Kemp's Purchase completely overlapped with the Arahura Purchase.

large and lucrative farming estates. They later denied the sale of the Main Divide. Ngāi Tahu sought a substantial reserve between the Waimakariri and Rakahuri (Ashley) rivers.[9]

Governor Grey was busy convincing his superiors in London that he had acquired a vast amount of land in the South Island, but he did not mention that he was unable to include adjacent Banks Peninsula in the purchase. Buying land on the peninsula was complicated by the presence of the French. Captain Jean Langlois had arrived in the late

1830s, before the signing of the treaty, and bought a small amount of land. Despite this, he sailed back to France boasting of his large purchase and full of plans for a French colony. When he returned in 1840, just after the treaty was signed, the colonists he brought with him were disappointed to find that their wide-ranging lands were much smaller than they had been led to believe and that they were only able to live there under the protection of Ngāi Tahu rangatira. When, from 1843 to 1845, the colonial administration investigated the series of old land claims, purchases made by Europeans before the signing of the treaty, the French were awarded a 30,000-acre (12,140-hectare) block on Banks Peninsula that was far larger than the amount they had purchased. After the French largely abandoned this block to the British once it became apparent that the French would not be able to establish a nationwide colony, Crown land purchasers used the French 'purchases' as a way to pressure Ngāi Tahu into selling at lower prices. The French and British had been competing for influence in the area, but by the mid-1840s the rivalry had simmered down into the neutrality of an entente. Ngāi Tahu's fortunes struggled as a result.[10]

Aware that Mantell had kept the purchase price at a bare minimum and provided the tiniest of reserves in Canterbury, Grey assigned him to purchase the Banks Peninsula lands. In 1849, under significant pressure from Mantell and restricted from selling for much higher prices to private individuals, Ngāi Tahu rangatira at Rāpaki sold the Port Cooper (Lyttelton) block of around 59,000 acres (23,875 hectares) for £200. A mere 866 acres (350 hectares) were reserved around Rāpaki; of this Mantell said only 60 acres (24 hectares) was 'arable land'. Mantell travelled next to neighbouring Koukourarata, where he was able to obtain 104,000 acres (42,087 hectares), the Port Levy block, for £250 and provide reserves totalling only 1361 acres (550 hectares).[11]

To complete his purchase of Banks Peninsula, Mantell travelled on towards Akaroa Harbour. There the rangatira stridently rejected his offer of £150 with 1880 acres (761 hectares) reserved out of a total of approximately 88,500 acres (35,815 hectares). Despite the incomplete purchase, the British Parliament in London passed the Canterbury Association Lands Settlement Act in 1850, which empowered the association to sell an area of about 2.5 million acres (1,011,715 hectares) in Canterbury, including all of Banks Peninsula. In 1856 another Crown

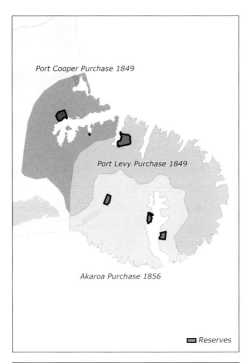

Port Cooper Purchase 1849

Port Levy Purchase 1849

Akaroa Purchase 1856

▨ Reserves

On Banks Peninsula, Ngāi Tahu were under severe pressure to sell because the Crown erroneously claimed that the French had already bought the land.

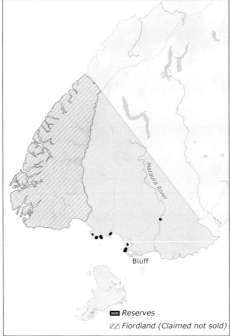

Mataura River

Bluff

▨ Reserves
▨ Fiordland (Claimed not sold)

In the Murihiku Purchase, Ngāi Tahu claimed that they had never sold Fiordland.

land purchaser, William Hamilton, was commissioned to complete the purchase at Akaroa. The Crown had attempted to buy the Akaroa block back in 1849 for the same price but with 1880 acres (760 hectares) reserved. The rangatira of Akaroa thought they could get a better deal if they waited but ended up worse off. Hamilton himself admitted that the reserves were barely sufficient.

In 1853 Murihiku, in the very south of Te Wai Pounamu, was the target: as instructed, Mantell bought, for £2,600, some 7,257,500 acres (2,937,000 hectares) and reserved 4875 acres (1973 hectares). Ngāi Tahu had sought additional reserves, most significantly at the sacred Rarotoka (Centre Island), the exclusion of Fiordland and a higher purchase price.

The purchasing continued in 1857: 2,137,500 acres (865,000 hectares) of North Canterbury for £500 without any reserves. Ngāi Tahu requested reserves at Motunau and Hurunui for their stock. Settlement had already begun in the area because the Crown had erroneously believed they had purchased the land from Te Rauparaha. Farmers had cut Ngāi Tahu off from their access to mahinga kai.

For the North Canterbury Purchase, no reserves were provided because the Crown had already sold all the land to settlers.

In much the same way, Ngāi Tahu were pressured to sell land at Kaikōura in 1858: around 2,817,000 acres (1,140,000 hectares) for £300 with 5558 acres (2250 hectares) reserved. Ngāi Tahu claimed they sought £5,000 and 100,000 acres (40,468 hectares) of reserves. The Crown purchaser bragged to his superiors that the reserves at Kaikōura were of the 'most useless and worthless description'.[12] The Ngāi Tahu residents of Kaikōura had to buy land back from the Crown to accommodate their cattle and horses.[13]

In 1860 the focus moved to the West Coast. The Arahura Deed, handled by James Mackay, consisted of the sale, for £300, of 6,946,000 acres (2,810,000 hectares), with 6724 acres (2720 hectares) reserved and ownership of the Arahura River from its source in the Main Divide to the Tasman Sea. Ngāi Tahu claimed a higher purchase price and significantly larger reserves, especially up the Arahura River so that they could maintain their access to what was arguably their most precious resource, pounamu. Against Mackay's wishes, they maintained that they wanted a reserve at Māwhera, on the present-day site of Greymouth. Although they were successful in acquiring Māwhera as a reserve, it was also coveted by Pākehā leaseholders who rented the lands from the

Reserves
Reserve requested

With the Kaikoura Purchase, Ngāi Tahu requested a large reserve in the middle of the block, between the Kahutara and Tutaeputaputa rivers.

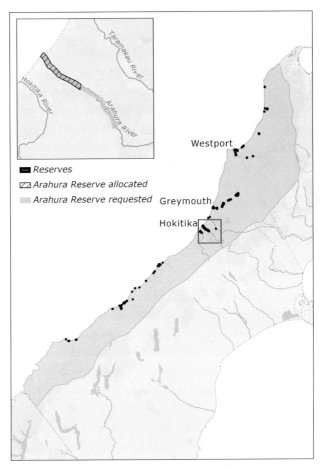

For the Arahura Purchase on the West Coast Ngāi Tahu asked for a reserve covering the entire Arahura River to its origin at Mount Tuhua, but this was not provided.

Poutini Ngāi Tahu owners. The Westland and Nelson Native Reserves Act, passed in 1887, provided 21-year leases with automatic renewal for the leaseholders at the exact same 'peppercorn rental' rates.[14]

The final Te Wai Pounamu purchase was that of Rakiura (Stewart Island) in 1864 (see map on p. 150). Around 420,000 acres (170,000 hectares) was purchased for £6,000, with nine reserves amounting to 935 acres (378 hectares) reserved. The land included a number of islands where Ngāi Tahu harvested tītī (muttonbirds). A third of the purchase was provided in cash, a third for specific individuals and the remaining third was to be invested for education and other purchases. It was the closest that any of the Crown purchases came to representing a 'fair deal', although it did mistakenly include a number of important Tītī Islands that should have been reserved.[15]

The Banks Peninsula purchases – Port Cooper and Port Levy in 1849 and Akaroa in 1856 – were later categorised as one purchase and as a result the 10 purchases became eight. Along with the restrictions on access to mahinga kai, these have become known as the nine tall trees of Te Kerēme, the Ngāi Tahu claim.

Thanks to marginal and minuscule reserves, and the denial of access to the food sources they had relied upon for centuries, within a generation of the first land sale Ngāi Tahu were left landless and impoverished while settlers were provided with cheap and wide-ranging estates throughout the region.[16] The weka and other birds hunted in the inland areas of the Ngāi Tahu rohe were no longer available as pastoralists established their farms and put up fencing. The eels that were a staple of the Ngāi Tahu diet were starved of their traditional ecosystem as farmers drained the swamps on their newly acquired properties. Access to large water bodies such as lakes Te Waihora (Ellesmere) and Wairewa (Forsyth) was cut off due to the sale of adjacent waterfront lands to the Crown and later to farmers. Te Waihora, one of the largest lakes in New Zealand, was known as Te Kete-o-Rākaihautū (the fish basket of Rākaihautū) and the loss of its abundant seafood resources and birds was a particularly severe blow to the prosperity of local Ngāi Tahu. The forests contained a number of resources, including birds such as manu-kiwi, kākā, tūī, kererū, kākāpō, makomako and others, as well as a number of plants: karaka, kōtukutuku, miro, mataī, rimu, kahikatea, koromiko, hīnau, tōtara, tī, pikopiko, katoke, kāuru, mamaku and others. Other resources lost were those gathered for weaving, tool-making and artistic endeavours, such as kareao, toetoe, pīngao, harakeke, kiekie, raupō and kuta. Last but not least, there was the loss of once abundant pūhā and watercress.[17]

The first formal expression of Ngāi Tahu land grievance came in the form of a letter from rangatira Matiaha Tiramōrehu to Lieutenant-Governor Edward Eyre, asking him to designate adequate land reserves, according to the specifications of the land purchases. (Tiramōrehu and other leaders had already approached Eyre in person in Akaroa the year before.) Ngāi Tahu took their first case to the Native Land Court in 1868 but received from Judge Francis Fenton 'only paltry additional rights' and were left with 'a deep sense of injustice'.[18] Later that year they tried to challenge the judgement in the Supreme Court but were thwarted when the government immediately passed the Ngaitahu Reference Validation Act, which prevented their claims from being heard by putting them 'beyond the reach of litigation'.[19] In February 1879 Premier Sir George Grey established a royal commission, headed by Thomas Smith and Francis Nairn, to investigate the Otago, Kemp, Murihiku and Akaroa purchases. The Smith–Nairn Commission began public hearings in May and over the next two years accumulated a great deal of evidence. But in April 1880 Native Minister John Bryce, part of a newly formed government, halted the funding for the inquiry, which could not complete its work in Murihiku. Although the commission issued a report in January 1881, which criticised much of what had gone on, this languished until 1882, when Bryce dismissed its work as 'altogether unnecessary'.[20] After continued efforts by Ngāi Tahu parliamentarians H. K. Taiaroa and then Tame Parata, asking what had happened to the Smith–Nairn report, in May 1886 the government appointed Alexander Mackay as a royal commissioner to investigate settling claims by granting more land. His 1887 report recommended the return of more than 200,000 acres (81,000 hectares), but following a change of government this was criticised and undermined by a joint parliamentary select committee. As a result of a second such committee in 1889, in 1890 Mackay was again made a royal commissioner to travel around the South Island, documenting the economic situation of Ngāi Tahu. Mackay's report of May 1891, which described widespread poverty and deprivation, recommended the return of land and the payment of compensation, but with no result. In 1906, the South Island Landless Native Act allocated 4064 'landless natives' (not all Ngāi Tahu) 142,465 acres (57,650 hectares) of land, mainly inaccessible mountainous bush country that would have been impossible to farm without substantial capital. Each person was allowed only 50 acres (20 hectares).

Ngāi Tahu continued to petition the government throughout the late nineteenth and early twentieth centuries. In 1920 a Native Land Claims Royal Commission, chaired by Native Land Court Chief Judge Robert Jones, reported on only one of the ten 1844–64 purchases, Kemp's of 1848. Jones's 1920 report recommended that £354,000 be paid as compensation, but again nothing happened. In 1944, thanks to Peter

Fraser's Labour government, the Ngaitahu Claim Settlement Act paid the iwi an annual sum of £10,000 for 30 years: this was intended to finally settle all claims about the Kemp purchase. Many members of Ngāi Tahu regarded this small amount, which quickly devalued with inflation, as a temporary measure. Some leaders, especially those who had negotiated the compensation, were initially pleased with the settlement but later considered that the compensation had been forced upon Ngāi Tahu. The iwi continued to petition the government regarding its claims through the body established to distribute the payments, first the Ngai Tahu Trust Board, set up in 1946, and from 1955 the Ngai Tahu Maori Trust Board.[21]

As Te Maire Tau has noted, 'Ngāi Tahu's response to the loss of land was to organise themselves into hapū and village rūnanga' from the late 1800s onwards. These rūnanga sought redress from the government and organised themselves to tackle the resolution of the Ngāi Tahu claim.[22] Marae across the large Ngāi Tahu region worked together but, owing to lack of funding, there was no unifying structure. In 1929 the first Ngaitahu Trust Board was set up 'to administer all funds held by it for the benefit of the ... tribe and was charged with continuing negotiations with the Crown for settlement of the Claim. The Trust Board was also able to buy and sell property, erect buildings, farm and administer lands it owned, and lend money.'[23] The 1944 settlement led to the 1946 Ngaitahu Trust Board Act, which reconstituted the board and authorised it to administer the money. The legislation was, however, limited in its recognition of Ngāi Tahu rangatiratanga.[24] Like all other Māori trust boards of the time, Ngāi Tahu's would ultimately be accountable to a minister of the Crown rather than to the members of the iwi. The 1955 Maori Trust Boards Act applied Ngāi Tahu's board structure to some other Māori groups around the country. By the early 1980s trust board members were considering developing a governing structure that would incorporate input from Ngāi Tahu rūnanga.[25]

CHAPTER 2

Ngāi Tahu takes action

The modern Treaty of Waitangi claims process began in the 1970s, although its roots go back further to other attempts by Māori to have their historical claims addressed by the Crown. By the 1970s Māori protest was quite widespread and diverse – conservative, liberal and radical factions often worked together, but also alone. Their efforts culminated in the 1975 Māori land march (hīkoi), organised by a group of Māori and some Pākehā activists, which focused on halting the alienation of land and resolving claims.[1] Māori MPs and political figures outside of Parliament were also pushing the government to deal with historical redress for Māori claims. Led by Labour Maori Affairs Minister Matiu Rata, and supported by Ngai Tahu Maori Trust Board chairman Frank Winter, they helped to establish the Waitangi Tribunal via the Treaty of Waitangi Act in 1975. The tribunal was a permanent commission of inquiry authorised to investigate breaches of the principles of the Treaty of Waitangi – but only those that had occurred after 1975 – and make recommendations to the government. Shortly after the tribunal was set up, the National Party, led by Robert Muldoon, won the general election; the result was limited funding and political support for the tribunal.[2] However, despite the limits placed on the Waitangi Tribunal in its first decade of existence, some early findings were particularly important, such as the historical context in which the treaty was signed, recognition of the Māori text and the different Māori and European understandings of the treaty, especially regarding sovereignty or rangatiratanga.[3]

Pressure from Māori MPs, Māori activists and especially from new Ngai Tahu Maori Trust Board chairman Tipene O'Regan made the extension of the Waitangi Tribunal's powers to investigate historical grievances a part of Labour's policy platform in the 1984 snap election, which it won. The Treaty of Waitangi Amendment Act passed in 1985 allowed for the tribunal to inquire into Māori grievances against the Crown dating back to the treaty signing on 6 February 1840. But the Labour government that introduced legislation to increase the investigative reach of the Waitangi Tribunal also embarked on a neoliberal economic agenda that clashed with its intention to resolve Māori grievances.[4] In 1986 Parliament passed the State Owned Enterprises (SOE) Act, which sought to corporatise or privatise some of the most valuable Crown assets and land administered by government departments.[5] In addition to the economic changes that were introduced during the second half of the 1980s, Labour was also intent on reforming the New Zealand political structure. Legislation was increasingly being written with the Treaty of Waitangi incorporated into its structure to ensure that the government would not be breaching treaty principles. Such legislation included the State Owned Enterprises Act and the Environment Act in 1986, the Conservation Act 1987 (which established the Department of Conservation (DOC)), the Māori Language Act of the same year and, in 1989, the Education and Māori Fisheries Acts.

But the privatisation policies implemented during this period were focused solely on economic rationalism, and originally failed to include any recognition of Māori claims, despite the fact that the government had finally recognised the right of Māori to a fair hearing of their historical grievances. Any land or resources that had been acquired by the Crown in a way that breached the Treaty of Waitangi, but had been sold into private hands, were completely off limits in the claims process.[6] Māori claimants could only receive government-owned lands and resources as compensation. This clash between recognition of historical treaty rights for Māori and the need and desire to privatise the economy was embodied in Ngāi Tahu's first claim to the newly empowered Waitangi Tribunal.

In August 1986 Rakiihia Tau Snr, on behalf of the Ngai Tahu Maori Trust Board, submitted a claim to the Waitangi Tribunal about the government's announcement that it would transfer Crown land interests to SOEs. Ngāi Tahu's concerns about and actions relating to the privatisation of SOEs, along with those of other iwi and hapū, and the New Zealand Maori Council (NZMC), eventually led to a series of victories for Māori in the courts in relation to SOE lands, fisheries and forests, including the famous 1987 *NZMC v Attorney-General* or 'lands' case. The Crown was forced to negotiate with the victorious Māori litigants to establish safeguards for those assets, which included binding powers that the Waitangi Tribunal could use to force the return of SOE lands, forests and financial compensation. These powers were contained in the Treaty of Waitangi (State Enterprises) Act 1988 and the Crown Forest Assets Act 1989. The focus of these cases was on Māori nationally but generally they were led, certainly in terms of the evidence provided in court, by Ngāi Tahu, especially for SOE lands and fisheries.[7]

The 1986 *Te Weehi v Regional Fisheries Officer* case was more directly relevant to Ngāi Tahu since it related to customary fisheries interests in North Canterbury but also had national ramifications for Māori rights to fisheries. In 1986 Tom Te Weehi had been convicted by the District Court for taking undersized pāua in the Motunau rivermouth area but he challenged the decision in the High Court. Te Weehi had received permission from Ngāi Tūāhuriri upoko Rakiihia Tau Snr to take the pāua and based his appeal on customary treaty rights that he claimed had never been extinguished. The judge found that Te Weehi was exercising a customary fishing right and this exempted him from certain fishing law requirements. As Tau later put it, 'Te Weehi was found not guilty of taking paua from Motunau in excess of fishing regulations that none of us were aware of.' The absurdity of the laws restricting Ngāi Tahu's access to mahinga kai was embodied in regulations that were not well publicised even in the 1980s. Tau confidently asserted that 'our ancestors reserved our mahinga kai in the Kemp's Deed of Sale and Purchase'. The High Court judgement advanced the fisheries claims that were then making their way through the courts and Tau rightly saw a possibility of funding emerging from the possible fruits of those legal endeavours.

While Ngāi Tahu fought the Crown with others in court, they also continued to present their claim in the Waitangi Tribunal. After the first claim by Tau related to SOEs, seven further amendments to their statement of claim were made over the next year and a half, setting out Ngāi Tahu's grievances arising from land purchases and the lack of reserves provided by the Crown, and the loss of access to mahinga kai, including both sea and inland fisheries.[8] Tau was the deputy chairman of the Ngai Tahu Maori Trust Board and the head (upoko) of the Ngāi Tūāhuriri hapū of Ngāi Tahu based around Tuahiwi Marae near Kaiapoi, north of Christchurch. He and Tipene O'Regan, as chair of the trust board, formed an effective partnership in leading the Ngāi Tahu claim in the 1980s. O'Regan also chaired the Māwhera Incorporation, a Ngāi Tahu landowners' trust on the West Coast of the South Island set up in 1976.[9] From August 1987 to October 1989 the Ngāi Tahu claim was heard by the Waitangi Tribunal around various marae and other South Island venues. Ngāi Tahu whānui knew about the history of their claim, but their story was not as well known throughout the country. The Waitangi Tribunal provided an opportunity to educate not only Pākehā society, but also North Island Māori, about Te Kerēme. It also provided an avenue for direct communication with the Crown, a chance for Ngāi Tahu grievances to truly be heard.

Until the Ngāi Tahu claim, the tribunal had inquired into and reported on claims by individual claimants, but the increasing number of claims filed since the 1985 amendment meant an alternative system was needed. When a claim is accepted by the tribunal for determination, it is assigned a Wai number. The inquiry into the Ngāi Tahu grievance would be one of the first to investigate multiple claims, although there was still a unifying effort through the original Wai 27 number for the first recorded Ngāi Tahu claim. This had originally consisted of a series of different Wai claims for the different regions representing the different land purchases, so organising it helped to unite the iwi.

The Waitangi Tribunal's Ngāi Tahu hearing was led by the inquiry's presiding officer, the Waitangi Tribunal deputy chair and Maori Land Court judge, Ashley McHugh. He was joined by some very important figures in Māoridom – Bishop Manahuia Bennett, Sir Monita Delamere, Sir Hugh Kawharu and Georgina Te Heuheu – as well as knowledgeable Pākehā, Professor Gordon Orr and Sir Desmond Sullivan. Kawharu was an Oxford scholar who had written a book on Māori land tenure. Delamere was an experienced Māori incorporation manager.

Many people turned out for the first hearing of the claim, which took place at Tuahiwi Marae on 17 August 1987. Among the large crowd was an unexpected group claiming interest in the north-west and north-east of Ngāi Tahu's region of interest, the Interim Committee of the Kurahaupo Waka Trust (Kurahaupō-Rangitāne) (see p. 15–16). Their arrival delayed the beginning of the hearings, which was in fact a boon, since the number of people present meant that, after the opening of the claim and the pōwhiri for the tribunal and other visitors at Tuahiwi, the venue was shifted to the assembly hall at Rangiora High School.

At the opening of the hearing the Rangitāne speaker stood up to oppose the Ngāi Tahu claim and contested the iwi boundaries. They laid a koha upon the marae, which was returned to them. The challenge had been laid down by both sides, and this would not be the last time that cross-claim interests with the iwi and hapū of Te Tau Ihu (northern South Island) became an issue for Ngāi Tahu negotiators. The tribunal accepted their right to be heard in the inquiry but recommended that another body should determine the boundaries between Ngāi Tahu and their northern neighbours. Ultimately, the matter was referred to the Maori Land Court and later the Maori Appellate Court, which in 1990 delivered an opinion in favour of Ngāi Tahu.

The first hearing day, like all those that came after it, began and ended with a karakia. After the prayer McHugh made some short introductory comments in te reo Māori to set the scene:

> He ra tino nui tenei ki a Ngāi Tahu. Te Roopu Whakamana i Te Tiriti kua eke nei ki te whakarongo ki a koe Ngāi Tahu mo nga mahi ki a koutou i mua noa atu. I ahatia i era wa, a, me pewheatia inaianei. Kua tae mai ki te whakarongo ki o auetanga. Inatata nei whakatatutia e te Kooti Piira, te tumuaki ko Ta Rapene Kuki, i ki ia ko nga taonga o Te Tiriti o Waitangi i mea; Te Maori me Te Pakeha i runga i te Tiriti kia kotahi, kia ngawari me te tino whakapono. Koia nei nga korero a Ta Rapene Kuki: Tera whakahau ehara i te mahi iti, tino nui rawa atu te uaua. Ki te taka ki raro o nga whakahaere, ahakoa he aha te wa, te whakahau ma te Kooti kia whakahonoretia.

> This is a very important day for Ngāi Tahu. This tribunal is about to hear from Ngāi Tahu what happened in the past, what was done

about it and what must be done now. We are ready to listen to your grievances. Recently in the Court of Appeal decision, the president, Sir Robin Cooke, stated that the principles of the Treaty of Waitangi required the Maori and Pakeha Treaty partners to act towards each other reasonably and with the utmost good faith. Sir Robin Cooke said: That duty is no light one. It is infinitely more than a formality. If a breach of the duty is demonstrated at any time, the duty of the court will be to insist that it be honoured.[10]

The chairperson's words were meant as much to put the Crown on notice as to reassure the Ngāi Tahu communities in the audience, and around the country and indeed even the world. In addition to the claimants, cross-claimants from Te Tau Ihu, the tribes of the northern South Island that included Rangitāne, and various Crown representatives, two non-government organisations with an interest in environmental and recreational issues – the Royal Forest and Bird Protection Society (Forest & Bird) and Federated Mountain Clubs (FMC) – were also involved. These two organisations would prove determined and stubborn opponents of the Ngāi Tahu claim, and of the settlement negotiations.

Because Ngāi Tahu's region of interest took up most of the South Island, their claim was of interest to many, especially those in the conservation sector. Rik Tau related how a number of 'European organisations' wanted to know what Ngāi Tahu were claiming and, more significantly, whether their claim would affect their property rights. He described a 'continuous round of public meetings for the next three years to explain very clearly with my public utterances that we were not claiming privately owned lands held by individuals, as our claim was not to create further injustices by righting past injustices'. He always emphasised at public meetings that 'only the Government could right the wrong, as they held or claimed ownership of all the family jewels of New Zealand'. The Waitangi Tribunal would later experience the repercussions of attempting to include private lands in resolution of treaty claims.[11] In 1992 its *Te Roroa Report* recommended the Crown's purchase of farmer Allan Titford's lands in Northland because of the egregious manner in which they were acquired. The Crown would eventually do so but not before also passing the Treaty of Waitangi Amendment Act 1993, which forbade any finding by the tribunal to recommend the return of private lands to claimants.[12]

Ngāi Tahu realised the importance of keeping media onside, particularly in this period where there was a relative monopoly on news. Luckily for Ngāi Tahu, Bill Gillies from Rāpaki was a friend of esteemed journalist and media personality Brian Priestley, who advised on how to address the media and control the narrative. After Tau's lawyer David Palmer met with the *Press*, journalist Jane England was attached to the Ngāi Tahu negotiators as their reporter. As Tau noted, they discussed their strategies and public relations obligations with England and 'that removed a lot of racial media reporting, guesswork and speculation by outside media personnel... Jane attended our strategy meetings and was treated as a member of our family.'[13]

Some Waitangi Tribunal hearings are conducted in an adversarial manner with stringent cross-examination by lawyers; others have a more inquisitorial angle. At most hearings the evidence of kaumātua is rarely questioned, out of respect, and that principle applied to the Ngāi Tahu hearing. Although expert evidence from the Crown, Ngāi Tahu and the tribunal was cross-examined, the inquiry was far more inquisitorial in nature. An interesting aspect was a father–daughter duo who represented opposing sides: Gordon Stewart Parsonson for the Crown and Ann Parsonson for Ngāi Tahu.[14] There was so much history to explore that, in contrast to other hearings, the Crown and Ngāi Tahu technical witnesses, who were mainly historians, did not so much rebut one another throughout the hearing as provide different parts of the story. This would not become the norm for all hearings. Only a few years later, during the Waitangi Tribunal's Muriwhenua (top of the North Island) land hearings, the approach was far more adversarial.

The tribunal held a total of 26 hearings spread over approximately 24 weeks and covering many of Ngāi Tahu's claims: land, fisheries, legal personality and ancillary claims. The Crown and technical witnesses in the tribunal had to have all evidence read aloud in full, but many of the reports were hundreds of pages long and this took up a lot of time. In future inquiries, large reports would be received as read and only summaries provided orally.

Before turning to the negotiations themselves, it is important to recognise the challenges of funding the process. Tau recalled how, after the claim was submitted, he worried constantly about funding the expertise necessary to defend the claim, much less the negotiations that would follow. Lawyers and historians were paid, and their help was sorely needed and appreciated. But there were countless volunteers who gave their time in the wharekai, helped with logistical issues like transport and opened homes and marae for manuhiri or whānau.[15] Although there was some minimal funding from the Crown, it covered only a minute portion of the total cost.[16]

From 1986 to 1990 the Ngai Tahu Maori Trust Board was also carrying the major burden of funding the Māori fisheries litigation and negotiation, although these were dramatically eased as a consequence of the 1989 Interim Fisheries Settlement. Towards the end of the Waitangi Tribunal hearings and into the early years of the negotiations, the board was in a tenuous financial position. As a consequence of political pressure in the waning days of the fourth Labour government, the board's bankers withdrew their services. Following an encounter with economist and consultant Graham Kitson, who had Ngāi Tahu whakapapa links, O'Regan was introduced to Japanese businessman, Masashi Yamada. On the strength of a handshake, Yamada loaned Ngāi Tahu about $800,000 when the tribe was nearly broke. This financial infusion of funding allowed the iwi to maximise their use of the land-banking arrangements and fisheries settlements that followed.

At the conclusion of Ngāi Tahu's Waitangi Tribunal hearings in October 1989, McHugh expressed concerns about the continuing alienation of Crown land in the South Island. Tau and O'Regan brought his comments to the attention of the Crown and asked that a system be established where the Ngai Tahu Maori Trust Board would be consulted before any Crown land was alienated.[17] By mid-December 1989 the solicitor-general and acting deputy-director general of lands, following discussions with Tau and O'Regan, proposed an early warning system (or land-bank) under which the board would be notified before any alienation of Crown land in the Ngāi Tahu rohe. The system was originally confined to Department of Crown Lands land but O'Regan was told that other Crown agencies would also be included. If the Crown land was not subject to offer-back requirements under the Public Works Act 1981 (where the previous landowner was first offered an opportunity to purchase the land if it had been acquired for a public work), a board representative would be informed of the pending sale,[18] and the board would then have to decide whether it wanted to retain (bank) the land as part of a future settlement. O'Regan had sought a blanket ban on the sale of all Crown land in the Ngāi Tahu rohe but he understood that the early warning system was a fair compromise. The Crown provided funding for the board to employ a specialist to help with its selection of properties.[19]

In the first year of operation, 1990, there were some difficulties. Some government departments ignored the new directive to warn the board before disposing of their surplus assets. They were also concerned that they would not be compensated for the loss of revenue from the sale. Eventually individual departments and SOEs were paid full market value for the revenue they lost when placing Crown properties in Ngāi Tahu's land-bank and, later, other land-banks.[20]

Both before and during their negotiations with the Crown, Ngāi Tahu were concerned that there were still enough Crown assets available to compensate Ngāi Tahu, particularly in the face of widespread government privatisation. The planned privatisation of Electricorp in 1990 led O'Regan to press the Crown not to conduct the sale without first consulting Ngāi Tahu, who were still bitter about the sale of the Housing Corporation without prior notification to the Ngai Tahu Maori Trust Board. They had not used litigation but decided to co-operate with the Crown's process and submit a commercial bid. There was a veiled threat that if the sale of Electricorp proceeded in the same way, then litigation would certainly follow. This attitude was in tune with Ngāi Tahu's eagerness to play the Crown at its own game. O'Regan also reminded Prime Minister Geoffrey Palmer that Ngāi Tahu would be interested in receiving SOE shares as part of their future settlement but they had been repeatedly ignored when approaching ministers. Ngāi Tahu made it clear that if the Crown persisted with the sale of Electricorp without consulting the iwi it would be in breach of the principles of the Treaty of Waitangi yet again.[21]

The formation of the Waitangi Tribunal and the court cases establishing the Treaty of Waitangi within New Zealand's legal framework were important in pushing the government to negotiate settlements with iwi, but the tribunal could not negotiate for the Crown: it could largely only make recommendations. It was up to the government to negotiate and until the late 1980s it had not made any substantial efforts to begin doing so. Until late 1988, the Labour government maintained that the settlements of the past for major Māori grievances were full and final and would not be reopened. But Māori groups, the tribunal,

the courts and internal factions within the Labour Party led by Koro
Wetere and Geoffrey Palmer changed the government's mind and pushed
it to negotiate.[22] These events prompted the Labour government to
create, in 1988, the first official government policy unit charged directly
with dealing with treaty breaches, the Treaty of Waitangi Policy Unit.[23]
From the very beginning the Crown Law Office played a significant role
in assisting the unit to develop treaty policy advice for the government
and gradually other departments also began to play a part – Treasury (in
relation to fiscal matters), DOC, the Department of the Prime Minister
and Cabinet, and Manatū Māori (later Te Puni Kōkiri). Although the unit
was originally meant only to advise the government on treaty matters,
its officials were quickly drawn into involvement in direct negotiations.

Te Tai Poutini – the Arahura River was sacred to Ngāi Tahu because of the pounamu found on its banks. The riverbed was meant to be reserved to the iwi in the Arahura Purchase.

In this bird's-eye view of southern Banks Peninsula, Wairewa (Lake Forsyth) is in the foreground, Te Waihora (Lake Ellesmere) in the centre, Kaitorete Spit to the left and the Southern Alps in the background. The lakebed of Te Waihora and Kaitorete Spit were returned in the settlement.

The important urupa of Rarotoka (Centre Island) was returned in the settlement with blue water title down to the foreshore and seabed.

Whenua Hou (Codfish Island) is an important taonga for Ngāi Tahu. A co-management system was established in the settlement. Te Pou Hou, Te Pou Neherā and Te Pou Haumi, Waikoropūpū (Sealers Bay), Whenua Hou, 2017.

The Tītī Islands, which constitute the longest uninterrupted food-gathering economy in Aotearoa New Zealand. As here on Timore, houses have been built on some islands to provide shelter in the unforgiving autumn when the annual gathering of tītī (muttonbirds) takes place. The Crown was meant to reserve all of the islands in the Rakiura Purchase but only reserved some. The return of the Crown Tītī Islands without marginal strips was a non-negotiable aspect of the settlement.

Putauhinu, with Pohowaitai and Tamaitemioka in the background. South-east of Rakiura (Stewart Island), some Tītī Islands are much smaller than others. Each island is owned by a specific set of families based around the Ngāi Tahu rohe.

Tūtaepatu Lagoon was returned in the June 1996 interim settlement. It is an important mahinga kai for the Ngāi Tūāhuriri hapū based at Tuahiwi.

In November 1997 the Prime Minister presented a collection of pounamu, including this hei tiki, to Ngāi Tahu as a koha to cement the signing of the deed of settlement for Te Kerēme.

Sir Tipene O'Regan and Doug Graham at the initialling of the deed of settlement in Wellington, September 1997.

Sir Tipene O'Regan, Anake Goodall, Jim Bolger and Doug Graham at the signing of the Ngāi Tahu deed of settlement at Takahanga Marae in Kaikōura on 21 November 1997.

The Crown paepae for the signing of the Ngāi Tahu deed of settlement at Takahanga Marae. Front row: Eru Manuera, Doug Graham, Jim Bolger, John Clarke and Bill English.

Sir Tipene O'Regan and Prime Minister Jim Bolger hongi at Takahanga Marae.

Ngāi Tahu whānau walking up the steps outside Parliament House for the final reading of the Ngāi Tahu Claims Settlement Bill on 30 September 1998.

Doug Graham in Parliament for the final reading of the Ngāi Tahu Claims Settlement Bill.

Ngāi Tahu whānau in the public gallery react to speeches in Parliament during the passing of the Ngāi Tahu Claims Settlement Act.
Front row: Sir Tipene O'Regan, Mark Solomon, Edward Ellison and Mataawiki Wakefield. **Middle row:** Rakiihia Tau Jnr, Sid Ashton, David Higgins, Trevor Howse and Manu Manihera (partly obscured).

Richard Wallace and kaumātua on the wharenui steps at the Crown apology to Ngāi Tahu at Ōnuku Marae on 29 November 1998.

Georgina Te Heu Heu, Jenny Shipley, Burton Shipley and Doug Graham
wait to come onto the marae at Ōnuku.

Sir Tipene O'Regan speaking at the pōwhiri before the official Crown apology.

Kai Wero Peter Brennan meeting the official party at the Ōnuku Marae entrance.

Rakiihia Tau Snr, the original Ngāi Tahu claimant, at Ōnuku Marae.

CHAPTER 3

The negotiating principles

After hearing Ngāi Tahu's claims from 1987 to 1989, the Waitangi Tribunal released the *Ngai Tahu Land Report* in February 1991. It covered the major land purchases made between 1844 and 1864 and the restrictions on access to mahinga kai. The tribunal validated Ngāi Tahu's claims in relation to the lack of reserves, schools and hospitals and the miserly prices paid for land. It found in favour of the iwi in all its claims to mahinga kai. However, it rejected Ngāi Tahu's claims in specific instances, citing a lack of direct written contemporary evidence, for example, in the claims to the Otago tenths, the 'hole in the middle' (the claim that the Main Divide had not been sold) and Fiordland. Overwhelmingly, though, the tribunal found in favour of Te Kerēme – the Ngāi Tahu claim. There would be three more reports. The second and third, both produced in 1992, addressed Ngāi Tahu's legal personality and sea fisheries claims. The fourth and final report, released in 1995, covered the ancillary claims that grew out of the original claim.

The first phase of Ngāi Tahu's negotiations, which started soon after the report was published, ran from 1991 to 1994. In this period Ngāi Tahu would experience the frustrations of dealing with a government that was largely developing policy ad hoc. The Crown would counter that putting a full policy in place would either be regarded as a decree from above or would involve years of consultation. Ngāi Tahu also met resistance to key elements of the redress they sought. A central point of disagreement was the extent to which Māori autonomy would be acknowledged within the settlement. Ngāi Tahu framed their negotiations with the Crown as an attempt to reassert rangatiratanga. The Crown's view was that, as in the 1940s, redress would be provided in the form of money, but the recognition of autonomy was not negotiable. Unlike the 1940s policies, however, the 1989 Principles for Crown Action, as limited as they may have been in the view of some activists and academics, did include the return of land. Led by Mike Moore, Labour lost the 1990 election in a landslide to Jim Bolger and National.[1] It was now up to the Crown officials who had begun the process under Labour to continue their work under National.

Despite claims to the contrary in his autobiography, Jim Bolger had been critical of the legislative and judicial advances made in the 1980s and it was not apparent that he would continue the work.[2] His first minister of Māori affairs, Winston Peters, was not very encouraging for those who appreciated the increasing significance of the Treaty of Waitangi within New Zealand's legislative and legal systems. Peters had gained a great measure of popularity by appealing to the entrenched supporters of a monocultural New Zealand. He was originally placed in charge of all treaty negotiations, including those that had begun with Waikato–Tainui, but never became actively involved.

After Peters was dismissed from Cabinet in October 1991,[3] Minister of Justice Doug Graham, who was responsible for the Treaty of Waitangi Policy Unit because it was within his department, was appointed minister in charge of treaty negotiations. Although more encouraging than Peters, Graham had, in 1985, voted against providing the tribunal with powers to inquire into historical claims, and so it was not guaranteed that he would be willing to continue the work begun under Labour. He later stated that he only voted against the legislation because as a backbencher he had to follow his party.[4]

The first year of Ngāi Tahu negotiations under National was largely characterised by the development of the Crown position on the *Ngai Tahu Land Report*. The most concerning matter for Ngāi Tahu was trying to maintain the Crown's asset base by preventing it from selling off any more Crown lands as well as developing negotiating principles and kick-starting talks about creating a legal personality for the tribe that was divorced from the old Maori Trust Board model.

The Ngāi Tahu negotiations were marked by layers of bureaucracy and many different parties that the Crown negotiators had to consult before they could make a decision. And a limited amount of policy on treaty-related conservation issues prevented any quick resolutions.

By the time the Ngāi Tahu report was released, the policy unit had marginally increased in size but the coordination of treaty policy across the different Crown agencies and departments was proving challenging. Both the Crown and Ngāi Tahu accepted the general thrust of the report as a basis for the negotiations. Each had their problems with some of the tribunal's findings but agreed to set their disagreements aside.[5] The report was the largest and most comprehensive the tribunal had so far produced and analysing it extended past the middle of 1991 as officials from the Crown Law Office, Treasury, Manatū Māori and DOC became involved.[6]

While most departments analysed the report and attempted to hypothesise about the likely consequences of its findings, Treasury's lens was one of fiscal conservatism – the question of repaying Ngāi Tahu's outstanding costs from the tribunal hearings and providing the bare minimum of funding for the iwi to begin the negotiations with the Crown. To cover their costs, Ngāi Tahu were forced to sell their Christchurch property on Armagh Street tenanted by NZ Post and to stop educational grants; it did not print annual reports in 1991.[7] Treasury wanted to limit the repayment of costs but was overruled by the combined weight of the Treaty of Waitangi Policy Unit and Manatū Māori.[8] This was only the first disagreement between the unit (later the Office of Treaty Settlements) and Treasury officials during the Ngāi Tahu negotiations.[9]

In July 1991 five Crown working parties were formed to analyse how to approach the negotiations with Ngāi Tahu. The purpose of the working party considering reserves not awarded was to decide what land and resources were available in compensation for grievances related to the Otago reserves. At this stage redress was, in theory, going to be more directly connected to the specific claim and breach of treaty principles. It reported several anomalies related to the purchase but the most significant was the fact that more land had been taken than was actually bought. The deed of sale allowed for an area of 161,875 hectares (400,000 acres) but 215,985 hectares (533,700 acres) was taken, an increase of more than 54,000 hectares (133,700 acres). This, the working party noted, 'could not have been paid for except by dilution of the original per acre purchase price. There seems to be an injustice here which is

actually "bigger" than the lack of provisions of tenths [i.e. the reserves].'
This illegal increase was one of the main strengths of the Ngāi Tahu
claim. Although most of the purchase area for the entire claim was
rural, about 12.5 per cent of the Otago claim was now in urban or semi-
urban development and it would be difficult to provide land in this area.
The 'compensatory land' would likely come from other more rural areas.
Using the notion of a tenths requirement, the Otago reserves would have
been short by about 17,000 hectares (42,000 acres) of land. The only
major asset available for compensation would be exotic (mostly pine)
forests, including both the land and the trees. It was estimated that of the
Crown forests already sold, the land remaining in Crown ownership was
worth $10 million, and the value of unsold forests, both land and trees,
was approximately $20 million. Other potential sources of assets were
commercial and industrial land, some of which was already also in the
land-bank. Government departments, Crown agencies and SOEs could
also contribute. The working party on health and education endowments
canvassed the different types of Crown lands available for redress but
made little comment except to say that the report clearly showed schools
and hospitals had been promised in the purchase.[10]

Most of the discussions that followed the report's release concentrated
on the contents of a future settlement, but there was still clearly limited
clarity on the distribution of settlements to Māoridom as a whole.
One Crown official noted that Ngāi Tahu were essentially a minority
group within the South Island because of migrations by North Island
Māori to the South Island for work after the Second World War. At this
early point it was still not evident that redress would flow to centralised
iwi rūnanga in their home territory and that it would be up to tribal
members to register and potentially see the benefits.[11]

The Crown had planned to begin negotiations soon after the *Ngai
Tahu Land Report* appeared but it quickly became apparent that more
time would be needed for analysis. Treasury wanted the negotiations
to be delayed until at least a preliminary strategy for them was formed.
Treasury agreed to accept the general thrust of the report and to state
that although there would be aspects on which Ngāi Tahu and the Crown
might disagree, this should not prevent constructive negotiations.[12]

There were also areas about which the tribunal report had not made
specific recommendations but which were a part of the negotiation process.

This included the return of Milford airport in Fiordland. Just as the negotiations were beginning, the Ministry of Transport was seeking to privatise its airports. A Cabinet paper on the subject made no mention of a Māori, let alone a Ngāi Tahu interest, in Milford. The ministry stressed that it was only the business, and not the land, that was being sold. This was self-evident since the airport was located on national park land. A new interdepartmental working party focused solely on Milford airport, organised to coordinate between government departments, believed that 'in order to show good faith to the claimants, and to ensure that the Crown has a full basket from which to negotiate remedies, and to ensure that the claimants receive an adequate economic base, the business of the aerodrome should be available to the Crown to offer to the claimants as a viable income stream'. This reflected some of the competing interests and motivations driving different departments within the Crown.[13]

The final Cabinet report to guide the Crown's negotiations with Ngāi Tahu covered swathes of the tribunal's recommendations and the formation of new working groups for these issues in early September 1991. The Crown was especially concerned about the creation of precedents on larger settlement issues but also about recommendations in the report on such specific matters as the Tītī Islands. The report canvassed different approaches to a potential settlement. Ngāi Tahu had publicly indicated that theirs would be geared to the magnitude of their proven grievances. The Crown noted that, of an estimated 526,000 hectares (1.3 million acres) of reserves not awarded, considerable proportions were prime land, with an estimated unimproved value of $250 million. Officials thought that Ngāi Tahu would not rigidly adhere to a reparations-based approach during negotiations because they understood that there was a limit on the public purse. The Cabinet report severely criticised Treasury's purely needs-based attitude to compensation: 'If this approach were to be followed, the Crown would have to get an accurate population census of the tribe, assess each individual's need and compensate accordingly. A host of variables confront the programming of a just calculation in a case such as this, and the assessment of "what might have been" is highly subjective.' (The first major problem was the lack of accurate

statistics on the Ngāi Tahu population: the Iwi Population Estimate of
Ngāi Tahu as at June 1990 was between 7000 and 9000 but the figure
was closer to 60,000.) As the report noted, 'For example, the Crown
cannot assess what the tribal needs, as opposed to their aspirations are.
Nor is it possible to devise a formula which could differentiate the two.
Indeed, the socio-economic needs of Ngāi Tahu are the same as any
NZer.' Treasury's approach 'ignore[s] the fact that Ngāi Tahu have been
discriminated against in the past, and that opportunities have been
taken from them because of the malpractice of the Crown. To ignore
that fact compounds the Crown's breaches, rather than redresses them.'
The Crown advocated a restoration-based approach which would take
'into account the magnitude of the tribe's past dispossession, focus upon
the current needs and aspirations of the people, and restore the socio-
economic position of the tribe'.[14]

But not all government departments agreed with the Cabinet paper.
Manatū Māori pointed out that further Ngāi Tahu positions on mahinga
kai, ancillary claims and other related issues would need to be known
before policy could be developed. The ministry also noted that some of
the tribunal's recommendations might not actually address Ngāi Tahu's
grievances, such as vesting pounamu in the iwi without giving them a
way to mine it in the future or vesting the lakebed of Te Waihora without
ensuring that Ngāi Tahu had an exclusive right to fish eel.[15] Manatū Māori
was also concerned about the effects on third parties of such moves as
the raising of Te Waihora to restore mahinga kai or vesting all pounamu
in Ngāi Tahu. This raised the possibility of significant Pākehā opposition.

In September DOC raised the issue of public consultations about
a series of possible transferrals of Crown property and their effect,[16]
and in October there was a general meeting between officials from the
Treaty of Waitangi Policy Unit and DOC, and Ngāi Tahu negotiators,
who conveyed to DOC their concerns about the ownership of sacred
sites and the mining of pounamu, and the importance of Rarotoka
Island (near Rakiura), Whenua Hou (Codfish Island) and the Crown
Tītī Islands.[17] DOC was in many ways allied philosophically with third-
party environmental and recreational groups who were to prove very
challenging in advancing the negotiations.

Early in the negotiations both the Crown and Ngāi Tahu realised
that a public relations strategy was essential to counteracting any

false information; this applied to other government departments as well as third parties such as environmental and recreational groups. There was clearly still a lot of confusion about the practicalities and effects of providing redress to Ngāi Tahu. As one worried Crown official asked, 'How are all New Zealanders' rights to be addressed [in a future settlement]?'[18] As a knowledgeable Māori DOC official stated in November 1991, the concern about the negotiations was 'arising in significant part from a lack of knowledge or information... I believe we need to deal with this and deal with it urgently, and I suggest that in the very near future, i.e. within the next week or two, we arrange a small informal meeting with representatives of some of the main groups at which we can talk to them about the negotiating process we are following, and allay some of their fears about "hidden agendas", "secret deals", etc.'[19] The challenge, as Minister of Conservation Denis Marshall soon found out, was allaying those fears while at the same time emphasising the scope and extent of Ngāi Tahu's loss.[20] Public relations were so important that the Ngai Tahu Maori Trust Board talked about developing its own strategy parallel to that of the Crown.[21] The question began to be asked: what happens when outcomes have been negotiated, but are no longer adhered to when they reach third-party consultations? Does that negate the whole point of direct negotiations? That challenge would certainly be daunting.

Ngāi Tahu had to attempt to convince many sectors of the general public of the justice of their case, but perhaps the most challenging was the conservation movement and those groups representing recreational interests. Some DOC officials had foreseen the difficulties that would arise but they were seemingly in a minority.[22] Conservationists who supported Ngāi Tahu, such as Dr Henrik Moller of the University of Otago, who had been involved with the iwi in studies of muttonbirding in the Tītī Islands, were targeted by conservation groups in the media.[23] Government officials were also frustrated when conservation groups asked for consultation but then failed to participate in it.

Forest & Bird, Public Access New Zealand (PANZ), FMC and, at first, Fish and Game felt that the conservation estate alone (rather than non-conservation land) was going to be used to address settlements, but this was not the case.[24] The other predominant fear related to Ngāi Tahu participation in the management of conservation areas; it was felt this would curb access to the public. Tangata whenua participation in the management of conservation areas was often misconstrued as being another part of the privatisation process and Ngāi Tahu as merely another private interest. In early 1992 FMC wrote to Douglas Graham that 'No-one would suggest giving control of our public conservation parks to a private group, e.g. Helicopter Line, or Fiordland Travel.'[25] This lack of understanding about Ngāi Tahu's treaty rights was reinforced by FMC later in the year when they again wrote to Graham: 'Ngāi Tahu have [had] no strong visible relationship with conservation lands during European times. Their relationship to these lands before settlement is unprovable, and for much of the inland estate, appears minimal.'[26] FMC emphasised the subjective nature of Ngāi Tahu's historical claims, despite the undeniable archaeological proof of their continued and sustained use of the inland South Island.[27] FMC continued, 'Other NZers have fought and won the preservation of these lands. Their mana, including their desire to see these lands protected in perpetuity, deserves precedence.'[28] In late November 1993 the TV news show *Frontline* presented a programme about treaty settlement negotiations and the potential use of national parks. The programme sparked a flurry of letters from concerned New Zealanders, all of them opposing the use of any conservation land in a possible settlement. Many referred to the need to maintain the principle that New Zealanders were one people.[29]

In the 1993 annual report to the Ngai Tahu Maori Trust Board, O'Regan noted that Ngāi Tahu had become a particular focus of 'Green' and 'Public Access' lobbies. He noticed 'the marked contrast to the positions taken by the conservation lobbies in other countries with similar situations, such as Canada and Australia'. In this O'Regan was correct.[30] 'The positions adopted by the Green lobbies, in respect of National Parks, pastoral leases, Crown lands, coastlines and fisheries have been consistently hostile to Maori and generally bitter and hostile to Ngai Tahu. It is my belief that our own conservation ethics are generally superior to those adopted by the Pakeha cultural models.' O'Regan did recognise that Pākehā cultural models would be used and claimed that Ngāi Tahu had to face a large and daunting public relations challenge in combating the lobbies. 'For the moment, all I can say is that the political pressure of those lobbies has been a significant factor in slowing resolution of quite important issues.'[31]

In the midst of a constant stream of criticism of the negotiation process by most conservation groups there were a few examples of support from this sector. After the release of the first tribunal report in 1991, the North Canterbury Conservation Board had backed the return of Te Waihora (Lake Ellesmere) to Ngāi Tahu.[32] One letter of support seemed quite progressive but was in fact more of a realpolitik response to the challenges of using conservation land. In 1992 the conservation and environmental organisations Greenpeace New Zealand, the Maruia Society, Friends of the Earth and the Wellington Rainforest Action Group wrote a combined letter to Graham, which he then passed on to O'Regan:

> Genuine recognition of the Treaty of Waitangi and the claims which flow from it is a challenge that faces all NZ society, environmentalists or not. The principal challenge, of course, is to recognise the injustice of past action and the need to settle past grievances in a fair and just manner. The challenge specifically to conservationists and the environmental movement is to recognise that Maori are not merely another interest group to be consulted, but partners with the Crown through the Treaty. For example, it is for Maori, not the environmental movement, to decide what mechanism adequately recognises their mana under the Treaty. It means a recognition that where land has been unjustly confiscated or appropriated in the past, returning it to Maori is not a question of privatisation, but rather a question of returning it to its rightful owners.[33]

This type of thinking was the exception among New Zealand conservation groups in this early period of treaty settlements. Rather than a principled action by the progressive wing of a conservation group, this was a tactical letter. Its writers had decided that rather than directly tackling the government as FMC had, it was better to maintain the conversation with the government and also, if necessary, with Ngāi Tahu. Behind the scenes, some seemingly supportive conservation organisations continued to work to ensure that as little critical conservation land as possible was included and they were quite successful.[34]

CHAPTER 4

The negotiations begin

Ngāi Tahu's negotiations formally began in September 1991, seven months after the release of the Waitangi Tribunal's *Ngai Tahu Land Report*, and there were monthly meetings until the negotiations broke down in mid-1994. These were formal gatherings led by each side's main negotiator: Tipene O'Regan for Ngāi Tahu and Doug Graham for the Crown. The named claimant for Ngāi Tahu's Waitangi Tribunal claim, Rakiihia Tau Snr, was a co-negotiator. Other members of the A Team were Kuao Langsbury, Trevor Howse, Charles Crofts and Edward Ellison. Shortly before the Crown's settlement offer was received in September 1996 Rakiihia Tau Snr was replaced by his son, Rakiihia Tau Jnr. Gabrielle Huria also joined the A Team late in the negotiations. The A Team was mandated by the Ngai Tahu Maori Trust Board (and at the end of the negotiations, Te Rūnanga o Ngāi Tahu) to manage the negotiation process and negotiate directly with government ministers and resolve major negotiating differences. The B Team worked with and advised the A Team on all matters relating to the negotiations and dealt directly with high-level officials in various Crown departments and agencies including the Treaty of Waitangi Policy Unit/Office of Treaty Settlements, the Crown Law Office, Treasury, DOC and the Department of the Prime Minister and Cabinet. The B Team overall negotiating group included prominent lawyer Nick Davidson, from Bell Gully Buddle Weir, who became Ngāi Tahu's lead legal consultant when Paul Temm stepped aside after acting as lead counsel during the tribunal hearings.

Later in the negotiations, during the breakdown period, another lawyer from Bell Gully, Christopher Finlayson, led the litigation strategy.[1] Also appointed was commercial development consultant Stephen Jennings, an economist for Credit Suisse First Boston. He was aided by two other Credit Suisse consultants – Paul Baines, who replaced him in 1993, and Richard Meade. Sid Ashton, the secretary of the Ngāi Tahu Maori Trust Board since the mid-1970s, also played a major role,[2] as he had in Ngāi Tahu's Waitangi Tribunal hearings in the late 1980s. Anake Goodall was the claims manager and by the end of the negotiation was a key part of the final push to a settlement.

Later in the negotiation, as the two sides approached an agreement, a series of specialist C Teams carried out the detailed research and clause-by-clause negotiation of the various sections of the draft heads of agreement and deed of settlement. The C Team actively supported the B Team and was itself advised by kaumātua, kuia and many other tribal experts. The leaders of the various Cultural Redress teams (focused on the return of particular sites of cultural significance such as the Tītī Islands, Rarotoka Island and pounamu) included Diane Crengle, Justine Inns, Jan West and Sandra Cook. Te Maire Tau led the Apology/Historical Account team while Tony Sewell was the leader for the Economic Redress groups. A number of other advisers were used on a case-by-case basis to help each team.[3]

The Crown's A Team consisted of Graham and Secretary of Justice David Oughton. Their B Team was initially made up of a diverse array of officials from various government departments and headed by the Treaty of Waitangi Policy Unit.[4] Later, Prime Minister Jim Bolger would play a key part in restarting discussions. Dozens of officials would come and go during the negotiations; Graham was the only constant on the Crown's side.[5]

The first meeting was held in mid-September 1991. Both Graham and O'Regan began by making conciliatory statements. Graham attested to the loss suffered by Ngāi Tahu through the thoughtlessness of the Crown but also through documented and malevolent Crown action, which had restricted the extent of Ngāi Tahu reserves and kept the prices paid at a minimum. Graham claimed that anyone who grasped Ngāi Tahu's loss would understand that a substantial settlement was going to be necessary. He invited Ngāi Tahu to sit with him to discuss matters 'calmly and rationally so that, eventually, there could be an understanding that was not only satisfactory to Ngāi Tahu, but to all New Zealand'. Unless this understanding was reached, the negotiations would have achieved nothing. Unlike many other nationalities, New Zealanders possessed an innate fairness and Graham believed that, if accompanied by honesty and divine assistance, fairness would help to resolve the problems before the negotiating teams. This emphasis on the will of God and the 'fairness' of New Zealanders would reappear throughout Graham's negotiations. O'Regan, speaking for Ngāi Tahu, stated that any settlement would have to be endorsed by their rūnanga. He welcomed the Crown's commitment and indicated that establishing the legal personality of Ngāi Tahu was one of the most important things necessary to kick-start the negotiations. The iwi sought a settlement that comprised resources, land ownership, areas of shared management and some cash as 'a lubricant for the business of development'.[6]

At the second meeting of Crown and Ngāi Tahu negotiators, the agenda revealed the breadth of issues that faced the negotiating groups: pounamu, Whenua Hou, Rarotoka Island, legal personality, the Railcorp agreement, the Crown Tītī Islands, ancillary claims, draft framework agreement, Māwhera perpetual leases, a formal apology, the Greenstone Valley, Milford airport, Te Waihora and third-party interests. Marathon sessions lay ahead. Ngāi Tahu were concerned that various issues were being isolated and the overall view lost.[7] Both sides were anxious about the principles that would guide the negotiations. Ngāi Tahu noted the difference between 'loss' and 'settlement' and felt it was important that the public needed to understand the scale of the Ngāi Tahu loss and see any settlement in this light. It was vital to work from the principles of the tribunal's report and for the Crown to acknowledge the harm done in the past. It was important, too, to restore Ngāi Tahu to the position that they might have enjoyed had the treaty principles not been breached. At the end of the meeting there was a discussion of the advantages and disadvantages of a 'grand slam' approach to settlement, in which all items would be progressively resolved and assets held in a 'container' for delivery in a total package. This had some characteristics of the fiscal envelope policy that would be released in 1995. Ngāi Tahu had, however, identified several difficulties with this approach, including the holding costs to both parties and the unique nature of each treaty breach.

Although the iwi understood the danger of settling in a completely unsystematic manner, it wanted to ensure that all claims were properly addressed. Some issues needed to be dealt with urgently and could be resolved quickly; others could not.

A critical issue early in the negotiations was the privatisation of the Crown's forestry assets. Ultimately the compromise contained within the Crown Forest Assets Act 1989 enabled the Crown to retain the land on which its forests grew but to sell the right to grow the trees – Crown forest licences. The land would be returned when licences expired, a percentage of the rentals out of the licences would be set aside for use when the relevant claimant group settled and financial compensation would also be paid. Some of these rentals were also used to fund claimant research. While it protected some Māori interests in the forests, the act also enabled the continuing disposal of Crown forestry assets. Tipene O'Regan and Nick Davidson had been key negotiators for Ngāi Tahu in 1989 when the Crown Forestry Rental Trust was established, but it was soon clear that it would not be an adequate vehicle to protect Ngāi Tahu's interests in the Crown's forestry assets. From the beginning, Ngāi Tahu stressed that they wanted forestry assets as a part of their final settlement and that no further forests in the Ngāi Tahu rohe should be privatised. This proved to be a particularly difficult task for the Crown, especially since Ngāi Tahu's rohe encompassed nearly half of the total land mass of New Zealand.

Ngāi Tahu requested that the Crown halt the sale of NZ Timberlands, an SOE created by the Crown in 1987 when it disestablished the Forest Service and separated conservation from plantation forest, since 25 per cent of the company's forests were located in Ngāi Tahu's rohe. Treasury was concerned that if an exception were made for Ngāi Tahu it would set a precedent for other claimants. Treasury also pointed out that agreements with all Māori were very difficult initially and that Ngāi Tahu had already begun participating in the negotiations. They also claimed that halting the sale would reduce the potential cash flow to the Crown Forestry Rental Trust, and this income was available for all iwi to use in progressing claims on Crown forest land through the Waitangi Tribunal. Treasury's main worry was that a declaration of the validity of Ngāi Tahu's claim would deter investors from purchasing 100 per cent of the shares in NZ Timberlands, as the Crown wished. In addition, because Southland forests comprised a quarter of the value of the forests to be sold, removing them from sale would make it impossible to sell all the shares in the company.[8]

At a meeting about the sale of NZ Timberlands' South Island interests held on 22 January 1992, Ngāi Tahu reiterated their concern that some or all of the forests would be sold quickly after indicative bids were submitted in mid-February. They asked either that the Crown stop the sales process completely, which was not going to happen, or, more likely, that a compromise was achieved in which part of the sales could proceed but more than half would be placed in a land-bank. They did not consider that their interests were covered by the Crown Forest Assets legislation because it applied only to an actual or potential claim that was related to specific forested lands and in a pre-tribunal situation. Forest assets were so crucial as a viable asset base that Ngāi Tahu were willing to go to the High Court, where their senior counsel assured them they would win. They claimed that they wanted to avoid confrontation but could not do this without at least some kind of compromise. The Crown's response was to remind Ngāi Tahu that the asset sales were not within Treasury's remit, but government policy that would have to be changed at Cabinet level.[9]

It was clear that the discussion was not really about the Crown forests legislation but about how to take Ngāi Tahu's interests into account in the sales process. Were the Crown's actions in the asset sales programme consistent with their treaty obligations in the context of the tribunal's report? Although Ngāi Tahu did not question the intent of the Crown negotiators and the 'genuineness' of the minister's assurance, they looked 'historically at the past incapacity of the government to deliver on intent'. They felt that, if they did go to the High Court for an interim order to halt proceedings, this would frighten off potential purchasers, and that a resulting ruling would apply to every Crown asset in the South Island. They would rather be involved in economic growth. However, O'Regan had a mandate to do whatever he needed on this issue, given the centrality of forests to their aspirations. If the government had to choose between the 'icon' of the 'integrity' of the sales process, and the treaty partnership, it should opt for the latter. Without some kind of legal protection of Ngāi Tahu's interests, they would be forced to gain their own. As a final response, the Crown negotiators undertook to brief the relevant ministers, stressed that negotiations should be conducted in an atmosphere of trust and good faith and emphasised the importance of ministerial assurances.[10] However, internal Crown memoranda revealed that the overwhelming motivating factor was completing the sale. In the eyes of certain Crown officials, even if Ngāi Tahu were adamant that they sought ownership of Crown forests, the tribunal report did not state that forestry redress had to be provided.[11] In fact, Crown forestry assets would become the most common form of redress in future treaty settlements.

As was often the case, Graham and the policy unit officials were caught between the demands of Ngāi Tahu negotiators and of Treasury. The Crown was not willing to give Ngāi Tahu most of its forestry assets in the South Island. Treasury did little to improve matters when they informed Ngāi Tahu adviser Stephen Jennings that the Crown was planning to sell NZ Timberlands' South Island interests to one bidder. Jennings pleaded with Treasury officials to delay the sale. (Ironically, later in the decade Jennings oversaw the privatisation of whole swathes of the Russian economy.)[12] Eventually some forestry assets were set aside for Ngāi Tahu, but only after persistent lobbying from Jennings, O'Regan and Ashton.[13]

Although the discussions at that point were mainly about exotic forests, mostly pine, Ngāi Tahu negotiators also made it clear that they were seeking the return of all indigenous production forests in their rohe, particularly the Westland production forests. They sought to regain 'the mana in these forests and the land on which they stand; ownership of the land, and of the pounamu beneath the surface of the land, on which these forests stand; a primary role in developing and applying sustainable management policies for these forests and within [this] context, the right to harvest resources from these forests'. These indigenous forests were of economic and cultural importance, the last remnants of mahinga kai. Ngāi Tahu were interested in processing all forest products on the West Coast to reduce unemployment in the region. They had 'severe reservations' about the unsustainable management regimes then being used; they would seek to restrict production until the proper conservation values had been met, but would honour current production commitments. The iwi was also interested in developing tourism enterprises. 'We regard the return of the indigenous forests and land, and an assured role in the development and sanctioning of related resource use policies, as important not only to the achievement of Ngāi Tahu's direct economic and cultural objectives with regard to these forests, but also to their sustainability, to the benefit of the wider public, in the longer-term.'[14] This was strong evidence that Ngāi Tahu were keeping in mind both third-party and general public interests.

Although Ngāi Tahu's land-bank system regarding the disposal of Crown properties continued under the National government, other Crown assets remained open to privatisation. The National Maori Congress was negotiating with the Crown on behalf of all iwi over the ongoing privatisation of Railcorp land, but Ngāi Tahu asked to be kept separate from those negotiations.[15] They would negotiate their own arrangement with Railcorp by early 1992. As far as Electricorp was concerned, the Crown sought out various iwi opinions in late 1991, including those of O'Regan, who in this context was presenting his own views and not those of Ngāi Tahu. He met with Treasury and Treaty of Waitangi Policy Unit officials to discuss the matter.

Ngāi Tahu wanted to be a part of the future ownership of whatever privatised entity emerged from the structural changes planned for Electricorp. O'Regan maintained, though, that if the Crown 'reneges on the general assumption of the Tribunal Report, Ngāi Tahu might "relitigate" the "hole in the middle" argument, which it thinks it would win' and that this would have major ramifications for the central South Island's electricity generating capacity, as Ngāi Tahu would claim the whole central catchment back. Otherwise, the main Ngāi Tahu interest in the central South Island was mahinga kai; they were interested in a 'reservation' concept, which would later become the nohoanga entitlements. More generally, Ngāi Tahu wanted a place at the allocation table, not to own all the water used in the hydro dams outright. One Crown official described O'Regan's general approach as one of '"generous inclusion" in enterprises with the state (e.g. SOE shares) [to show their] pragmatism, but not a pragmatism which will sell out environmental quality'. The Crown did not privatise Electricorp until later in the decade and the issue did not remain pressing throughout the first few years of negotiations.[16]

The final formal meeting of 1991 took place in late November. There was still substantial goodwill and a positive momentum driving the negotiations. Both sides signed a short framework agreement to set the tone for the discussions. This accepted the main thrust of the tribunal report, and highlighted the need to negotiate in good faith, to have a just, equitable and durable settlement and to conduct negotiations in such a way that both they and the resolution of grievances enhanced the mana of Ngāi Tahu and restored the honour of the Crown. Most importantly, it stated that some parts of the settlement could be dealt with before others.[17] Ngāi Tahu stressed the necessity to begin work on the public relations campaign because they were already experiencing a substantial Pākehā backlash. O'Regan would meet with third-party interests before Christmas in Christchurch. Ngāi Tahu were also still waiting for information regarding DOC, Government Property Services and other Crown lands. Positions on the Crown Tītī Islands, Te Waihora and Wairewa were being developed and the Ministry of Commerce reported that it would be difficult to do anything about the abuse of pounamu licences other than instituting better enforcement. Ngāi Tahu wanted to ensure that Timberlands sales would cease until the completion of negotiations and expressed their specific interest in two forests. Ngāi Tahu discussed the concept of treaty title in relation to certain DOC lands such as Aoraki/Mount Cook and acquiring Central Otago high-country leases, but the Crown was quite hesitant. The one major problem, the lack of progress on reserves not awarded, would remain a substantial sticking point for the rest of the negotiations.[18]

The extent of financial compensation and lands contained in Ngāi Tahu's land-bank were also prominent issues between 1991 and 1994 and began to be addressed early on. The first significant matter for Ngāi Tahu, though, was the creation of a legal entity that would enable them to control their own affairs. The trust board structure was now seen as impinging on Ngāi Tahu's rangatiratanga, because it was accountable to the Crown rather than to the people and marae of the iwi.

CHAPTER 5

Establishing Te Rūnanga o Ngāi Tahu and rangatiratanga

As a precursor to a more robust legal personality, at a hui at Arowhenua in 1988 some members had advocated forming an incorporated society of rūnanga. By the end of 1989 an incorporated society, Te Rūnanganui o Tahu, had been established 'to protect, to advance, to develop and to unify the interests of Ngāi Tahu in the true spirit of tino rangatiratanga implicit in the Treaty of Waitangi'.[1] It operated separately from but in concert with the trust board.

In 1990 the Labour government passed the Rūnanga Iwi Act, which gave established tribal authorities extensive governing powers. It was soon repealed by the incoming National government, which claimed that because too many Māori had severed their connections with their respective iwi the tribal authorities would not be representative of the majority of Māoridom. Ngāi Tahu were firmly opposed to the repeal of the legislation, noting that it had given Māori some recognition of tino rangatiratanga; they believed that the Rūnanga Iwi Act should be amended. After the repeal of the act, the Waitangi Tribunal and the Court of Appeal noted the Crown's lack of recognition of a legal personality for Ngāi Tahu and that recognising this would go some way towards restoring the guarantee of tino rangatiratanga that was inherent in the signing of the treaty.[2] Ngāi Tahu wanted a legal personality in order to ensure full control of their own social and economic affairs following settlement. The previous Māori trust boards had been subservient to the Crown: the most recent board had been unable to spend even $200 without ministerial approval.[3] Ngāi Tahu wanted a rūnanga-based organisation in which Ngāi Tahu leaders would be accountable first and foremost to their rūnanga, marae and the whānau.

In a mid-1991 memorandum to Doug Graham, O'Regan also emphasised that a legal personality would address what he referred to as the Crown's oft-cited nightmare of successive Ngāi Tahu generations returning to reassert their claim. Ngāi Tahu's negotiations did not address the spirit or intent of their 1944 settlement. This may have been a result of the tribunal's finding that the 1944 settlement was very limited in its scope and terms of reference, and of the Crown's earlier experience with the issue during Waikato–Tainui's negotiations in 1989 and 1990.[4] If Ngāi Tahu had stronger control of its fate, the eventual settlement would be more final. Ngāi Tahu emphatically did not want to follow the problematic post-settlement situations that had developed internationally such as the for-profit corporations that had arisen out of the 1971 settlement for indigenous people in Alaska.[5]

A draft Ngāi Tahu Rangatiratanga Recognition Bill to recognise Ngāi Tahu's legal personality was sent to the negotiators on 8 November 1991 and reviewed by the Ngāi Tahu team, which recommended significant revisions. The Crown was obviously uncomfortable about the use of the term rangatiratanga: Manatū Māori officials had changed the name to the 'Ngāi Tahu Bill'. Nick Davidson explained that the title contained the term for a specific purpose, and that its meaning was both literal and necessary. The recitals, a condensed history of Ngāi Tahu's attempts to have its rangatiratanga recognised over the years, formed a key part of the legislation, placing it in its historical perspective, and the Crown had omitted them from the draft.[6]

In the next draft of the bill, Manatū Māori had still not reinstated rangatiratanga in the title, and gave no explanation for the omission. Davidson wrote to both the secretary of justice and Manatū Māori to say that the changes he had provided the week before were absolutely necessary. Some recitals had been reinserted, but they bore only a slight resemblance to those originally provided by Ngāi Tahu. Graham advised Manatū Māori that, although Ngāi Tahu continued to assert that the term rangatiratanga was necessary in the recitals, title and purpose of the bill, he had convinced them to agree subsequently that the term kāwanatanga should also be included, so that self-determination would be balanced by

Crown governance. A reference to Article 1 and Article 2 of the Treaty of Waitangi would then be the best vehicle for this.[7]

The Crown Law Office, too, was particularly concerned about the use of the term rangatiratanga. Throughout all of its court proceedings with Māori claimants the Crown had argued that the executive alone, and not the courts, could determine treaty policy. One official feared that if tino rangatiratanga were guaranteed to Ngāi Tahu within their rohe, they would challenge the Crown in the courts over the use and ownership of resources. In light of the recent court's support for some Māori claimants, Crown Law considered it best to oppose the use of the term rangatiratanga. It also noted that the tribunal had not recommended the Crown recognise Ngāi Tahu's rangatiratanga specifically through legislation. Although the Crown could, and at times did, ignore the Waitangi Tribunal's recommendations, it could also, when necessary, use these to its own advantage. Crown Law believed the establishment of a legal personality was possible without the use of the term rangatiratanga.[8]

Another Crown Law Office official also felt that Ngāi Tahu's proposed bill went far beyond what was needed to establish the iwi's legal personality. There were legal and constitutional implications in using the term rangatiratanga. A Crown affirmation of Ngāi Tahu's rangatiratanga could be interpreted by the courts as giving the iwi the right to regulate its own laws and justice system, which would create serious constitutional issues. She understood that the Crown should not be seen as imposing upon Ngāi Tahu in any way, but some accountability measures were required. Some government MPs had criticised the notion of the 'principles of the Treaty of Waitangi' and she thought that rangatiratanga would face even more opposition. At every monthly meeting until the end of 1991, Ngāi Tahu negotiators underlined that the inclusion of direct references to rangatiratanga was essential in their legal personality legislation, and especially the reference to Article 2 of the Treaty of Waitangi in te reo Māori.[9]

The Solicitor-General, John McGrath, was concerned about including a term such as rangatiratanga in legislation when the negotiating parties had not agreed on a definition of the word. With the support of Treaty of Waitangi Policy Unit officials, McGrath recommended that Crown and Māoridom consult, in a similar way to the treaty negotiations, to determine a proper definition. As one observer said, however, 'it must be noted that Ngāi Tahu's meaning of rangatiratanga may not accord with views held by other iwi'.[10]

After meeting with Graham on 4 December 1991, O'Regan sought to address the Crown's concerns about Ngāi Tahu's draft bill. Anxiety regarding 'justiciability [the limits on legal issues over which a court can exercise its judicial authority] and self-government' would be dealt with by deleting the first part of the bill's long title, which read: 'To recognise the tino rangatiratanga of Ngāi Tahu Whānui.' Also to be deleted would be one of the recitals, which stated that 'Ngāi Tahu asserts that its tino rangatiratanga resides in its papatipu rūnanga represented in Te Rūnanganui o Tahu Incorporated'. There must be no change, however, for the first two recitals, which stated that 'the tino rangatiratanga of Ngāi Tahu existed prior to Ngāi Tahu signing the Treaty of Waitangi in 1840' and 'the Treaty of Waitangi confirmed and guaranteed the tino rangatiratanga of Ngāi Tahu': they could not be deleted because Ngāi Tahu could not have signed the treaty if it did not hold tino rangatiratanga over the land and its people. O'Regan also pointed out that the Treaty of Waitangi confirmed and guaranteed the tino rangatiratanga by stating this in the Māori version. O'Regan also wondered whether a more 'bare bones' piece of legislation could address their legal personality or if there should be a deed between Ngāi Tahu and the Crown that acknowledged Ngāi Tahu's rangatiratanga outside Parliament and would therefore be non-justiciable. Graham told O'Regan that the legal personality bill would not be introduced to Parliament before the end of the year because the Crown needed to have discussions with Crown Law and Parliamentary Counsel.[11]

A special meeting was arranged for 10 February 1992 to focus on the development of Ngāi Tahu's legal personality legislation and specifically the term rangatiratanga. Nick Davidson thought he was showing up for a private gathering with, at most, one or two Crown Law Office officials, but instead he arrived, alone, to find a room full of Crown officials, including representatives from the recently established Te Puni Kōkiri, the Ministry of Māori Development. Davidson felt ambushed. In his view, the only negative reactions to Ngāi Tahu's proposals came from Te Puni Kōkiri, which repeatedly rejected the use of the term rangatiratanga, and not the Crown Law Office. Te Puni Kōkiri contended that there was no way to specifically define rangatiratanga, whereas Ngāi Tahu negotiators had stated that they would provide their own definition, which was not contingent on acceptance by all Māoridom. Later in the meeting, Te Puni Kōkiri emphasised, too, that Māori participation in conservation and management decisions should be kept to a minimum.[12] At the regular monthly meeting in March 1992 between the Crown and Ngāi Tahu, the CEO of Te Puni Kōkiri, Wira Gardiner, reported that, due to staff turnover at the ministry, little work had been done on Ngāi Tahu's legal personality legislation.[13] By the third and fourth draft, the bill did not contain a single reference to rangatiratanga.[14] It would be another four years until Parliament recognised Ngāi Tahu's legal personality. This delay stemmed largely from dissension within Ngāi Tahu and the stalling power of the parliamentary select committee process.

Although the first kanohi ki te kanohi (face-to-face) meeting of Ngāi Tahu's formal direct negotiations with the Crown only took place late in September 1991, the year had been marked by a heightened sense of urgency and activity following the February release of the tribunal report. Both Ngāi Tahu and the Crown were kept extremely busy considering its findings and implications for the negotiation. The Crown's asset sales also continued at a fast pace, as the government shifted from Labour to National, and Ngāi Tahu did all it could to maintain the Crown's asset base even before the direct negotiations began. The privatisation of airports, forests and power stations kept Ngāi Tahu on its toes. The potential inclusion of conservation lands in a future settlement also began to come to the fore in 1991. All these practical aspects of the negotiations would take somewhat of a backseat as 1992 began and negotiations moved to a much more conceptual level. Ngāi Tahu wanted to measure their quantifiable losses and compare them to any proposed settlement offered by the Crown. Perhaps more than any other issue in the entire negotiation, the economics of a Ngāi Tahu settlement would challenge negotiators from both sides.

CHAPTER 6

The economics of Ngāi Tahu's settlement

Central to the tensions that arose during the negotiations was the question of how the total value of the settlements would be ascertained and dealt with. Whereas the Crown initially took the view that the settlements of the 1940s only required updating in a financial sense because the annual payments had quickly eroded with inflation, negotiators for Ngāi Tahu believed that the amount returned to them had to reflect the estimated current value of what they had lost. Although they understood that full reimbursement was impossible, they believed that some rationalisation or formula was necessary. The negotiation established some of the basic ways in which the settlement would compensate for past loss, and the extent to which it was intended to improve Ngāi Tahu's socio-economic position, through better education and employment. Generally all New Zealand treaty settlements have been estimated as less than 1 per cent of the value of the assets that were improperly acquired.[1] For Ngāi Tahu, the question was whether the amount offered was sufficient to secure agreement to the Crown's requirement that treaty settlements be a full and final settlement of their historical claims. The Crown's focus was not only on limiting the amount made available, but on doing so in a way that set acceptable precedents for future settlements.

Ngāi Tahu's valuation studies arrived at various estimates for the value of the reserves that were never granted by the Crown during the land purchases of 1844–64. Each estimate was in the billions. In the first half of 1992 Ngāi Tahu continued to negotiate with the Crown about how their settlement should be valued. The Crown's position was based on the assumption that the settlements remained a political decision because it was impossible for treaty grievances to be fully compensated. This symbolised the dominance of the Crown's kāwanatanga over the rangatiratanga asserted by Ngāi Tahu. It was another settlement – the fisheries settlement, signed in September 1992 – that ultimately set the benchmark for the settlements with Ngāi Tahu (and with Waikato–Tainui). After the fisheries settlement, the Crown developed its policy for establishing the total sum available for all treaty settlements, which became known as the fiscal envelope. Later, after this policy was officially dropped, the Crown focused on using overall financial limits to determine how treaty settlements might be related to one other. As the term 'fiscal policy' was gradually phased out, the Crown began to refer to the financial redress available for a settling group as the quantum policy.

Not only did the amount set aside for the fisheries settlement become the maximum amount the Crown would offer for Ngāi Tahu (and Waikato–Tainui), but it would also become entrenched in the relativity clauses that established how these settlements would be related to future settlements. The quantification of loss and the development of the fiscal envelope policy were among the major questions addressed throughout the Ngāi Tahu negotiations.

Ngāi Tahu and the Crown began their negotiations with the intention of quickly arriving at a settlement. Because the Crown pressed Ngāi Tahu to make an opening proposal, the iwi commissioned considerable research to establish the value of the tribe's loss. The Crown did not believe that research was necessary, because of the political nature of the agreement, but agreed to consider the results of Ngāi Tahu's investigations. However, it continued its own research into the matter.

The working party on reserves not awarded canvassed the amount of land available to fulfil the notion of a tenth of the area sold. This was estimated at approximately 1.3 million hectares (3.4 million acres) but the amount of land available in the Crown's residual estate, the conservation estate, Crown assets like Railcorp, Crown-owned buildings of government departments and SOEs was less than 161,875 hectares

(400,000 acres), so other avenues would have to be investigated if the Crown were to accept the idea of tenths. (It refused to do so because it would be liable for sums it could not afford.) Interestingly enough, in this report the value, in 1991 dollars, of the remaining land noted above in Ngāi Tahu's rohe was approximately $170 million. That figure was reduced to 66 per cent, to cover assets that Ngāi Tahu would reject, approximately $100 million. This was the figure the Crown would stick to until negotiations broke down in late 1994. A Department of Survey and Land Information official recommended that more information be garnered from government departments, Crown agencies and SOEs regarding their assets in the Ngāi Tahu rohe to make up the shortfall because the amount of Crown lands and the conservation estate available was insufficient to provide for a well-balanced portfolio.[2]

Although the Waitangi Tribunal report was a thorough examination of Ngāi Tahu's claims against the Crown, in order to allow for a negotiated settlement it contained no specific recommendations for settling the iwi's economic loss. During the tribunal hearings Ngāi Tahu had argued that the Crown had promised to reserve a tenth of the land that was sold. The tribunal was unable to locate specific written evidence of this but nonetheless found that the Crown had breached treaty principles by providing insufficient reserves – approximately 9915 hectares (24,500 acres) out of a total of approximately 13,760,000 hectares (34 million acres), sold between 1844 and 1864. Although the tribunal did not specifically find that a tenth of the total land area sold by Ngāi Tahu should have been reserved for them, it did note that had 1,376,000 hectares (3.4 million acres) been reserved it 'would have been greatly to their advantage'.[3] It was on these findings that Ngāi Tahu based their negotiating principles. At the centre of these was establishing the value of their loss as the current value of one-tenth of the land sold. The main point of contention was whether the Crown had been obligated to provide this proportion for Ngāi Tahu's use. Internally Ngāi Tahu negotiators had calculated the value of 1,376,000 hectares (3.4 million acres) at approximately $1.3 billion. This figure was too high for the Crown and even what Ngāi Tahu perceived to be a significant compromise was rejected because the amount of compensation was still far too large. The Crown had opposed Ngāi Tahu's arguments on tenths during the tribunal hearings and they continued to do so during the negotiations.

Ngāi Tahu's case focused on the loss of property rights. They sought compensation for a number of grievances. The largest, economically, related to the difference between the reserves that were awarded, approximately 9915 hectares (24,500 acres) and those reserves that Ngāi Tahu argued should have been awarded, approximately 1,376,000 hectares (3.4 million acres). Ngāi Tahu also pointed to the significant gap between their expectations for payment at the time and the marginal amounts paid by the Crown, redress for insufficient health and educational endowments and restricted access to mahinga kai.[4] The iwi strove to establish a baseline for the value of its historical loss but this was difficult to do. Ngāi Tahu engaged Malcolm Hanna, a valuation consultant, to produce an assessment. His preliminary report found the total unimproved value of the eight land blocks was $13 billion in 1990 terms. In his following report on the principles and procedures for the assessment of compensation for land claims, he did not think the Crown would fall in with the idea of tenths. Ngāi Tahu could obtain the largest sum by using the Public Works Act to provide compensation for land not provided as reserves. Since this legislation applied to land that was taken by the Crown, Hanna recommended using the difference between reserves actually awarded and those Ngāi Tahu believed they should have been awarded to calculate the compensation. Hanna acknowledged that the Crown would not be likely to agree to that calculation.[5]

Although the negotiations overall were primarily conducted through Treaty of Waitangi Policy Unit officials, discussions about the quantification of Ngāi Tahu's loss were managed primarily by Treasury. Its role was to limit the fiscal impacts of treaty settlement on the financial state of the government as a whole.[6] Treasury concentrated on restoring the capacity of Ngāi Tahu on a 'needs' basis: it sought to determine how much compensation would be necessary to take the whole iwi out of poverty.[7] Ngāi Tahu felt their view on property rights was economically conservative because it did not take into account other factors like opportunity costs, but Treasury refused to recognise this rationale. Initially, Graham approved of some level of quantification, what was referred to during meetings and correspondence as the 'peg in the ground', but he continually stressed that Cabinet would be looking for a political decision on the total claim rather than examining and quantifying each grievance.

Treasury's focus on needs inevitably shifted the historical focus away from tenths and on to calculations of what 'needs' might actually represent. Treasury was interested in developing a demographic and socio-economic picture of Ngāi Tahu. O'Regan forwarded two limited studies, which were carried out 'before the worst effects of restructuring were visited on our people... Recent policy has substantially increased unemployment and disadvantage in housing, further education and health. As yet we have not fully documented these effects. We are still reeling from their impact.'[8] The neoliberal economic reforms of the mid- to late 1980s undertaken by the fourth Labour government continued under National in the 1990s. These increased Māori unemployment, and affected Māori involvement in both the economic and political spheres. As Cybele Locke has noted, the reforms were felt more harshly by Māori (and Pacific Islanders) than by Pākehā New Zealanders. In 1992 Māori unemployment was at 25.8 per cent while the Pākehā unemployment rate was 8.1 per cent.[9] O'Regan took the chance to show Treasury the historical continuity of dispossession that bound the current Ngāi Tahu generation to the grievances of the past.

Ngāi Tahu insisted on using a rights-based rather than a needs-based approach. As O'Regan put it, 'We could see the "Needs" argument coming some three years ago.' Other commentators have agreed. In the words of historian Michael Belgrave, Treasury 'emphasised the re-establishment of the tribal estate as the primary focus of settlements' and suggested that 'redress could be achieved relatively inexpensively'.[10] O'Regan had to hold discussions with Treasury to convince them that Ngāi Tahu had a large population. Under Treasury's proposed needs-based model, the more Ngāi Tahu people there were, the greater the compensation would be. In a bid to avoid fighting an unwinnable war over what Ngāi Tahu needs were, O'Regan recommended hiring a mutually acceptable person to define them.[11]

Discussions about the quantification of Ngāi Tahu's loss also continued within the Treaty of Waitangi Policy Unit.[12] Officials conceded that estimating the dimensions of the 'redress envelope' would be difficult. There was no clear-cut methodology for determining what would be appropriate.[13] One official attempted to bridge the gap between the Treasury and Ngāi Tahu positions by emphasising the need for restoration, drawing Cabinet's attention, in a memo, to the 1839 instructions from the Colonial Secretary, Lord Normanby, to Hobson, explicitly telling him not to enter into any contracts with Māori that would be injurious to them. The writer sought to restore Ngāi Tahu to the position it may have been in had treaty breaches not occurred, by 're-affirming it with an economic base and thus enhancing its rangatiratanga'.[14]

Treasury had some substantial criticisms of this approach, considering that it would 'imply the Crown aims to provide redress to a value equivalent to the estimated total loss incurred by Ngāi Tahu' when it 'has no accurate idea of the size of that loss or, indeed, whether it can be estimated on anything other than a highly subjective basis'. 'Because the order of magnitude is likely to be very large relative to the Crown's ability to pay', it would risk 'committing itself to achieve an unobtainable objective'.[15]

Despite Treasury's comments, Ngāi Tahu merely wanted an agreement with the Crown on the extent of their loss. Only then would it be possible to begin justifying whatever gap existed between the value of Ngāi Tahu's total loss and the compensation. By dismissing Ngāi Tahu's dollar estimation of its own loss as based on 'highly subjective ... historical research', Treasury attempted to cast doubt on both the severity and the veracity of Ngāi Tahu's deprivation.

Detailed economic analysis marked the investigation of the quantification of loss. As Jennings wrote to his Treasury counterpart, 'the objective of the exercise should be to calculate the value in present day terms of the reserves not awarded plus the cumulative foregone income over the period since reserves were denied'. One approach offered, for the lands that were not reserved, was adjusting for inflation to current values and adding an estimate of cumulative earnings, but this, as Jennings understated, would rely 'on a significant number of difficult-to-validate assumptions'. An alternative approach would begin by identifying the value of the land Ngāi Tahu would hold now if reserves had been awarded and held until that day.[16]

As O'Regan commented to other Ngāi Tahu negotiators and advisers in October 1991, 'We are establishing a Rights base and the Crown is trying to establish a Needs base. We're avoiding population arguments and relying very much on the "present and future needs of Ngāi Tahu" line that the Tribunal developed. At the moment we don't think they can escape "10ths across the board".'[17] It was within the context of these 'rights' versus 'needs' debates that Ngāi Tahu made its first formal settlement proposal to the Crown.

The first meeting of 1992, on 4 February, reflected the concerns Ngāi Tahu had expressed as 1991 ended. Both parties began with the usual pleasantries about mutual goodwill and full-time commitment, but Ngāi Tahu remained very concerned with the sale of state and forestry assets in its rohe. A definition of pounamu had yet to be made and there were still options to sort through for the Crown Tītī Islands, Whenua Hou, Rarotoka Island, ancillary claims and mahinga kai. The Crown expressed its own concern at the measures of benefit to Ngāi Tahu individuals from the transfer of large state assets but Ngāi Tahu countered that they wanted to make sure any package would consider the maximum in job creation. As O'Regan said, 'Cabinet will have to see Ngāi Tahu are trying to reinforce their economic base and be confident that individuals will benefit.' Public relations were still stalled. Consultation with third-party interests had also begun and DOC had held two meetings with non-government organisations. Discussions about Whenua Hou had been encouraging and positive but there was caution about the proposal that would vest the entire Arahura catchment in Ngāi Tahu. The main areas of anxiety were conservation and access, which they felt would be ensured only under Crown ownership. They would prefer that SOE land be used as compensation rather than Crown land and assets. Ngāi Tahu confirmed that public access and conservation values would be maintained. Perhaps most ominously there was yet to be an agreement on the amount of reparation.[18]

Both sides continued to disagree over the basis for establishing financial redress. Ngāi Tahu felt that 'a needs-based solution would be more expensive to the Crown than a rights-based solution'. Although the Crown was generally uncomfortable with a valuation of Ngāi Tahu's loss, at this meeting Graham 'felt agreement was required as to what Ngāi Tahu have lost and advised that a prima facie position was probably all that was needed'.[19] These statements reflected the continuing emphasis that Ngāi Tahu placed on its rights-based solution, and the Crown's continuing hesitancy about estimating the value of the lands Ngāi Tahu had not been awarded in the mid-1800s.

Early in 1992 Graham asked that Ngāi Tahu provide a written proposal to the Crown that detailed Ngāi Tahu's preferences for settlement. Stephen Jennings suggested to Ngāi Tahu the different ways the proposal could be presented:

> We all agree that we need to vigorously resist Treasury's approach. At the same time, however, we must recognise that Treasury's advice to the Minister of Finance will have a major bearing on the Crown's final position regarding the reserves not awarded component of the settlement. It is important, therefore, that we monitor Treasury's needs-based work and try (behind the scenes) to influence the direction of that work. We should also provide Treasury with data they require where this will assist our ultimate end (e.g. data which increases the measured size of Ngāi Tahu).

Jennings was essentially advocating the control of the flow of information on which Treasury might base its calculations of Ngāi Tahu's needs. This would have included demographic data that detailed the population and incomes of Ngāi Tahu members. Jennings had worked for Treasury during the 1980s and may have believed that he could personally persuade officials. He pointed out, too, that Treasury's needs-based approach could result in a larger settlement than a rights-based approach if the benchmarks were tied to mean or median community income levels. A settlement of '$1.5 billion would be required to provide an annual per capita gain of $1,500 to 60,000 Ngāi Tahu, assuming a 6 percent after tax return on the total asset base received'. Treasury's attitude towards a settlement would also be influenced by their perception of Ngāi Tahu's financial accountability. But where to begin the bidding? $1.3 billion was the most conservative estimate established by Ngāi Tahu's valuation studies and Jennings recommended that figure as the opening bid.[20]

Ngāi Tahu made their settlement proposal in a letter from O'Regan to Graham on 7 February 1992. Seeking $1.3 billion as compensation for all of their claims, they stated that their approach to settlement was based on principles set out in the tribunal report that the 'Crown acted unconscionably and in repeated breach of the Treaty of Waitangi …

The tribe is clearly entitled to a very substantial redress from the Crown [whose] obligation to effect redress in this case is indeed a heavy one.' O'Regan also noted that the remaining lands in the Crown's possession would not provide Ngāi Tahu with an economic base, even if such a transfer were possible. O'Regan couched his statement in the language of the needs-based solutions that Treasury advocated, claiming that to achieve a final and durable settlement, the 'size and composition of the assets package will need to be such that the overriding objective of restoring Ngāi Tahu economic health and self-sufficiency is achieved'. The $1.3 billion was a 'very conservative valuation approach, based on current land values within Ngāi Tahu's rohe'. The capital value of the reserves that were not awarded was far larger since it included both the land and all the improvements such as buildings, farms, stock and crops. Because compensation of that magnitude would not be possible, Ngāi Tahu were requesting only the land value of the unawarded reserves. To make up the $1.3 billion settlement, the iwi envisioned having a diverse range of Crown assets such as forestry cutting rights and land, commercial property owned by the Crown, properties already in their land-bank, Landcorp land, SOE shares, Housing Corporation properties and mortgages, indigenous forests, coal mining licences, Crown pastoral leases and any remaining compensation as cash. Ngāi Tahu were also interested in purchasing shares in SOEs if they were privatised in the future, such as The Power Company Limited or Trans Power. The land owned by these SOEs was covered by the 1988 Treaty of Waitangi (State Enterprises) Act, but if the entire business was privatised or even partially privatised, as Mighty River Power would be in 2012, Ngāi Tahu were interested in purchasing shares. O'Regan said that Ngāi Tahu were willing to discuss any payment deferral mechanisms to accommodate the Crown's fiscal limitations.[21]

The Crown disagreed with the entire Ngāi Tahu proposal. An internal Crown memorandum signed by the justice secretary, but presumably with heavy Treasury input, said that the iwi's calculations had 'some serious limitations in terms of providing a practical basis for a settlement'. There was 'no objective way of establishing the extent to which the estimated current value of the reserves not awarded would have been similar if the land had been retained by Ngāi Tahu, instead of being developed by others'. Although estimating the value of the unawarded reserves was a difficult task, the Crown could have tried to average out the value of land and identify the value of areas where substantial Ngāi Tahu kāinga and mahinga kai sites existed. The estimated current market value of those lands would have been hard to calculate, but a lower baseline value could have been established to determine the least that the lands could have been worth without any development such as farming or housing subdivisions. Finally, the memo claimed that Ngāi Tahu's valuation of their loss 'takes no account of the value of any government assistance provided over the years specifically to assist Ngāi Tahu or Māori people' and 'some of the betterment of the original land that should have been reserved for the tribe, has been distributed indirectly to the tribe as a member of the various local communities which have benefited from the development of former Ngāi Tahu land'. From the Crown's point of view it was fiscally impossible to provide Ngāi Tahu with assets totalling $1.3 billion.[22] Ngāi Tahu's focus on the valuation of their loss was understandable, and whānau and marae had demanded a rationalisation regarding their settlement, but the Crown had to be realistic about what it could allow in terms of both the immediate financial consequences for its own balance sheets, and the precedent effect that such a large settlement could have. There had to be a compromise between the two positions.

On 11 February, only days after Ngāi Tahu's proposal was submitted, the two sides met for a formal negotiation session. Graham stated that the Crown could not provide $1.3 billion, and proposed $100 million. Ngāi Tahu rejected this offer. Graham insisted that there was no precedent for such negotiations and the tribunal's report had been rather vague regarding an economic base. 'Ngāi Tahu,' he said, 'have been deprived of opportunity and this now has to be corrected. To quantify this is extremely difficult.' A settlement would have to be reached that the Crown, Ngāi Tahu and the people of New Zealand believed was fair. Some compensation was necessary, but the practical and economic impact of the settlement on the country as a whole had to be taken into account:

> The Crown wishes to negotiate a figure which it believes is fair and will allow Ngāi Tahu the opportunity to develop in a productive stage and out of grievance mode. Ngāi Tahu has put forward a figure of $1.3 billion, which is said to be an understatement of the loss, but is beyond the Government's ability to pay. Combined wisdom is required

to reach a figure which may be based on nothing more than an inside feeling that it is fair ... There is concern as to what the Crown can do to restore its own honour and enhance Ngāi Tahu's mana so it has a base on which to build.

The Crown's response was reasonable. Ngāi Tahu responded that they were haunted by previous governments that had refused to deal with the claim. They were concerned that the guilty party, the Crown, was acting in the role of the judge: this sentiment would recur throughout the negotiations. Then there was the durability of what Ngāi Tahu perceived to be the Crown's financially limited settlement offer. Their 1944 settlement was also meant to be durable, but it was inadequate even before it was devalued by inflation. As a result, Ngāi Tahu remained cautious about the size of the Crown's offer.[23]

In a letter to Graham the day after the meeting, O'Regan said that the Crown's $100 million package was substantially below Ngāi Tahu's 'most reasonable expectations... We continue to believe that achieving the durability sought both by Ngāi Tahu and the Crown will depend on the adoption of a principled approach, based on the findings of the Waitangi Tribunal on "Reserves not Awarded" and linked to a mutually accepted valuation of Ngāi Tahu's loss.' In light of the significant gap between Ngāi Tahu and the Crown, the iwi would devote considerable effort to finding a level that would suit both parties, but warned that it still intended 'to review that identification against Ngāi Tahu's losses before making a formal response to your proposal'.[24]

According to Nick Davidson, he was told by a DOC official that the $100 million offer originated solely from Treasury. 'He seemed to indicate that we were about $350 million apart. He said that the Crown's initial offer of $100 million had not been at all well-handled. According to him the number had been dreamt up by Treasury. I had always tended to the view that it was a Doug Graham number.' When asked during a Cabinet committee meeting how the $100 million figure had been arrived at, a Treasury official had refused to provide an explanation. Finance Minister Ruth Richardson then allegedly became frustrated at the increased level of scrutiny. In the view of the DOC official, 'the episode in the Cabinet committee had been quite damaging to the Crown's internal processes. He put the blame at Treasury's doorstep.'[25]

Davidson later commented to the Ngāi Tahu negotiating team that Graham was also critical of Treasury:

> I felt that the tone of [Graham's] reference to [Treasury officials] was less than glowing. He then went into a diatribe about hordes of people carrying out complicated calculations and statistical analyses in order to reach doubtful conclusions about how much money it would take to restore the wellbeing of any individual. He thought that these sorts of exercises tended to do nothing but produce a figure which was in capital terms so excessive that it was irrelevant. At the end of the day, he said, it came down to the art of the politically possible.[26]

O'Regan wrote to Graham again on 27 February to make another proposal that would take into account the economic and fiscal constraints faced by the government. However, to ensure finality and durability, a substantial sum would still be required.[27] Ngāi Tahu's new proposal halved the $1.3 billion proposal to approximately $560 million in the same diverse set of assets as before. O'Regan struggled to understand why Ngāi Tahu were forced to bear the burden of New Zealand's 'unsatisfactory economic performance over the last 20 years' after the Crown had accepted most of the iwi's grievances. He alluded to the challenges of negotiating a treaty settlement given that New Zealand's economy had struggled since the 1970s,[28] but he believed that the Crown was forcing Ngāi Tahu to share 'a disproportionate burden of these economic costs' on top of the suffering experienced by individual tribal members from the neoliberal restructuring of the 1980s and 1990s. If Ngāi Tahu were being forced to bear the costs of New Zealand's economic situation, O'Regan also wanted them to gain from any future economic improvement. He suggested that the sum that Ngāi Tahu were paid yearly by the Crown would depend on New Zealand's gross domestic product (GDP) growth relative to the mean Organisation of Economic Cooperation and Development (OECD) GDP growth. There would be no payment if New Zealand's annual GDP growth was less than 40 per cent of the OECD rate; $50 million would be paid if New Zealand's GDP growth exceeded the OECD's. The new Ngāi Tahu offer entailed major concessions while recognising the Crown's economic constraints, but could still prove final and durable.[29] Ngāi Tahu negotiators never received a written response to either of their February 1992 proposals.[30]

Until June that year, Ngāi Tahu and Crown negotiators argued over the reliability of Ngāi Tahu's estimates of its historical loss. A Crown-appointed valuer from Valuation New Zealand investigated the value of the reserves that were not awarded,[31] but the exercise was marked by ongoing disagreements on the relative reliability of information sources and the methodology used to arrive at an estimate.[32] For the Ngāi Tahu valuation expert, some of the key components focused on trying to establish land values at the time of purchase, the influence of wool prices and the presence of gold mining.[33] The Valuation New Zealand expert wanted to minimise the number of contextual factors and downplayed the low prices the Crown paid for Ngāi Tahu land.[34] The Crown generally ignored the results of the investigation, which arrived at a value of Ngāi Tahu loss set in the billions.

The different positions of Ngāi Tahu and the Crown were set out in correspondence between O'Regan and Graham in April 1992. On the 15th Graham said that the Crown had been asked to respond to Ngāi Tahu's letters of 7 and 27 February, but held that these 'do not in fact set out how the compensation referred to in them has been quantified or the methodology used. It must be apparent to all parties that not only is that a difficult issue in itself but the contribution any methodology might make to a justification of a final settlement package is questionable.' Whatever methodology was used would most likely provide 'little more than a guideline', especially 'when the package is likely to involve non-monetary considerations such as the restoration of Rangatiratanga or the cultural and spiritual aspects such as the mountain tops. Thus the contribution to an economic base is only part of the whole. It is the whole package which the Crown believes needs to be weighed in this balance and found to be fair and, therefore, durable...' Graham thought that 'endless research and analysis' on numbers of Ngāi Tahu whānui 'may well be of little help when set against the ability of the Crown to require predominantly this generation to carry the burden of the settlement taking into account that the cause of action was not of its making.'[35]

This position exasperated O'Regan, as it may well have done any tribal leader attempting to negotiate. He defended the need for an agreed valuation methodology when arriving at a suitable and agreed figure for compensation. It was necessary to derive a measure of Ngāi Tahu's loss, and to the number of Ngāi Tahu for whom the settlement would need to cater. 'In taking a settlement to our people the Ngāi Tahu negotiators need to be able to explain how that settlement compares with the loss that Ngāi Tahu has suffered; that is, on the size of the concession that they are making in accepting any given settlement... Similarly, we assume that the Crown's ability to explain and justify any settlement to the wider public will be enhanced if the Crown can illustrate its relation to a sound analytical assessment of loss and/or of a sustainable economic base for Ngāi Tahu.'[36]

In June 1992 the Treaty of Waitangi Policy Unit attempted to put together an offer that doubled the $100 million settlement, but Treasury offered little support. Both the policy unit and Te Puni Kōkiri agreed with a paper commissioned by the unit from economist Brian Easton, which found that the new offer would help Ngāi Tahu to solidify an economic base. Easton argued that any economic liabilities would be counteracted by increased investment, which would mean more jobs for the South Island. Treasury, however, argued that the new package would not represent 'a durable or equitable' settlement. It noted that, in the past, settlements had not proved full and final, but neglected to say that this may have been because the Crown was unwilling to provide any substantial compensation and because Ngāi Tahu's 1944 settlement had been largely perceived as imposed.[37] Treasury questioned how Ngāi Tahu were going to distribute their compensation, what the socio-economic status of the community was relative to the rest of the Māori population and why the assets Ngāi Tahu would receive in the fisheries settlement were not included in the assessment. In the cover letter to Graham, policy unit officials expressed some frustration at Treasury's observations. It was, they said, far from clear how the fisheries settlement would be distributed (it had not yet been finalised) and that Ngāi Tahu's fisheries claims were completely separate from these land-based claims. They wrote that 'on a preliminary view Treasury's arguments re durability mean in the final analysis that in their eyes a settlement is impossible'. The Cabinet Strategy Committee took Treasury's advice and rejected the $200 million proposal.[38]

On 21 September 1992, Cabinet agreed to the establishment of a Treaty of Waitangi Settlement Fund and set an undefined cap on the total amount of money available for all treaty settlements.[39] The pan-Māori fisheries settlement, often referred to as the Sealord Deal, was signed two days later on 23 September 1992. Although Māori had been guaranteed their lands, forests and fisheries under the treaty, their control was greatly reduced over the years as commercial fisheries were legally regulated. Māori made various claims to resolve this grievance and in 1989 an interim agreement was reached, stemming from the implementation of the new quota-based commercial fisheries system introduced by the fourth Labour government. The second part of the deal, in 1992, marked full and final settlement of Māori commercial sea fishing claims under the treaty. It was confirmed in December that year with the passing of the Treaty of Waitangi (Fisheries Claims) Settlement Act. Coupled with the interim $20 million fisheries settlement of 1989, the settlement was worth a total of $170 million. This amount would be deducted from the settlement fund (although the size of the fund would not be decided until December 1994).[40] The $170 million figure would become the upper limit benchmark for treaty settlements. Following the signing of the fisheries settlement, that amount began to appear in the minutes of meetings between the Treaty of Waitangi Policy Unit and Ngāi Tahu advisers (and with their Waikato–Tainui equivalents).[41]

The negotiations had effectively stalled following Cabinet's rejection of the enlarged offer, and the Crown and Ngāi Tahu remained far apart on the size of the settlement. The Crown had refused to respond to Ngāi Tahu's 27 February paper and it rejected a position paper in late June. Ngāi Tahu felt that this denied both the findings of the tribunal report and of the joint valuation exercise undertaken in the first half of 1992. Subsequently, they began exploring other avenues of compensation, namely mandatory orders under the Crown Forest Assets Act, as well as common law action regarding the Banks Peninsula purchases. They felt the research undertaken for the tribunal report had revealed new information that was vivid proof of 'unconscionable, coercive, and constituted equitable fraud' in the acquisition of Banks Peninsula. It was estimated that approximately $310 million of compensation could be garnered from common law action. Ngāi Tahu's legal advisers had also advised that the iwi would be able to benefit from a tribunal recommendation to revert all Crown forest licensed land to Ngāi Tahu. This was estimated to be worth $350 million. As an internal Ngāi Tahu memorandum noted, it was 'considered appropriate' to bring both these matters to the Crown's attention again, 'not as a direct threat or veiled threat, but in order that [it was] aware of avenues which are open to Ngāi Tahu in the unfortunate event of a negotiated settlement not being concluded.' And the negotiators could not ignore the combined figure of $660 million, which was based on 'detailed research and stringent analysis' by the legal advisers.[42]

Ngāi Tahu eventually became so frustrated at having to spend inordinate amounts of time halting the sale of state assets, and specifically the Crown exotic forests, that it informed the Crown in July 1992 that it would soon be ready to file proceedings in the Waitangi Tribunal or the High Court regarding all Crown forest land remaining in its rohe, as well as the alleged unlawful purchase of Banks Peninsula. Graham requested Crown Law's advice on Ngāi Tahu's chances in court. One Crown Law official commented that he could not be sure of the accuracy of Ngāi Tahu's $350 million valuation of the forests. Another opinion, given to Treasury in July 1992, said there could be no way of definitely predicting whether Ngāi Tahu's application to the court or the tribunal would be successful. The solicitor-general believed they were bluffing; if they were so sure of their case, they should present their evidence. Crown Law's final comment was that 'it may be time to consider whether if Ngāi Tahu declines this invitation they should be advised that on this issue they have cried "wolf" too often and that the Crown is prepared to have these matters dealt with either before the Tribunal or the Courts'. A member of the Treaty of Waitangi Policy Unit thought that Ngāi Tahu stood a 'better than even chance of succeeding should the matter go to Court'. However, she noted, once the remedies claim reached the tribunal for determination, the Crown could try to make submissions on quantification, 'and it then becomes anyone's guess'.[43]

Graham and his officials did not even want Ngāi Tahu to take the forum for discussion back to the tribunal, much less the courts. The Crown opposed such action because the tribunal would have to make binding orders for the Crown to return the forests and provide additional financial compensation as set out under the Crown Forest Assets Act. The tribunal seemed to want no part of the decision relating to the settlement amount, and Graham and his officials wanted to avoid returning to the tribunal because it would indicate to other claimants and the public that the negotiations were failing. They knew, too, that the tribunal could only generally advise the government. If it had used its mandatory powers of resumption, the government would have presumably legislated those away. After the rejection of both their settlement proposals, Ngāi Tahu were eager to return to the tribunal.[44] When Graham edited the minutes of a late October 1992 meeting he erased some key aspects of Ngāi Tahu's frustration with agencies and the process. Ngāi Tahu had wanted the minutes to record that 'there has been a serious breakdown in communications between the Landcorp chairperson and the Board, which is affecting Landcorp's operation'.[45] Although 1992 had been incredibly busy for Ngāi Tahu negotiators, by the end of the year they seemed no closer to settlement.

CHAPTER 7

The gradual breakdown of 1992–94

The gradual breakdown of Ngāi Tahu's negotiations with the Crown began in early 1992 when the two sides could not even come close to an agreement on the financial scope of the settlement, and spread over two years as both sides tried to remain in direct negotiation. It was felt that discussions, no matter how acrimonious, were better than adversarial litigious relations. The challenges that led to the collapse of the settlement negotiation were embodied in three different forms: the Crown's internal development of Treaty of Waitangi settlement policy, third-party interests slowing down the resolution of conservation-related redress, and debate from within Ngāi Tahu about the mandate of the negotiating team and the structure of the future tribal organisation, Te Rūnanga o Ngāi Tahu.

The idea of an overall fiscal limit for all settlements which, as we have seen, first appeared in a Cabinet paper two days before the signing of the fisheries settlement, had always been significant for the Crown because of the financial impact treaty settlements could have on the whole country. Graham had formally introduced Ngāi Tahu to the fiscal envelope concept at an intense weekend negotiating session held in Wellington in early August 1992 to break the deadlock that had developed over the quantification issues. There was no support from Ngāi Tahu negotiators.[1] Following the fisheries settlement in September, the Crown embarked on a two-year internal development of a treaty settlement policy. After mid-1992 there was very little for the Crown and Ngāi Tahu to negotiate and the monthly meetings became repetitive. As one Ngāi Tahu adviser quipped in February 1993, 'It was apparent that ToWPU [Treaty of Waitangi Policy Unit] is virtually defunct in relation to our negotiation, other than as a means of co-ordinating the Crown Team to attend meetings. (What meetings?).' Another adviser described the discussions with Graham as 'prayer meetings'.[2]

Nearly a year after Ngāi Tahu sent their first proposal to the Crown, O'Regan wrote to Graham in early February 1993 expressing disappointment with the pace of negotiations and the lack of agreement, and essentially offering that same proposal again. He also conveyed Ngāi Tahu's objection to the envelope approach the Crown was developing to settle treaty claims. Graham had begun the negotiations by stating that he did not want to engage in a sort of 'Dutch auction'. O'Regan accused both the minister and the Crown of creating a negotiation process that was far worse: he called it a 'lolly scramble'. In O'Regan's view the Crown was forcing Māori into conflict with each other by pitting iwi against iwi for the limited overall financial compensation that was available. He also accused the Crown of assuming the same colonial positions as government officials Walter Mantell and James Mackay in the nineteenth century.[3] Although there was only a measured response to O'Regan's letter from Graham, Crown officials who had been working very hard to persuade ministers to be more generous were disappointed by Ngāi Tahu's allegations.[4] As O'Regan told the *New Zealand Herald*, although he did not believe that Graham had developed the fiscal envelope policy as a divide and conquer tactic, a distinction had to be made between the 'honourable motives of one individual Cabinet minister and the behaviour of the State machine'. Former Minister of Māori Affairs and fisheries co-negotiator Matiu Rata did not think that limits on compensation would ensure finality. As he pointed out, 'the package idea was referred to in the settlement deed of the Sealord fisheries claim, but the Government had not discussed it with Māori groups'.[5]

At a formal Ngāi Tahu–Crown negotiation session in late March 1993, the Crown explained that there was still work to be done on the envelope. According to the minutes, 'Ngāi Tahu again complained at the lack of consultation over the envelope concept and reminded the Crown of its Treaty obligations "actively to protect" Ngāi Tahu's interests.' The envelope might not be 'an effective tool for use in the settlement of claims, particularly if it is to include wāhi tapu and fiscally neutral matters. Consultation should take place if the envelope is to be more than an internal management mechanism for the Crown.'[6] Ngāi Tahu were generally concerned about the Crown's unilateral development of the envelope concept, but especially about the aspects that did not involve compensation. The Crown argued that developing the policy would have taken even longer if nationwide consultation with Māori had been required. Ngāi Tahu charged that since the policy was a tool for the settlement of claims, all iwi should be consulted regarding its development. The Ngāi Tahu negotiators were also under increasing pressure from their own constituency. In some ways Ngāi Tahu negotiators had dug themselves a hole by creating such high expectations for their members. Government policy cannot always be developed with the help of those it affects most, but in this case the completely internal process was particularly difficult for Māori negotiators.

The Crown's focus on policy development led to the cancellation of the May 1993 meeting, which annoyed the Ngāi Tahu negotiation team. There could be discussions about specific redress and conservation matters, but the Crown maintained that Cabinet was still analysing the fiscal issues related to settlements. In the first meeting of July the Crown stressed that Cabinet was making good progress on the envelope. They could only repeat this at the end of month meeting and right up to the 1993 election on 6 November. In October O'Regan told Graham that, since the Crown seemed to be dragging its feet on its own fiscal settlement policies, there were other non-fiscal matters that could be resolved in the meantime. Although Ngāi Tahu had previously eschewed partial settlements, they began warming to the idea once it became evident that a large and durable settlement was not imminent. Graham replied that if aspects of a partial settlement could be agreed on, he would endeavour to take such an offer to Cabinet as soon as possible after the election.[7] At the end of 1993, O'Regan's annual report to the Ngai Tahu Maori Trust Board summarised the recent difficulties the negotiating group had experienced with the Crown. 'The Crown's inability to make up its own mind about the issue of quantum on a basis which is even morally defensible, let alone financially defensible, has been a huge problem...' The one small note of optimism was that the improvement in the economy could favour a more reasonable fiscal approach by the Crown.[8]

In mid-February 1994 Graham and Māori Affairs Minister John Luxton held a hui in Rotorua to introduce the fiscal envelope policy to a large gathering of Māori leaders, but there was no press coverage. The Crown did not invite Ngāi Tahu, who learnt about the hui through other channels. In the end, trust board member Charles Crofts and secretary Sid Ashton were able to attend. Graham announced that the fiscal limit for treaty settlements would be $1 billion for all claims, including the fisheries settlements negotiated in 1989 and 1992. The envelope concept was a mechanism for the Crown's own fiscal management. It did not seek the agreement of Māori to either the idea or the total amount of compensation proposed. Nonetheless, the Crown did say that the envelope would need to be large enough to result in fair and durable settlements that would provide certainty to all parties. The settlements would also need to be fair between individual claimants and the Crown, and between claimants themselves. All Māori leaders who attended rejected the notion of a fiscal limit for treaty settlements.[9]

The Crown set aside the work commissioned by Ngāi Tahu to estimate the value of its loss. The fisheries settlement and the envelope policy would establish a new benchmark and set a fiscal cap, divorced from iwi estimates of loss. Waikato–Tainui would have to cope with the precedent of the fisheries settlement, and the gradual development of the envelope policy, just as Ngāi Tahu did. Like O'Regan, Waikato–Tainui chief negotiator Robert Mahuta was also a co-negotiator on behalf of Māori for the fisheries settlement.

With the big-picture economic issues stalled, Ngāi Tahu looked to other areas of the negotiation. The properties contained in Ngāi Tahu's land-bank, and all other land-banks, were generally restricted to Crown land. Early in the negotiation process, Ngāi Tahu expressed an interest in the purchase of a private asset, the Elfin Bay Station high-country pastoral lease on the shores of Whakatipu wai-māori (Lake Wakatipu). In May 1992 the lease was advertised for sale.[10] In June Ngāi Tahu requested the purchase of Elfin Bay Station and an adjoining high-country pastoral lease, Greenstone Station. The Crown agreed. At the time of purchase Ngāi Tahu expected the high-country pastoral leases to immediately be transferred to the Ngai Tahu Maori Trust Board. Ngāi Tahu raised the precedent of the transfer of the decommissioned army base at Hopuhopu near Ngāruawāhia to the Tainui Maori Trust Board in 1991, but the Crown maintained that the leases and Hopuhopu were different kinds of assets. As a result the leases would be placed in the land-bank and transferred upon settlement.[11]

As the Greenstone Station pastoral lease was being purchased by the Crown for inclusion in the Ngāi Tahu land-bank in June 1992, the minister of conservation sought to retire 4534 hectares (11,200 acres) into the conservation estate. Although Ngāi Tahu were hesitant, they agreed.[12] Despite Ngāi Tahu's support for increasing the conservation and recreation values at Greenstone Station by agreeing to the retirement of a large area to the DOC estate, several conservation and sports recreation groups continued to fear the iwi's motives. The Otago Fish and Game Council expressed its opposition to the transfer of the lease for Greenstone Station because of the potential negative implications for trout angling. The Otago Conservation Board charged that Ngāi Tahu would erode the conservation values of the area around the station.[13] The South Otago branch of the New Zealand Deerstalkers Association asked that the Crown purchase the entire Greenstone Station for recreational sports interests.[14] The Southland Fish and Game Council was more moderate, asking to be kept informed of developments in relation to recreational fishing access in the Southland section of Elfin Bay Station.[15] These third-party interests would play a significant role in delaying agreement on the return of the high-country leases, and all other conservation aspects of Ngāi Tahu's settlement negotiations.

In July 1992, following the inclusion of the Elfin Bay and Greenstone Station leases in the Ngāi Tahu land-bank, the Crown sought to have a $40 million cap placed on the total value of Crown properties in the land-bank. This coincided with the debates regarding the overall quantum of Ngāi Tahu's settlement that were explored in Chapter 6. Ngāi Tahu initially opposed the $40 million limit, but ultimately agreed to it.[16]

Then, in July 1992, Ngāi Tahu requested the purchase of Routeburn Station, a high-country pastoral lease adjacent to Elfin Bay and Greenstone.[17] The Crown made the purchase of Routeburn Station contingent on the reduction of the land-bank cap from $40 million to $35 million, and an undertaking from Ngāi Tahu that they would request no further private pastoral leases for the land-bank. Although Ngāi Tahu considered the Crown's request for the land-bank limit arbitrary, they again agreed.[18] In August 1992, the cap was reduced to $35 million and Routeburn Station was added to the land-bank.[19]

In October 1992 Treaty of Waitangi Policy Unit officials met representatives of two major sports recreation organisations, Hugh Barr, president of Federated Mountain Clubs (FMC), and Bryce Johnson, chairman of the New Zealand Fish and Game Council. There was, Barr said, great concern about the use of Greenstone Valley, Elfin Bay and Routeburn stations as treaty settlement redress. He wanted the government to recategorise the land making up the stations into three new categories: farming, conservation and recreational. Both Barr and Johnson sought an active role in consulting with DOC to determine the proportion of the new land categories within the three high-country stations. As one of the policy unit officials reported to his superiors, Barr and Johnson 'maintained that they did not want to interfere with the resolution of Ngāi Tahu's grievances where this concerns commercial interests. They do, however, want to have a chance to represent their constituents' interests (and what they see as the wider public interest).' The unit staff made it clear to Barr and Johnson that Ngāi Tahu had always insisted that they would not restrict public access to areas of conservation/recreation value. (It is important to note that there is generally no public access on pastoral leases.) They also pointed out that Ngāi Tahu were bound by the same public access provisions as previous lessees. Ngāi Tahu had a strong commitment to conservation principles and had wanted to set up joint management projects with the Crown to put these into effect.[20]

The officials recommended that Fish and Game and FMC write directly to DOC and the policy unit, explaining that they had undertaken assessment work on the areas in question, and that they wished to be part of consultation to determine which parts of the high-country leases in question the Crown would retain for conservation/recreation purposes and public access rights. Despite the Crown's assurances, however, Barr and Johnson remained sceptical of Ngāi Tahu's motivations.[21] Following the meeting, Johnson wrote to Graham asking that conservation and sports recreation organisations be consulted before any settlement offers were made to Ngāi Tahu.[22]

In July 1993, as a result of political pressure from conservation and sports recreation advocates both within and outside government, DOC produced a report that recommended the retirement of a large proportion of the three high-country pastoral leases into the conservation estate because they were high-value conservation lands and unsuitable for pastoral grazing. Ngāi Tahu were concerned that, after the retirement of 4534 hectares (11,200 acres) from Greenstone Station, further sections of the property would now be similarly affected. As the policy unit told Graham, DOC had removed 'discussion of certain options, namely conditional vesting of land title and unconditional vesting of land title ... from the draft of the report.' 'While this rewrite may suit the views of the NGOs, it may not suit those of iwi.'[23]

Ngāi Tahu felt that the pressure from DOC had undermined their aspirations for Greenstone Valley tourism development. In O'Regan's words, 'Ngāi Tahu appreciate the conservation values but not the proposals contained in the report. They are aware of the botanical values but are concerned that the protection of red tussock will damage the economic viability of the area; if so, they would require compensation.'[24] When he complained to Graham that Ngāi Tahu would not accept the three high-country pastoral leases unless they were a viable farming unit, the minister replied that the Crown had originally intended to transfer the lease to Ngāi Tahu but that conservation groups had to be consulted.[25] Despite the report, in 1993 and 1994 conservation and sports recreation interests continued to press the government over the use of the three high-country leases.

Although the Crown/Ngāi Tahu negotiations were at a standstill, to conservation and sports recreation organisations a settlement always seemed imminent. They continually highlighted the need for further consultation, no matter how much the Crown conferred with them – and from the evidence it seems there was wide consultation.[26] Among other organisations that were vocal in their opposition to the use of the high-country pastoral leases were Forest & Bird and Public Access

New Zealand. Graham spoke to members of the latter and corresponded with their director, Bruce Mason.[27] Ngāi Tahu had concerns about the effect that this group could have on the high-country pastoral leases aspect of any final settlement.[28]

Ngāi Tahu told the Crown that the public consultation process had been hijacked by special interest groups, but these made the same comments about Ngāi Tahu. In April 1992 Catherine (Cath) Wallace, chair of the umbrella group Environment and Conservation Organisations of New Zealand, specifically asked Graham that Ngāi Tahu not be present at future public consultation.[29] By 1994 Ngāi Tahu negotiators felt that a disproportionate amount of time at consultations was being given to speakers who opposed them.[30] Negotiator Edward Ellison asked Sid Ashton to investigate the alleged racist tendencies of the Otago Fish and Game Council because of their opposition to the transfer of the three high-country pastoral leases.[31] At the June 1994 negotiation meeting, Ngāi Tahu made known their strong reservations about the manner in which the North Canterbury and Southland Conservation Boards ran their public consultations; the iwi preferred that these be conducted by a body with 'less vested interest'.[32] When the negotiations broke down in late 1994, the three high-country leases remained in the land-bank.

Although the land-bank established in late 1989 and early 1990 was advantageous for Ngāi Tahu, its overall effectiveness was still limited nearly two years later. In late 1991 the iwi had told the Crown that in some cases it was pressured to release Crown land for alienation due to political and commercial pressure. An example was the surplus Railcorp lands at Christchurch Railway Station, which were proposed for commercial development. Ngāi Tahu's land-bank was also restricted to specific government departments and agencies such as the Department of Survey and Land Information, the Ministry of Transport, DOC, the Ministry of Education, the Ministry of Social Welfare, and Landcorp. Ngāi Tahu wanted an early warning system for all Crown land and other assets in the Ngāi Tahu rohe. The Crown responded by creating, and making available, a database of all Crown lands and assets in the Ngāi Tahu rohe, but it was incomplete. Throughout its negotiations the iwi continued to press the Crown for further financial information regarding the land and assets it held. Historian Alan Ward has suggested that all treaty claimants were given limited information.[33]

The land-bank was also susceptible to subversion as a result of the offer-back procedures contained within the system. In one 1991 case a Survey and Land Information property was offered back to the original owners under Section 40 of the Public Works Act 1981, but the offer-back was refused. Shortly thereafter the original owners reversed their position, bought the property back and quickly sold it on to a private buyer. Ngāi Tahu believed there had been a 'measure of active collusion' involved in the transaction.[34]

By mid-1993 Ngāi Tahu were concerned that the Crown valuation of the properties offered for inclusion in the land-bank often differed significantly from the market values, to the detriment of the iwi. Ngāi Tahu sought an amendment to the land-bank system so that they could have input into the valuation of properties intended for transfer. They also wished to be involved in the management of land-bank properties, which were managed solely by Survey and Land Information until settlement and final transfer to the Crown.[35] The Crown left open the possibility of new mutually agreed valuations of land-bank properties upon settlement, but did not agree that Ngāi Tahu should be involved in management before transfer. It claimed that Ngāi Tahu's land-bank arrangements were superior to all others, and uniquely generous, because they were able to move properties in and out of their land-bank. As well, Ngāi Tahu could add any property in their rohe to their land-bank, whereas all other negotiating groups had to prove that the property they wanted had special importance.[36]

Ngāi Tahu's acquisition of the high-country pastoral leases was part of their claim to the 'hole in the middle', as was their pursuit of many other site-specific areas, such as the Arahura River. The Waitangi Tribunal had found that the Crown had breached the treaty by 'failing to meet the wishes of Ngāi Tahu to retain ownership of the pounamu in and adjacent to the Arahura and its tributaries', and had recommended that the river and all its tributaries be vested in the Māwhera Incorporation or another body nominated by Ngāi Tahu.[37] The Arahura Valley has traditionally been one of the iwi's principal sources of pounamu, representing power and survival and recognised as both a sacred object and a valuable commodity.[38] Despite the tribunal's recommendation, the process of vesting the Arahura was complicated by conservation interests both inside and outside government. The Crown and Ngāi Tahu had largely agreed that it would be more cost-efficient to identify the catchment area of the Arahura River and its tributaries and transfer that to the iwi, while ensuring the maintenance of conservation values and public access. But when DOC consulted with conservation groups, there was opposition based on anxiety about the preservation of conservation values and public access.[39]

After public consultation DOC, in an October 1992 report, recommended the establishment of a reserve governed by the Reserves Act 1977. Ngāi Tahu did not want this. As O'Regan suggested, it incorporated 'effective powers of confiscation'. He believed that:

> a formula governed by the Reserves Act which would make us tenants, subject to ejection under the current or future legislation, would be demeaning in the extreme and is quite inappropriate. It is our belief that the Tribunal recommendation to return the title, which is itself a reflection of the importance placed by the Tribunal on this taoka,[40] can be achieved at the same time as providing for the Crown's objectives of maintenance of conservation values and public rights of access. This issue lies at the heart of the restoration of the Crown's mana.[41]

By linking the Crown's mana to Ngāi Tahu's rangatiratanga, O'Regan was conveying their intimate connection under the Treaty of Waitangi and clarifying 'there could be few more tangible ways to confirm Ngāi Tahu's Tino Rangatiratanga' than by vesting the Arahura catchment in the iwi.[42] But DOC's reserve idea became entrenched by the Crown, and Ngāi Tahu remained opposed. In March 1993 they reaffirmed their desire for the river and its tributaries to be vested in the Māwhera Incorporation. The Crown maintained that the reserve status was the only option available.[43]

The Waitangi Tribunal also recommended a survey of the entire river and its tributaries. Once Ngāi Tahu and the Crown reached an impasse on the matter of vesting, Ngāi Tahu continued to request a survey of the area. When the Crown complained that the cost of this would be prohibitive, Ngāi Tahu responded that a survey would be unnecessary if the entire catchment were transferred to the Māwhera Incorporation as the Tribunal had recommended.[44] For the rest of 1993 and until the breakdown of the negotiations in November 1994, the opposing Crown and Ngāi Tahu positions on the Arahura River remained firm.

The Tītī Islands have been an important part of the Ngāi Tahu economy for centuries. The tītī or muttonbirds that were, and continue to be, harvested on the islands were not only a traditional food source but also a tradable commodity.[45] When Rakiura was sold in 1864, 18 of the closest neighbouring islands were reserved from the purchase for Ngāi Tahu. They became known as the beneficial Tītī Islands. The Crown took ownership of the remaining 18 islands, which became known as the Crown Tītī Islands. The Waitangi Tribunal found that the Crown should have reserved all of the islands near Rakiura, and recommended that 'beneficial ownership of the Crown Tītī Islands be vested in such persons or bodies as may be nominated by Ngāi Tahu and be subject to a similar management as the beneficial Tītī Islands'. Whenua Hou is the ancestral home of Rakiura Ngāi Tahu and was one of the original stopping-off places for southern Ngāi Tahu on their way to the Tītī Islands. During the tribunal hearings Rakiura Ngāi Tahu did not deny that Whenua Hou was included in the purchase of Rakiura, but they complained about being denied access to it. The tribunal recommended that 'subject to prior notification and to arrangements with conservation authorities, free access be available to Rakiura Māori to visit the island but consistent at all times with the security of wild-life'.[46] These two different sets of tribunal recommendations reflected the different forms of land-based redress that Ngāi Tahu and the Crown would develop together.

The return of the Crown Tītī Islands was one of the most integral aspects of the claim, especially for Rakiura Ngāi Tahu.[47] Although the Waitangi Tribunal had not recommended returning Whenua Hou to Ngāi

Tahu, O'Regan argued that its restitution would reaffirm the Crown's commitment to recognising the iwi's rangatiratanga. He wished to establish what he termed a 'joint title' approach in which the Crown and Ngāi Tahu would share title to important sites such as Whenua Hou.[48]

In late 1991, there was initially some limited support from DOC for the joint title approach, but only if Ngāi Tahu also agreed to co-manage the Crown Tītī Islands. But Ngāi Tahu's participation was limited to an advisory capacity, with DOC having primary control.[49] When the Crown consulted with third-party conservation organisations there was positive support for a Ngāi Tahu advisory role at Whenua Hou, but opposition to the joint title approach.[50] In June 1992 DOC formally proposed the establishment of a reserves board for Whenua Hou with a majority of the places on it kept for Rakiura Ngāi Tahu; Ngāi Tahu continued to push for joint title.[51]

O'Regan considered that this approach 'may well be relevant across a much wider spectrum of settlement within Ngāi Tahu's rohe. We believe the Australian and Canadian models in this area are instructive and find it difficult to understand why NZ should find it so difficult.'[52] (Ngāi Tahu used developments in Canada and Australia throughout the negotiations as precedents for recognising the rangatiratanga of indigenous groups, but the idea did not gain much traction with the Crown.) The Crown wanted Ngāi Tahu to have no more than an advisory role at the conservation board or reserves board level. In March 1993 O'Regan noted that Ngāi Tahu continued 'to be interested in the concept of shared title, for example, as for Ayers Rock [Uluru] in Australia',[53] and he tried to show that Ngāi Tahu were not trying to challenge DOC's role. 'In the case of the wider conservation estate this would not mean operational control or co-management as management is the business of the DoC. Ngāi Tahu would, however, seek control of the Ngāi Tahu cultural context, ie, names etc.' The Crown maintained that their co-management proposal for Whenua Hou was fully consistent with the tribunal's recommendations and that the concept of joint title would not be investigated further.[54]

Whenua Hou was not available for transfer or a joint title approach, but the Crown Tītī Islands were, though it was unclear how the transfer would be achieved. At first DOC proposed that the islands be co-managed by the Crown and Ngāi Tahu, but the iwi continued to seek fee-simple ownership as was the case with the beneficial Tītī Islands and rejected the concept.[55] The Crown then accepted that there would be a transfer. It envisioned Ngāi Tahu managing the Crown Tītī Islands in the same manner as it did the beneficial islands.[56] In large part, Ngāi Tahu and the Crown were in agreement regarding the vesting of the Crown Tītī Islands,[57] with the iwi asking only that they be vested without a marginal strip. From Ngāi Tahu's perspective, marginal strips were created when the Crown disposed of land, but returning land in a treaty settlement was a different matter. Many of the islands had steep seashore cliffs containing important tītī nesting sites which would be covered by the marginal strips. Ngāi Tahu also preferred the return of land without any Crown encumbrances. The Crown cautiously agreed to Ngāi Tahu's proposal but made it clear that the matter would have to be determined by public consultation.[58]

The Ngāi Tahu negotiators had developed a draft deed for the management structure that would govern the Tītī Islands,[59] and the Crown wanted to release this to another conservation organisation as well as the Southland Conservation Board and Forest & Bird. Ngāi Tahu were concerned that Forest & Bird would oppose the waiving of the marginal strip and derail the agreement, but the Crown felt that releasing the deed would allow it to allay any Forest & Bird concerns.[60]

The Crown's consultation with the Southland Conservation Board regarding the proposal for a reserves board at Whenua Hou and the transfer of freehold title to the Crown Tītī Islands proved partially successful: the board supported the proposals by a slim margin. Ngāi Tahu wanted to go ahead but Graham still required the minister of conservation's backing.[61] As the negotiations came to a halt in mid-1994, the two parties began to explore a possible interim settlement. Ngāi Tahu wanted to include Whenua Hou and the Crown Tītī Islands in the interim settlement, but the conservation minister was against this, citing the narrow support of the Southland Conservation Board. He was also concerned about the waiving of the marginal strip. The Crown refused to include either the Crown Tītī Islands or Whenua Hou in the November 1994 interim settlement (see Chapter 8) because it was still considering Ngāi Tahu's proposals for those two areas of redress. The Crown's position on Whenua Hou and the Crown Tītī Islands contributed to Ngāi Tahu's rejection of the interim settlement in late 1994, and the subsequent breakdown of the negotiations.[62]

—

The third major force leading to the breakdown of the negotiations was the steady internal opposition from dissident groups within Ngāi Tahu. This delayed the legal personality legislation for many years, but it also affected the overall negotiations, as the formerly rock-solid mandate was chipped away by continuing criticisms. This antipathy to the Ngāi Tahu negotiators started to manifest itself early in 1992. The Treaty of Waitangi Policy Unit began to receive letters from dissident groups within some West Coast and Southland hapū, identifying themselves as Ngāti Māmoe, Tuhuru and Waitaha, who claimed that the trust board had not involved them in discussions about developing a legal personality.[63] O'Regan was worried that, after all the trouble of fighting off external challenges, Ngāi Tahu would now have to combat challenges from within. 'I believe that the Government would run a mile from recognition of Ngāi Tahu if there was open internal dispute. Indeed, there is grave danger that a settlement could not be achieved by Ngāi Tahu with these parties rampaging through the process – leaving aside the legal personality legislation.'[64] Up to this point, the Crown had been negotiating with those they thought were the recognised leaders of the tribe. Now it began to state openly that it would negotiate only with the larger group, and that it was for the iwi to sort out its internal problems.[65]

The representative for the Tuhuru dissident group, Eli Weepu, contacted Graham and policy unit officials to request legal personality legislation for Ngāi Tahu on the West Coast as Tai Poutini Tangata Whenua.[66] Tuhuru had a competing view of rangatiratanga and believed that the Ngāi Tahu leadership had undermined their autonomy. They rejected Ngāi Tahu's mandate to negotiate for them.[67] But others from the West Coast were more supportive. At a meeting of Te Rūnanganui o Tahu at Takahanga Marae in Kaikōura in April 1992, Te Koeti Turanga, based in Westland, indicated that they supported the negotiators but that they wished ultimate authority to reside in Te Tai Poutini and not in Christchurch. O'Regan stressed that their assets needed to be held collectively to preserve their unified strength.[68] In August 1992 lawyers for Tuhuru notified the Ngai Tahu Maori Trust Board that they would be taking their case to the Maori Land Court to determine the issue of mana whenua on the West Coast. The court rejected their case.[69] Tuhuru then turned to the Waitangi Tribunal and requested an immediate hearing regarding the legal personality legislation, but their claim did not meet the criteria for urgency.[70]

Trust board representatives reported back to the iwi that the legal personality bill had been presented to hapū around the South Island and North Island at 10 hui and that, apart from some Ngāti Māmoe, Tuhuru and Waitaha critics, it had been well received.[71] The first hui was held in Hokitika but those Tuhuru opposed to the Ngāi Tahu negotiators did not appear.[72] At the Ngāi Tahu hui-ā-tau (annual meeting) held at Takahanga Marae in Kaikōura in November 1992, a large majority supported the introduction of the Te Runanga o Ngai Tahu Bill to Parliament.[73] The Crown's position on Tuhuru was that Ngāi Tahu negotiators had a mandate to negotiate, and they expressed their preference for meeting with them.[74] A policy unit paper prepared for Cabinet in early September 1992 sought permission to introduce legislation regarding Ngāi Tahu's legal personality, emphasising that this would give the Crown some certainty about who was negotiating, and a sense of finality to the settlement.[75]

The internal opposition that delayed agreement on Ngāi Tahu's legal personality was assisted by Ngāi Tahu MPs Sandra Lee and Whetu Tirikatene-Sullivan, who held up the legislation in Parliament.[76] Lee, who was the Auckland Central MP for the Alliance Party from 1993 to 2001, was affiliated to Ngāti Māmoe and Ngāi Tahu, but not involved in the trust board. Tirikatene-Sullivan, also of Ngāi Tahu, was a Labour MP who held the Southern Māori seat from 1967 to 1996. Her father, Sir Eruera Tirikatene, had been the main negotiator of the 1944 settlement negotiations. The vehement opposition of both women to O'Regan and the trust board was caused by a combination of personality clashes and differing leadership styles. Tirikatene-Sullivan sought to defend the legacy of her father's 1940s negotiations, while Lee seemed to bristle at the neoliberal basis and corporate structure of settlement negotiations and the future management of settlement assets. O'Regan attempted to appeal to Tirikatene-Sullivan directly to support the legislation but she maintained her opposition for many years.[77]

O'Regan addressed the issue of legal personality in letters to Graham but there was little that the minister could do. He had introduced the legislation to Parliament but could not force it through on his own. In March 1993 the Te Runanga o Ngai Tahu Bill was accorded urgency,[78] and on 27 July it was introduced to Parliament by Minister of Māori Affairs Doug Kidd. He noted that the Waitangi Tribunal's hearings on the Ngāi Tahu claim had led to the introduction of the bill, explained the limits of the current Maori Trust Board legislation and outlined the push by Ngāi Tahu to take control of their own destiny. He stated, too, that there was opposition to the bill from within Ngāi Tahu and that the central issue was one of effective representation.[79]

A number of MPs spoke about the details and consequences of the bill, including Tirikatene-Sullivan, Graham, MP for Western Maori Koro Wetere, MP for Tongariro (and brother of Winston Peters) Ian Peters, MP for Northern Maori Bruce Gregory, MP for Eastern Maori Peter Tapsell and MP for Nelson John Blincoe. All who spoke supported the bill in one way or another, although many had concerns. Among these concerns were support for the bill from Ngāi Tahu tribal members, the inclusion of Waitaha in addition to Ngāi Tahu and Ngāti Māmoe as those represented by Te Rūnanga, Māori living in the Ngāi Tahu rohe who were not Ngāi Tahu themselves, and the need for national legislation to reform the Maori Trust Boards Act.

Tirikatene-Sullivan spoke first. Although she supported the bill, she detailed a number of anxieties about it. She recounted the debate regarding the Te Runanga o Ngai Tahu Bill's predecessors – the 1944 Ngaitahu Claim Settlement Act and the 1946 Ngaitahu Trust Board Act. By the 1990s it was generally accepted that the 1940s settlement had not been sufficiently discussed to garner the true approval of the Ngāi Tahu community. She vigorously countered that perception: Eruera Tirikatene had held approximately 80 meetings up and down the South Island to debate the merits of that settlement. Tirikatene-Sullivan had attended each of these as 'a precocious child who took shorthand in Maori and English'. She expressed frustration that she had not been kept informed of the bill's contents, having only received a copy shortly before it was introduced to Parliament. She had attended meetings in Island Bay in

Wellington, and at Takahanga Marae in Kaikōura, which sought the approval of Ngāi Tahu members for the proposed bill, but she complained that it would have been difficult for her to provide her support as she had not perused the bill's contents. At the least, as the MP for Southern Maori and a part of the Labour Opposition, her approval was required before a private bill could be introduced.[80]

It would have been no surprise to anyone in Parliament, and to a number of Ngāi Tahu tribal members, including the negotiating team, who were in the visitors' gallery, that Tirikatene-Sullivan did not see eye to eye with most of the iwi leadership, but she was genuinely surprised to have been vilified as an 'enemy of Ngāitahu'. Even more concerning was what she referred to as 'an entirely incorrect impression that I was holding up the introduction of this bill into Parliament'. Nonetheless, such important legislation needed a high level of scrutiny, led by the Māori Affairs Select Committee. She then shared concerns about the bill from her colleague Sandra Lee, who could not be in Parliament. These included the exclusion of Waitaha from the noted ancestral bases of tribal identity (unlike Ngāti Māmoe and Ngāi Tahu), transparency in all of Te Rūnanga o Ngāi Tahu's affairs, effective representation and what she perceived as a concentration of power in the actual territory of Ngāi Tahu in the South Island rather than the majority of tribal members who lived outside the rohe. The first three points were fair, but regarding the last point, where else would Ngāi Tahu focus its efforts than on its own lands as it strove to re-establish the heart of its people, the marae and kāinga of Te Wai Pounamu? Tirikatene-Sullivan finished by paying tribute to the named tribunal claimant for Ngāi Tahu, Rakiihia Tau Snr, as a fellow follower of Rātana, but did not mention any of the other iwi negotiators.[81]

Doug Graham spoke briefly next, touching on the difficult negotiations of the last two years and the patience of generations of Ngāi Tahu who had fought for tribal recognition. He was followed by Koro Wetere, who pointed out that some aspects of the bill were similar to the repealed 1990 Runanga Iwi Act and particularly noted the consultation that Ngāi Tahu leaders had already had with their people, and the further consultation that would ensue under the select committee. There were Ngāi Tahu opponents of the bill, but that was not a surprise. A similar view was presented by the next speaker, Ian Peters, who above all hoped for what he termed a fair result. Bruce Gregory presented a number of factual questions about Ngāi Tahu history but otherwise supported the endeavour.[82]

The second to last speaker, Peter Tapsell, applauded the bill, although he lamented that a similar review of all other Māori trust boards was not completed before iwi-specific legislation was prepared for Ngāi Tahu. His perspective was of pan-Māoridom focused on a national identity rather than the tribal-based authority that the Crown continued to support. It was a fair concern, but the bill was the result of Ngāi Tahu's Waitangi Tribunal hearings and so a more specific product of those discussions, such as a legal personality for Te Rūnanga o Ngāi Tahu, was understandable. Finally, John Blincoe began his speech with what seemed like support for the bill, but he then pivoted to the use of conservation land for redress, revealing, in his advocacy, the power of the conservation lobby.[83]

Once the bill was introduced to Parliament, parts of the legislation came under review in the Māori Affairs Select Committee, of which both Tirikatene-Sullivan and Lee were members.[84] The former supported the bill, with some concerns. Lee, however, went a step further and submitted a claim to the Waitangi Tribunal on behalf of Ngāti Waewae interests from the West Coast/Te Tai Poutini on behalf of descendants of Tuhuru regarding the development of and consultation about the bill.[85] She did this even before the select committee heard evidence, and as a spokeswoman for opponents of the bill before the 1993 election, and part of a claim related to the bill in the Waitangi Tribunal, it could not be said that she was an unbiased committee member. In a meeting with the Crown, Ngāi Tahu negotiators noted that Lee's role in delaying the legislation represented a conflict of interest, but the Crown said there was 'no deliberate attempt … to delay passage of the bill' though it could not guarantee that it would be passed even in 1994.[86] As a result of that negotiating session, Graham wrote to the incoming chair of the Māori Affairs Committee, Koro Wetere, for his help in reviewing the bill and sending it back to Parliament as soon as possible.[87]

In March 1994 Tirikatene-Sullivan and Lee were invited to a meeting with members of a Ngāi Tahu hapū, Ngāi Tūāhuriri, at the Tuahiwi Marae to discuss negotiations and the legal personality legislation. Both women expressed their disappointment at the haste with which the bill was progressed. O'Regan and the Ngai Tahu Maori Trust Board, on the other hand, were tired of the consistent delays. O'Regan believed that Tirikatene-Sullivan and Lee had given some misinformation to John Crofts, a representative of Ngāi Tūāhuriri, who subsequently sent a letter to the Treaty of Waitangi Policy Unit asking that the legislation be delayed. The following day O'Regan had a meeting with other trust board members to organise a retraction of the letter. O'Regan tried to explain to the board that the legal personality was the platform upon which Ngāi Tahu would build its settlement and regain a measure of rangatiratanga.[88] The letter to the Crown had done irreparable damage to advancing the legislation through Parliament. When O'Regan wrote to Graham in May regarding the delays to the legislation, the minister replied that the situation had not been created by the Crown but by internal divisions within Ngāi Tahu.[89] Although Graham was quite willing to support the bill, ministers and officials could also use these internal divisions to justify whatever delays occurred on other issues, such as the financial dimensions of the settlement.

In early 1994 an internal review of the structure of Ngāi Tahu's negotiations had emerged as a topic of discussion at the Ngāi Tahu hui-ā-tau. Credit Suisse First Boston's role in Ngāi Tahu's negotiations, and in the privatisation of the Electricity Corporation, had come under some criticism by members of the trust board. Ngāi Tahu asked accountant (and future mayor) Garry Moore and solicitor Mark Knowles, both from Christchurch, to provide advice not only on this potential conflict of interest but also on the structure of negotiations in general. With marginal progress and significant pressure on the negotiators, legal remedies as alternatives were increasingly being considered.[90]

Moore and Knowles' report criticised both the Crown and specifically Graham for their role in the lack of progress but also the high cost of advisers to the Ngāi Tahu negotiators. Although the report was meant to remain an internal document, it was quickly leaked to the press. Ngāi Tahu negotiators and advisers, who were paid for their work, came under considerable pressure from claimants regarding their alleged financial gain from the negotiating process. Graham was particularly concerned that Moore and Knowles had not been properly identified at a formal Crown–Ngāi Tahu meeting that they both attended. The incident only added to Crown–Ngāi Tahu tensions, and exacerbated the divisions within the iwi.[91] By November 1994 the negotiations between the Crown and Ngāi Tahu broke down, and would not resume until 1996.

It is unclear if there was any credible alternative to the Crown's policy development process. Legislating the process may have caused even more lengthy delays. Would Labour in Opposition have been a constructive co-author of the new process or would they have reverted to the kind of anti-Māori political point-scoring that has marked so much of New Zealand's political history? Could the consultation have included significant sections of the Māori community? Certainly, but there was always going to have to be some kind of regimented process for the Crown to settle claims; the ad hoc nature of negotiations could not continue. Ngāi Tahu were effectively kept in the dark about most of the process and certainly during the gradual release of the process framework to a select group of Māori organisations.

The opposition from third-party interests, most notably from conservationists and public access advocates, was somewhat more surprising. In other jurisdictions, such as Canada, indigenous people have generally been able to rely on the support of conservationists. Although the image of an indigenous person always being in favour of conservation in a Western sense is stereotypical and offensive, the experiences of Māori claimants in the first Waitangi Tribunal showed significant overlap with environmentalists. This was certainly the case in the ground-breaking 1983 report on claims regarding polluted shellfish beds at Motonui, Waitara in Taranaki, the 1984 report on sewage pollution in the Kaituna River around Rotorua and the 1985 report on iron tailings in Manukau Harbour.[92] By the time Ngāi Tahu's negotiations were well under way it was clear that conservationist groups in the South Island had different conceptions about the involvement of iwi and hapū. Finally, the distinct challenges from within Ngāi Tahu would have been perhaps as expected as the Crown's tactics. Challenges to mandates have marked all treaty settlement negotiations and Ngāi Tahu's was no different. The Crown's requirement for an iwi-level organisation with which to negotiate has prevented hapū negotiations in all major tribal settlements.

CHAPTER 8

Collapse, late 1994–early 1996

The negotiations reached their nadir late in 1994. While Waikato–Tainui approached the signing of a heads of agreement, Ngāi Tahu's negotiations began to sink under the pressure of such a wide variety of claims. Waikato–Tainui's claim, in contrast, addressed only militarily induced land confiscation, and was therefore easier to address.

Unsurprisingly, Ngāi Tahu negotiators rejected the Crown's partial settlement offer, which had been influenced heavily by the largely negative advice of DOC and Treasury. Ngāi Tahu's legal advisers were then instructed to file a number of different lawsuits challenging the Crown on a variety of different fronts, including DOC concessions for whale-watching, Coalcorp and Landcorp business developments, and even the Department of Justice for a lack of funding for the Waitangi Tribunal. They also sought binding recommendations from the tribunal for all the extensive commercial forestry assets of the Crown in its rohe. The conciliation of negotiations gave way to the adversarial nature of litigation.

The Crown's experiences could not be described as smooth sailing. After barely getting Waikato–Tainui to sign following surrender on a number of different concessions, including a relativity clause, interest payments on the unpaid sum and an apology from Queen Elizabeth II, the Crown found its newly released treaty settlement policy under attack from all corners – even from Waikato–Tainui. Ngāi Tahu was able to bide its time as the northern group was criticised by various Māori communities for having acquiesced to the Crown's financial constraints. Nonetheless, by the end of 1995 it was clear that the drama over the Crown's fiscal envelope policy had passed and Ngāi Tahu would have to deal with the precedents set. The breakdown had provided Ngāi Tahu with its required leverage in the negotiations, but there remained much relationship mending to be done.

As 1994 began Ngāi Tahu negotiators were, understandably, feeling cynical and sceptical. As a result of direct protest actions involving Ngāti Haua at Whangape, Northland over the sale of part of an ancestral maunga, Whakararo, there had been substantial anti-Māori sentiment expressed in the media. Graham had written a few articles to present the Crown position. As O'Regan remarked in mid-January, 'I have to say that no matter how good and positive it all sounds, I believe Graham is "softening up" the public for his "envelope" policy and you will be aware how damaging that will be to the Ngāi Tahu interest. I suspect that when Ngāi Tahu rejects the Crown offer, he wants to be in a position to have the public feast on those "greedy and ungrateful" Ngāi Tahu.' He thought that was a month or so away. After asking the negotiators to 'read the present stuff and inform yourself of the state of play', he concluded, 'It's going to be a rough year.'[1]

While the Crown developed its policy, pressure was also increasingly being placed on Ngāi Tahu by internal dissension from Whetu Tirikatene-Sullivan and Sandra Lee and from the conservation movement. Some Pākehā backlash was to be expected, but the opposition from these two groups caught some Ngāi Tahu negotiators by surprise. They began to believe that the Crown wanted to conclude Waikato–Tainui's confiscation-based treaty claim before a purchase-based one such as Ngāi Tahu's. O'Regan said as much at one of the Crown and Ngāi Tahu's monthly meetings in early 1994. Although Graham quickly denied the charge, it is not difficult to see how Ngāi Tahu negotiators may have reached that conclusion because of the constant delays in their negotiating process. In fact the Waikato–Tainui negotiations were not guaranteed to conclude first; that was certainly not assured in early 1994.[2]

Following the pan-Māori meeting held in February 1994 by Graham and Luxton, coverage of pan-Māori, Sealord-like settlements increased in the media and they were discussed at length at a meeting of various Māori trust boards on 2 June.[3] O'Regan had gambled on the idea once already and was firmly opposed to any pan-Māori settlement. He stated his opposition at a meeting with the Crown later that month; Graham, too, was uninterested in the concept.[4]

There were few points of agreement at the early May 1994 negotiation meeting, which concluded with Graham offering O'Regan a partial settlement. This included some of the specific conservation-related aspects of the claim, such as limited title to Rarotoka Island, Tūtaepatu Lagoon (a culturally significant area north of Christchurch) and $10 million worth of land-banked properties, which were included in the interim offer in exchange for a revised early warning system and land-bank structure. Largely due to DOC opposition, title to Rarotoka Island was to include a marginal strip (which Ngāi Tahu rejected), Whenua Hou and the Crown Tītī Islands were excluded and access to pounamu was far from guaranteed. Ngāi Tahu's land-bank was the first of its kind and had the unique ability to add and remove properties. Treasury sought to bring the iwi down to the same standards as other claimants but this would take away the only benefit that Ngāi Tahu was gaining from the Crown other than a separate land-banking agreement with Railcorp.[5]

Ngāi Tahu further explored the limits of the partial settlement at the July 1994 meeting. They specifically wanted the four Aoraki Crown forests and the mountain top itself handed over to Ngāi Tahu as a part of the on-account settlement, but the Crown refused. The tension between the two sides was clear in the increased number of disagreements over the drafts of meeting minutes. O'Regan's minutes had Graham stating that 'the Crown wanted to give Ngāi Tahu a bit of a base but would not want to do more than that' and that he thought that the select committee was 'unfocused'. The Crown did not accept this version.[6]

As Waikato–Tainui proceeded to sign its heads of agreement in late December 1994, Ngāi Tahu's negotiations completely broke down. The beginning of the end can be pinpointed to early August 1994 when the Crown asked that their monthly meetings be delayed until the announcement of the Crown's new treaty settlement policy at the end of the year. In November 1994 came an interim settlement, which the negotiators took back to the iwi and it was rejected. It proposed that Ngāi Tahu receive freehold title to Rarotoka Island but with the imposition of a marginal strip,[7] Tūtaepatu Lagoon and $10 million worth of land-banked properties in exchange for a revised land-bank system.[8] Ngāi Tahu were certainly not averse to the idea of an interim settlement, having long advocated that a series of interim settlements would be better than the idea of a full and final settlement, but they regarded this offer as less than adequate.[9]

Both the Treaty of Waitangi Policy Unit and Te Puni Kōkiri had struggled to convince Treasury that the terms of the interim offer were beneficial to the Crown. They pointed out that the interim offer addressed all Treasury's problems regarding the conditions of acceptance of the interim settlement. These problems related mainly to the condition that Ngāi Tahu waive all other forms of redress, such as approaching the Waitangi Tribunal or Court of Appeal. Treasury had recommended that Graham not propose the interim settlement because it would not provide the finality or certainty the Crown wanted. As the policy unit and Te Puni Kōkiri emphasised, backing the interim settlement would give the Crown negotiators a chance to show that the extended negotiations had produced some tangible result. In a rare move, Cabinet approved the interim settlement and merely acknowledged Treasury's reservations.[10]

Like Treasury, Ngāi Tahu did not approve the on-account settlement offer, and for the same reason: the lack of 'certainty' it would provide. Ngāi Tahu's reservations related to the limited offer, which had neglected such matters as the importance of the iwi's unique land-banking system, Whenua Hou and the Crown Tītī Islands and had not provided enough concessions on pounamu, Rarotoka Island and title to the Arahura Valley. The islands and title to the Arahura Valley reflected DOC's reservations rather than Treasury's concerns.[11] DOC would begin to play a prominent role in Ngāi Tahu's negotiations from 1994, taking on the role often played by Treasury as key internal government critic of the treaty settlement process.

In 1995 Graham and O'Regan exchanged a number of letters regarding the difficulty of dealing with conservation interests. Graham tried to say merely that conservation interests had to be dealt with; O'Regan said that Ngāi Tahu's treaty rights should not be trampled on by conservationists because of alleged 'public interest'. He specifically noted Ngāi Tahu's concession of agreeing to the retirement of land from the Greenstone Station lease.[12] Graham's difficulties were exacerbated by the continuing hard line held by conservationists in 1995, despite the release of government policy stating that only small and discrete sites of conservation lands were available for settlements.[13] The negotiations officially broke down in December 1994.[14] Ngāi Tahu would state that the Crown had unilaterally cut off the negotiations during the breakdown from the end of 1994 until the start of 1996.[15] In the meantime the Crown planned to release its proposals for the settlement of treaty claims, timed to coincide with the signing of Waikato–Tainui's settlement.

The Crown's fiscal limit on the total value of treaty settlements had been rejected in many ways by Ngāi Tahu, Waikato–Tainui and other Māori groups by December 1994, but the Bolger government received its first official rejection when the Māori Queen, Te Arikinui Dame Te Atairangikaahu, and paramount Ngāti Tūwharetoa leader Sir Hepi Te Heu Heu refused to attend the Crown's presentation of its treaty settlement policy at Premier House on 7 December 1994. Although Waikato–Tainui was in the middle of intense negotiations with the Crown, Tainui Maori Trust Board members publicly criticised the $1 billion cap while acknowledging the courage of the Crown for attempting to settle Māori grievances. Waikato–Tainui chief negotiator Robert Mahuta stated that if the government wanted the settlements to be full and final then the Crown would need to increase the limit. The *New Zealand Herald* editorial criticised the manner in which the fiscal envelope policy was forced on Māori. A diverse group of different political stripes and authors opposed the fiscal cap in mid-December 1994: Labour treaty issues spokesperson David Caygill, Alliance co-leader Sandra Lee, National MP Michael Laws, author Alan Duff, former Prime Minister David Lange and National Party Māori vice-president Cliff Bidwell. The *Sunday Star Times* was one of the few newspapers that commended the Crown for at least building a starting point for negotiations.[16] The *National Business Review* also supported the Crown's new policy, although in its pages economist Gareth Morgan provided a stringent critique of the limits and unilateral development of the fiscal envelope early in February 1995.[17] Condemnation also came from figures as diverse as Moana Jackson and Winston Peters: one can struggle to ascertain who wrote what on the topic.[18]

A pan-Māori hui held in Tūrangi on 29 January 1995 at the behest of Sir Hepi Te Heu Heu concluded with all present endorsing Sir Hepi's motion to reject the Crown's proposals.[19] The mood of the Tūrangi hui echoed the hostile tone that marked the Crown's fiscal envelope hui, which were held throughout the country in the first half of 1995, fronted mainly by Te Puni Kōkiri staff, led by CEO Wira Gardiner. The hui rejected the Crown's proposals for settlement in sometimes forceful and dramatic ways.[20]

The Crown's proposed fiscal limit was too small to cover all the treaty settlements that would need to be negotiated and it was officially abandoned in the coalition agreement that followed the 1996 election. Although the criticism of the fiscal limit was, and continues to be, reasonable, the media seemed to focus disproportionately on this, rather than the whole package of proposals. Other major issues were the lack of consultation with Māori during the development of the policy and the policy's focus on grievances stemming from confiscation rather than the Native Land Court, and the uncompromising position of the Crown, which refused to recognise ownership interest in natural resources (other than pounamu), and severely limited the transfer of conservation land.[21] Nonetheless, Crown officials who were involved in the Waikato–Tainui and Ngāi Tahu negotiations and general treaty settlement policy have maintained that another settlement after the fisheries settlement would not have been possible without a fiscal cap. Many noted that Treaty of Waitangi Policy Unit and Te Puni Kōkiri had recommended a considerably larger sum but Treasury advice dominated.[22]

In line with their opposition to the fiscal envelope Ngāi Tahu engaged in a series of lawsuits – at one point 12 concurrent actions were in place[23] – intended to undermine the overriding principle that the Crown should control the treaty settlement process. The option of returning to the courts had always remained open. There had been boundary disputes in the courts between Ngāi Tahu and Rangitāne and other northern South Island iwi and hapū, and also a series of lawsuits involving the Treaty of Waitangi Fisheries Commission. By the end of 1994, Ngāi Tahu had turned the focus of litigation towards the Crown.

The first court action concerned Ngāi Tahu's belief that they should have priority over the commercial rights attached to whales in the Kaikōura area. The Crown had given an undertaking that it would not issue any more pounamu licences, pending the transfer of ownership of pounamu to Ngāi Tahu, but as the negotiations dragged on this did not provide enough comfort. In early 1995 Ngāi Tahu filed proceedings against the Crown to restrain it from issuing these licences because it had not honoured its promise.[24] Although Ngāi Tahu were not successful in all areas of litigation, they received favourable judgements in both the pounamu and whale cases and were eventually able to force the Crown back to the negotiating table.

Ngāi Tahu wanted to visit all Landcorp farming properties in their part of the South Island in order to decide on their suitability for inclusion in their final settlement. The Crown felt that visiting five farms would be more 'reasonable'. After significant lobbying the Crown shared some information regarding stock numbers, but no valuations were offered since Treasury claimed these constituted sensitive commercial information. Ngāi Tahu also filed proceedings against the Crown in relation to the Coal Export Project being planned on the West Coast of the South Island. Coalcorp was developing coal mines focused specifically on the export market and Ngāi Tahu wanted their interests protected. In early 1995 they sought access to forestry assets held by the Crown Forestry Rental Trust.[25] Then, in June, they amended their claim to the Waitangi Tribunal in order to seek binding recommendations for the return of all SOE properties in the Ngāi Tahu rohe.[26] The Crown feared that the tribunal would use its binding powers to return Crown forests to Ngāi Tahu with a very significant financial award made possible under the terms of the Crown Forest Assets Act.

The option of taking their case back to the Waitangi Tribunal always remained a possibility for Ngāi Tahu; it had occasionally threatened to do so in 1991–92. The threat was finally carried out in late 1994 when a meeting with the tribunal was planned for early 1995. It was originally meant to be presided over by Judge Ashley McHugh, who had presided in the original inquiry and was seen by many as sympathetic to Ngāi Tahu, but at the last minute he was replaced by the chairperson of the Waitangi Tribunal, Chief Judge Eddie Durie. Citing a lack of funding and time, Durie would not hear the Ngāi Tahu case. The iwi subsequently filed proceedings against Durie for refusing to hear their urgent inquiry, and against the attorney-general for not providing enough funding for the Waitangi Tribunal.[27]

Durie clearly faced a very difficult decision. Ngāi Tahu had been one of the first major hearings of the post-1985 era and four separate reports had been published between 1991 and 1995 regarding their claims. The backlog of other claims was quite substantial and Durie considered that Ngāi Tahu had already been given a large amount of the tribunal's attention and resources. But, as the early November 1994 hui-ā-tau made clear, the majority of Ngāi Tahu beneficiaries felt that returning to the tribunal was the best course of action and a natural extension of the iwi's strategy.[28]

After the rejection of the Crown's interim settlement, the negotiations officially came to a halt. Graham and O'Regan began to argue both in the media and in private correspondence. The precedent had been set by Waikato–Tainui's eventual acceptance of the Crown's offer, and O'Regan and other Ngāi Tahu negotiators and advisers began to take notice of the fact early in 1995.[29]

In terms of the quantification of loss, the Waikato–Tainui heads of agreement indicated that both the Crown and Waikato–Tainui recognised that the tribe's loss was $12 billion,[30] but as Ngāi Tahu adviser Nick Davidson noted early in February 1995, the whole matter of loss and settlement amount was complicated:

> Perhaps Treasury's reluctance to accept the tenths proposition in the early stages of the Ngāi Tahu negotiation was driven by very pre-conceived notions on the part of the Crown negotiators as to what was affordable. I have heard it suggested that Treasury 'advice' (which as we know is never 'given' on Treaty matters) may have 'indicated' that any tribal settlement in excess of the $170 million attributed to the Fisheries settlement would be unacceptable. That might well be the 'rationale' for the $170 million figure reached with Tainui. In any event, if the myth that Tainui's loss is the largest

is allowed to persist, the potential for depicting Ngāi Tahu as the greediest will be enhanced.[31]

Ngāi Tahu's litigation was in nearly full force by the middle of 1995. The Crown and Ngāi Tahu were meeting only in the courts and trading blows through the media. Prime Minister Jim Bolger had decided that he should intervene to attempt to kick-start the negotiations and get Ngāi Tahu and the Crown out of the cycle of litigation. He phoned O'Regan to establish a line of communication outside the courtroom, a gesture that O'Regan appreciated. At the centre of O'Regan's argument, and the core of most of Ngāi Tahu's lawsuits, was the need for the Crown to stop selling off its assets. Bolger and O'Regan first met while attending the Rugby World Cup in South Africa in June 1995. Bolger asked O'Regan to make the trip on the prime minister's plane and they had ample time to discuss Ngāi Tahu's negotiations. During refuelling in Tierra Del Fuego, Bolger and O'Regan walked together on the runway and agreed on the very basics of the deal while the prime minister's primary adviser on the issue furiously took notes.[32] O'Regan and Bolger met again in early August. Bolger promised to champion the Ngāi Tahu bill through Parliament but refused to negotiate until Ngāi Tahu suspended its litigation. O'Regan was still quite set on maintaining the leverage of litigation and stated that the fisheries negotiations had also taken place under the spectre of litigation. When Bolger's adviser asked 'what would happen now? Would there be a pause in the litigation?' O'Regan replied that 'there would be no pause but there was nothing in place that could not be undone by a phone call if necessary'. O'Regan made it clear that before negotiations could restart the Ngāi Tahu bill would have to pass through Parliament.[33]

By September 1995 Nick Davidson was frank in assessing the post-Waikato–Tainui treaty settlement environment and asking whether the courts or the tribunal would provide significantly more in terms of settlement size or, in fact, anything at all. Because of its need for coalitions, the mixed member proportional (MMP) electoral system, introduced in 1993, could also possibly detrimentally affect the Crown's ability to settle large treaty claims. At worst, Davidson stressed, Ngāi Tahu would be able to park its litigation during the negotiations, and if they failed, the litigation would merely resume. (Ngāi Tahu's mahinga kai and ancillary claims could be parked because that was essentially what Waikato–Tainui had received as part of its settlement – the exclusion of the claim to the Waikato River and harbours.) Davidson also perceived that economic restructuring would further damage Ngāi Tahu and that restoration would be harder the longer the iwi waited for its perfect settlement.[34]

The litigation strategy was not universally accepted among the diverse Ngāi Tahu community. After litigation had stretched on for a year Richard Parata voiced his highly critical disapproval of this approach. Parata considered that the Privy Council and High Court would certainly decide on the basis of precedent. As Waikato–Tainui's settlement was nearly finalised, $170 million would be the realistic precedent. He also thought that Ngāi Tahu 'may have misinterpreted the break off of negotiations with the Crown'.

> Much weight has been put on the mischievous intent of the Crown rather than they were out of their depth and grossly inefficient. The Crown broke off negotiations because they could not answer all the complex issues presented by Ngāi Tahu. They needed to go to ground. As it turns out they made a mess of things with the 'Fiscal Envelope'. The point I am making is that Ngāi Tahu have the opportunity to capitalise on this position. ie Ngāi Tahu were the guinea pigs. Incidentally there is in Crown circles a lot of sympathy for Ngāi Tahu's position.

Parata further pointed out that, despite the series of judicial proceedings, the Crown never cut off Ngāi Tahu's main source of funding, the unique land-banking agreement. For Parata, this was a vivid example of the Crown's measured response to Ngāi Tahu's aggressive litigation strategy but he did not believe it would last forever. Not all Ngāi Tahu negotiators accepted Parata's opinion, but it would continue to gain traction. Rakiihia Tau Snr, however, defended the legal action as necessary because he had no trust in the political process. The courts were the only forum under which justice could be obtained and therefore the litigation needed to continue.[35]

The perception of a settlement with the Crown became more generally accepted as 1995 progressed. In December Ngāi Tahu economic adviser Richard Meade had lunch with a lawyer who had provided legal advice to certain Crown research institutes affected by the settlement. The lawyer thought Waikato–Tainui had got an excellent deal, such as some free improvements on the land, in the form of buildings, for example. According to Meade, the lawyer felt that Treasury was quite concerned about the precedent-setting nature of the Waikato–Tainui deal because it had had little to do with the settlement, and that the politicians, including Graham, 'were determined to drive the deal through...' 'While we might think the Tainui deal appears cheap, she thought Tainui had driven a hard bargain, and other iwi would be able to adopt a similarly hard approach when negotiating a settlement, by reference to the Tainui deal. Hope so.'[36]

By the end of 1995, that very litigious year, there was clearly more optimism about a potential settlement than there had been at the end of 1994. In the end Waikato–Tainui's benchmark would do more to define the trajectory of Ngāi Tahu's negotiations with the Crown, but the power of litigation cannot be discounted.

While Ngāi Tahu undertook litigation in the hope of re-energising its central negotiations, the Te Runanga o Ngai Tahu Bill continued slowly through Parliament. By late 1995 over 100 written and oral submissions offering support, desiring amendment and expressing outright opposition had been made to the Māori Affairs Committee, which had been examining the bill for over two years. Some substantial amendments were made, the most prominent of them the addition of Waitaha to Ngāi Tahu and Ngāti Māmoe as the foundational descent lines of the iwi. There had also been a change to the description of the takiwā (district or region) of each papatipu rūnanga or sub-council that would sit on Te Rūnanga o Ngāi Tahu. Originally these were printed in detail in the first schedule to the bill; in 1994 they were made more general by reference to the places on which they were centred. Then the Maori Affairs Committee pushed for detail to be provided for the takiwā that was adopted. The election of members to the 18 papatipu rūnanga that would make up Te Rūnanga o Ngāi Tahu was also added and clarified. Although O'Regan had advocated for a postal ballot, the Takahanga hui-ā-iwi back in April 1992 had decided that each local community would decide how it elected the members of their papatipu rūnanga. Critics of the bill such as Whetu Tirikatene-Sullivan and Sandra Lee were particularly keen that individual Ngāi Tahu members should be able to take a matter of representation to the Maori Land Court for determination. Although O'Regan and the negotiating team opposed this provision because of the control it gave to the Maori Land Court rather than Ngāi Tahu whānui, the select committee adopted that change.[37]

Committee members commented at some length about the manner in which the proceedings had been run for such an important bill. The chair in late 1995 – the role was held by a number of different MPs during the length of the bill's debate in Parliament – was Koro Wetere. When opening the deliberations on 13 December he was emphatic that any other Māori bill like this must not be brought before the House in such a manner. When the draft legislation was first introduced as a private bill, the Standing Orders were suspended, which meant that the committee had to go through the bill. If the Standing Orders had been followed then the consultation over the bill would have taken place outside Parliament. Wetere considered it 'most disgraceful ... not only to the Ngāi Tahu people but also the committee to be treated in that fashion'. In the words of the MP for Eastern Bay of Plenty, National's Tony Ryall, the committee had to be the judge of what were essentially 'family matters'. He thought it was unreasonable that such disagreements had to be resolved in front of outsiders.[38]

Matters became particularly heated when Sandra Lee accused not only O'Regan and the entire negotiating team, but also Wetere, of corruption. Her allegation that he, as a Labour MP, was doing the National government's bidding to obtain a knighthood was a particularly low point in the long debate over the bill. Lee was duly condemned by both Labour MPs such as the deputy leader of the Opposition, David Caygill, and National MPs such as Doug Kidd and Ryall. The opponents of the bill often touted the strength of their numbers in their submissions to the committee. Indeed, 84 per cent of the submissions opposed or criticised the original bill and both Tirikatene-Sullivan and Lee used that fact to great effect to show the strength of the opposition. Kidd noted that nearly every one of the opposing submissions was sent to Parliament from one fax machine, that belonging to Sandra Lee's Alliance Party.

Another committee member, United MP Pauline Gardiner, noted that it was not unusual for written submissions to 'have all been jacked up by one particular interest group or another ... one often has those who are most well organised coming to the fore'. Kidd described the process leading to the bill as one of 'multi-layered multilocation ... that went over a substantial period of time'. He felt that the bill's concepts had been discussed throughout the Ngāi Tahu rohe before its introduction to the House. Over 500 had attended the final hui at Takahanga, which supported the bill. He saw the clear will of the people of Ngāi Tahu. With that, the motion to move the bill back to Parliament was agreed to.[39]

Maintaining unofficial connections between Ngāi Tahu negotiators and Crown officials during the breakdown of the negotiations was important for keeping the lines of communication open. When the Treaty of Waitangi Policy Unit was reorganised as the Office of Treaty Settlements at the beginning of 1995, a new director was appointed who had previously worked at Te Puni Kōkiri. The director and Nick Davidson had held off-the-record discussions in the first half of the 1990s and they stayed in contact even during the period of intense litigation. On 13 February 1996, as the tide began to shift back towards negotiations, Davidson had lunch with the director. Davidson made it clear that the passage of the Ngāi Tahu bill, which would establish a legal personality for the tribe, was the most important aspect of the possibility of resuming negotiations. The director, who was very candid, thought Graham was still the most capable and liberal minister in terms of treaty settlement policy, despite his comments about the Ngāi Tahu negotiations throughout 1995. She said that Bolger and Bill Birch were keen to get the negotiations restarted, although she was wary of DOC's presence in the negotiations. Although she did not want DOC involved as a permanent part of the negotiating team, the department would certainly have to be consulted. She also mentioned separating ancillary and natural resources from mahinga kai to make settling easier, but Davidson was doubtful because he felt they were too interconnected. The director's eagerness to separate those claims was far from the official line then emerging from the Crown. Bolger and O'Regan had also met in February and the separation of the mahinga kai aspect of the claim was also a key point of that discussion.[40]

The Waikato–Tainui settlement had excluded natural resource and river issues and this seemed an attractive precedent for Ngāi Tahu. Compensation for the restriction of access to mahinga kai had been a difficult issue in the first part of the negotiations and O'Regan felt that a separation of natural resource and mahinga kai issues could help to advance the negotiations. One of Bolger's most senior advisers stressed, however, that the Waikato–Tainui negotiations were the exception and that all future negotiated settlements would be completely comprehensive to achieve the Crown's desired 'finality'.[41] Issues regarding finality could sometimes be an exercise in semantics as the Crown attempted to find the least oppressive way to achieve 'durability' without impinging on mana. The issue of finality would reappear numerous times before the end of the negotiations.

The Crown also began to build a new strategy from which to approach the negotiations in February 1996. Pounamu and Tūtaepatu Lagoon would be returned and the Ngāi Tahu bill would be immediately put through its final reading. It was also recognised that the Crown's policy on Whenua Hou, Rarotoka Island, the Crown Tītī Islands, Arahura and the Wakatipu stations would need to be altered in some way. Landcorp properties could become the subject of the land-bank system. But litigation would need to cease before negotiations could resume. Success would hinge on an agreement on the size of the settlement, and the use of specific components in a redress package such as an apology, cash, land-bank properties, a right of first refusal, Crown lands, forestry assets and possibly a relativity clause. Both the right of first refusal and the relativity clause were products of the Waikato–Tainui settlement. The former gave the settled group the first right for 150 years to purchase Crown lands when they were about to be privatised. The relativity clause was intended to maintain the value of the Waikato–Tainui settlement in relation to other claims. When the Crown imposed its $1 billion fiscal envelope limit on all treaty settlements, Waikato–Tainui forced an agreement that its amount would always maintain its value as 17 per cent of total settlement spending. For every dollar that the Crown spends over the $1 billion limit, Waikato–Tainui receives 17 cents. There was also still some question over whether the settlement should cover all aspects of the claim. The Waikato–Tainui settlement would not have been finalised the year before if the claim to the river had been included. At the end of February 1996 Cabinet indicated that a heads of agreement needed to be signed with Ngāi Tahu by September.[42]

Bolger met with O'Regan again on 7 March 1996 and, before what would be a tense and dramatic meeting began, the prime minister handed over a letter that set out the different areas on which the Crown and Ngāi Tahu would have to come together to reach a settlement before the end of the year. The first steps for recommencement of the negotiations were establishing the size of the settlement, the Ngāi Tahu bill, specific assets, the halting of all litigation and an agreed process in which there was minimal contact between the principals, O'Regan and Graham. O'Regan had also laid out what he saw as the Crown's culpability for the deterioration in relations between the two principals. Bolger countered that 'Frustration and disappointment have become strong emotions for all who have been involved in earlier rounds. It seems to me that this is a time to rekindle our relationship, to move forward with a renewed sense of determination, tempered by our past experiences, but focused on the importance of resolving with completeness and finality a large and significant set of historical Treaty claims.'[43] During the meeting O'Regan tried to remain as vague as possible regarding the amount of a possible settlement, but Bolger's advisers wanted to ensure it was clear that $170 million would be the maximum.

O'Regan and his advisers did not want to commit to anything by the end of the meeting, and Bolger's letter was the perfect excuse – its contents, they argued, would have to be considered first. Bolger nonetheless pressed O'Regan on the issue of a 'ball park' amount and O'Regan pushed back. Since Ngāi Tahu were still waiting for responses to their February letters of 1992 and 1993, the most important thing would be to get some agreement between Ngāi Tahu and Crown negotiators on what the quantum actually covered. For example, would it apply to non-fiscal elements or ancillary claims? If Ngāi Tahu were being urged to show some flexibility, then the same was to be expected from the Crown: both sides needed to shift from their positions. The meeting ended with O'Regan informing Bolger that there would be no chance for any real negotiations until the third reading of the Ngāi Tahu bill, a point conceded by the prime minister. O'Regan and other Ngāi Tahu negotiators later expressed their fear about the influence of Bolger's two senior advisers,[44] who would later earn the dubious distinction of being referred to by a Ngāi Tahu adviser as 'Halderman and Erhlichmann', referring to two of disgraced American President Richard Nixon's closest advisers.[45] But in the end these Crown officials played an integral part in the rapprochement.

Despite such contact at the highest of political levels, there still remained challenges on the ground. To the frustration of the Ngāi Tahu negotiators, DOC, while remaining firmly opposed to any accommodation on conservation, was attempting to privatise just such an area on the shores of Te Waihora. Only days after O'Regan's meeting with Bolger, Davidson received a phone call from a Crown official, worried about rumours she had heard that Ngāi Tahu planned to pursue additional litigation.[46] Davidson set her mind at rest.

In March 1996, as it became clear that a recommencement of negotiations was likely, Treasury and Crown Law debated the relativities between the payment given to Waikato–Tainui and the potential amount to be offered to Ngāi Tahu, and also the relativities between the two groups in terms of historical loss. There was also some lively debate between Te Puni Kōkiri and DOC officials over conservation matters and their potential for both fostering and endangering the development of goodwill between Crown and Ngāi Tahu negotiators. As far as the Lake Wakatipu high-country pastoral leases were concerned, Te Puni Kōkiri opposed a recent report by the commissioner for Crown lands, which stated that 90 per cent of the stations should be retired to the conservation estate. 'Such a recommendation appears not to take account of the Crown's objective to settle the Ngāi Tahu claim. This para[graph] should note why Ngāi Tahu regard the stations as important to their settlement, and any barriers to having them included? For example do they have high conservation values?' In the end, some significant conservation information was added to the final Cabinet paper to underscore the conservation implications for many of the specific redress issues. Due to the contradictory advice from Te Puni Kōkiri and DOC, Cabinet declined to make a decision on the high-country pastoral leases.[47] The recommendations of the report would later result in large areas of the pastoral leases being retired into the conservation estate.[48]

In contrast to conservation and public access groups, the South Island High Country Committee of Federated Farmers was particularly supportive of Ngāi Tahu as potential high-country lessees, especially since the three high-country pastoral leases had been commercial properties for many years. The committee felt that a regrettable racial element had been injected into the debate: 'Pastoral leases are being bought and sold all the time. Therefore, the hard question has to be asked, why is PANZ [Public Access New Zealand] mounting a petition against these transactions and not others? The answer is that PANZ senses a political advantage in exploiting fears and prejudices in relation to Māori and proposed treaty settlements.' The support of high-country farmers was perhaps not so surprising, considering their own connections with the high country which, as the Waitangi Tribunal had noted, was not so different from the connections to the land claimed by Ngāi Tahu. Individual high-country farmers, such as H. A. P. Barker of Queenstown, also expressed support for Ngāi Tahu.[49] Ngāi Tahu had invested a lot of time and effort in building and maintaining a positive relationship with Federated Farmers.

As negotiations slowly began again, both the Crown and Ngāi Tahu recognised that they would have to shift their positions on the Arahura River.[50] Ngāi Tahu understood that the Crown refused to vest the catchment, and that they would have to maximise their opportunities within the reserve status of the area. Conservation groups pressed for the classification of the Arahura River area as a scenic reserve, but Ngāi Tahu countered that if, against their wishes, the area was going to be classified as a reserve, it should be historic not scenic. Although both reserves have the same public access provisions under the Reserves Act 1977, historic reserves are not specifically designed for the use of the public.

The Crown also explored some variations in the settlement offer regarding Whenua Hou and the Crown Tītī Islands to obtain Ngāi Tahu's approval. DOC wanted the Cabinet paper being developed in March 1996 to highlight the significant public opposition to the islands proposals and that they were only passed by the Southland Conservation Board with a narrow majority.[51] Te Puni Kōkiri took a different approach. The ministry was keen to be 'involved in any inter-departmental discussions on these matters as our participation will assist in achieving a better outcome. For example, in the past we have contested several elements of the

Crown's present negotiating position (ownership of pounamu, Whenua Hou, Crown Tītī Islands, Rarotoka including [the] foreshore and seabed) which are only now being contemplated as part of the compromises necessary to reach a settlement.'[52] Te Puni Kōkiri believed that the right of first refusal and a relativity clause would be important factors for Ngāi Tahu because the gap between the redress they would receive and their loss would be much larger than for smaller claimant groups and thus the incentive to seek provisions such as those would be more important. DOC's concerns about the Southland Conservation Board consultation process were included in the final Cabinet paper, but it also set out the limitations of the previous interim settlement offer of November 1994.[53] The Office of Treaty Settlements advocated for revised positions that reflected Te Puni Kōkiri and Ngāi Tahu's concerns.

Regarding Whenua Hou, Ngāi Tahu sought equal representation on the reserves board and the development, with DOC, of clear protocols regarding visitation rights. When it came to the Crown Tītī Islands, fulfilling Ngāi Tahu's request to waive marginal strips was necessary to advance the negotiation process. The Whenua Hou proposal prepared for the formal recommencement of negotiations largely met with Ngāi Tahu approval. As well as being equally represented on the reserves board that would be established to better manage Whenua Hou, a consultative group of Rakiura Ngāi Tahu would be formed to advise the regional DOC conservator about entry permits. The fee simple title of the Crown Tītī Islands without a marginal strip requirement was offered back to Ngāi Tahu, but the islands would still be managed as a nature reserve.[54]

On the surface Crown/Ngāi Tahu relations were clearly improving. At the end of the month O'Regan sent a long letter to Bolger laying the path for a formal resumption of negotiations: 'I share your view that we should be far more concerned about the future possibilities than past problems and that it would not be productive to dwell on the unfortunate recent record of Crown/Ngāi Tahu negotiation. Beyond the necessary exhumation of factual content, I hope there will be no need for an examination of those records of the last few years – a task I would rather see left to historians. I, too, am committed to looking forward.' O'Regan was particularly concerned about pounamu; resolving that impasse would create substantial goodwill from the iwi. 'The Ngāi Tahu preference has always been for a negotiated settlement and, despite our somewhat dogged heritage, we remain committed to that objective.' Internally Ngāi Tahu were still only cautiously optimistic, but this dialogue with the Crown was far removed from the constant litigation of the year before.[55]

In April 1996 the Crown was finalising its negotiating policy with Ngāi Tahu and in the middle of the month the Te Runanga o Ngai Tahu Bill was finally put through its third reading. O'Regan thanked Bolger for his help: getting the bill through the House, and restarting the negotiations, had certainly not been easy. With the support of Bolger, Kidd and Graham, on 17 April 1996 the Te Runanga o Ngai Tahu Bill was given its final reading in Parliament.[56] When royal assent was given on 24 April 1996, the Ngai Tahu Maori Trust Board was dissolved and replaced with Te Rūnanga o Ngāi Tahu.[57] The new organisation was now accountable to the Ngāi Tahu rūnanga and people rather than to the Crown.

CHAPTER 9

Negotiations recommence

After the passage of the Te Runanga o Ngai Tahu Act in April 1996, there were still a number of road-blocks on the route to a formal recommencement of negotiations. Both sides were staggering under the detail of what would and would not be on the table. The senior Department of the Prime Minister and Cabinet officials who had played such a key role in rekindling the negotiations gradually took a step back as the Office of Treaty Settlements grabbed the reins. Although originally opposed by the Crown, an interim settlement was agreed in June 1996 to keep the momentum going and from then the two teams continued at breakneck pace, trying to achieve a heads of agreement before election day on 12 October.

The third-party interests that had played such a major part in delaying the negotiations were reduced to a few hard-core opponents led by Kevin Smith of Forest & Bird and Bruce Mason from Public Access New Zealand, who continued to oppose any negotiated outcome. By this time previous opponents, such as the powerful Fish and Game, had come around and their communication with their members and the wider public through media exposure was helpful in rationalising the settlement from the point of view of both the Crown and Ngāi Tahu. Pressure from third parties would significantly reduce the size of the high-country stations, but otherwise their efforts at limiting redress on the important Tītī Islands and Rarotoka Island were largely unsuccessful.

As a settlement grew close to fruition, work also began in earnest on the Ngāi Tahu historical account. Although the negotiations regarding this were not as complicated and extended as Waikato–Tainui's, there were still a number of points of disagreement over Ngāi Tahu's experience of colonisation. In this task both sides were helped by the Waitangi Tribunal's *Ngai Tahu Land Report*, although they sometimes held such divergent criticisms of the report that its use as an objective arbiter was nullified. Before that work could be done, the two sides still had to return to the negotiating table.

April to June 1996 was a period of transition. The monthly meetings had been ineffective from as far back as late 1992; the new structure would focus on officials, rather than the A Team negotiators, conducting the real substance of the negotiations and using the principals, O'Regan and Graham, only at pivotal points to break deadlocks. Nonetheless, by the time a meeting was held in late April O'Regan and Graham were not yet on speaking terms and O'Regan and Bolger were still the principals, despite the prime minister's advisers counselling against this.

When Bolger and O'Regan met they were still far apart on the issue of settlement amount. With regards to comprehensiveness O'Regan still doubted that all mahinga kai issues could be dealt with in the timeframe allotted. Ngāi Tahu wanted to ensure that their common law rights in relation to mahinga kai were not abrogated because of a rushed settlement of claims in this area. O'Regan had expressed a desire for a cash settlement that would be coupled with a right of first refusal, which Ngāi Tahu already enjoyed thanks to the land-bank. Bolger raised the issue of establishing a fair market value and suggested that some assets should be excluded. O'Regan, however, wanted access to all assets so that Ngāi Tahu could respond to changes in circumstances. When pushed on what specific assets Ngāi Tahu were interested in, O'Regan referred only to the high-country stations and the forests. He did agree that litigation would be suspended.[1]

Internally, Ngāi Tahu were still weighing their options, despite the suspension of all negotiations-related litigation. The uncertainty of an award of damages by the courts was gaining traction in debates among

Ngāi Tahu negotiators and advisers, and with it the possibility of a much larger settlement amount.[2] Sid Ashton, the inaugural CEO of Te Rūnanga o Ngāi Tahu, was opposed to continuing litigation because he did not expect it to obtain any more than a negotiated agreement would. If litigation went on there would be no funding for marae or educational grants, and success was not guaranteed.[3] The focus began to shift to the contents of a possible settlement. The Ngāi Tahu negotiators set out a possible framework of agreement and basis for reparations to settle the reserves not awarded aspect of the claim. Ngāi Tahu wanted a right of first refusal over water rights, SOE properties, DOC concessions and Crown assets except for Electricorp. Also included on a list were cash and interest plus the four Aoraki forests, some Landcorp financial instruments and Coalcorp properties.[4]

The Crown, for its part, would need all litigation to stop and Ngāi Tahu would have a right of first refusal over certain assets but not airports, indigenous forests or coal. Furthermore, the settlement would have to be comprehensive, with the same monetary amount as that received by Waikato–Tainui. O'Regan wanted Ngāi Tahu and the Crown to achieve 'clarity of definition as to what we are talking about before formal negotiations commence... A lack of clarity in the past has been a substantial obstacle to progress.' The right of first refusal was going to be a key part of the settlement because of the very 'modest quantum proposed' by the Crown. Declaring some items off limits from the beginning would, O'Regan suggested, be 'unhelpful'. Although he understood that some assets would be very difficult to value, he still thought there was room for further discussion. Litigation would be suspended in good time, but not until negotiations had truly recommenced.[5]

The key issues to recommencing negotiations centred on the Crown's desire to include all aspects of the Ngāi Tahu claim, while the iwi wanted mahinga kai and ancillary claims to remain separate. Ngāi Tahu still demanded a right of first refusal on all Crown assets, interest payments and a relativity clause, which the Crown opposed. There was also a need for a significant interim offer to show the Crown's commitment to the negotiations. Another issue was the impending closure of the House before the election: neither Ngāi Tahu nor the Crown wanted to deal with the uncertainty that could follow. The scope of extinguishment was an incredibly important aspect of settlement and was tied to the issue of finality. The Crown planned to extinguish all claims, even those yet to be made. This was a step further than just mahinga kai and ancillary claims. Ngāi Tahu were concerned that they would be 'forced to extinguish rights before they are fully identified' and therefore would have to forego them. The Crown acknowledged that there needed to be a distinction between historical and contemporary breaches. Ngāi Tahu were especially concerned about water rights, which were not on the negotiating table but could be available to claimants in the future. There also had to be some inclusion of the conservation estate but this would require lengthy public consultation.[6]

When negotiations began again the Crown negotiating team was led by an Office of Treaty Settlements official who had spent a number of years at Te Puni Kōkiri and Treasury. She was joined by a Crown Law Office official who had worked on treaty and especially Ngāi Tahu-related issues throughout the 1990s, and a Treasury official who would later become the director of the Office of Treaty Settlements. Although Sir Tipene O'Regan (he had been knighted in June 1994) and Rakiihia Tau Snr remained the Ngāi Tahu principals and were still intimately involved in the negotiations, they left the minutiae of negotiation to Ngāi Tahu officials. Claims manager Anake Goodall was joined by long-time legal adviser Nick Davidson, financial adviser Richard Meade and Sid Ashton.

Led by Anake Goodall for Ngāi Tahu and the new lead Office of Treaty Settlements official for the Crown, the two sides met four times between 10 and 16 May 1996 to see if it was worth restarting negotiations. The meetings focused on clarifying the points in Bolger's late March letter to Ngāi Tahu. They had agreed to suspend litigation but also wanted to ensure there were no surprises in the sale of Crown assets during negotiations. If this were not the case, Ngāi Tahu asked to be free to pursue litigation. The iwi also wanted mahinga kai and natural resource claims parked, but the Crown remained adamant that the Waikato–Tainui settlement was not the model. With regard to amount, 'there was considerable discussion as to what the Prime Minister had meant by the term "you won't get any more than Tainui" in his meeting with Sir Tipene of 7 May 1996, particularly on Ngāi Tahu's use of the term "the Tainui model".' The Crown confirmed the different aspects of the

Waikato–Tainui settlement: cash and assets to the value of $170 million, interest payments, a right of first refusal, a relativity clause and the gifting of Hopuhopu. 'Ngāi Tahu made it clear that it was difficult to accept this quantum given what they believe to be the relative size of loss compared with Waikato. [The] Crown reiterated that [the] total quantum was $170 million.' Only assets commonly traded in the commercial marketplace would be available. Not much was said about interest payments and the relativity clause except that Waikato–Tainui had got it as part of their settlement. When Ngāi Tahu expressed concern that the Arahura Valley had been bracketed with the high-country stations as too difficult to handle for the moment, the Crown agreed to separate it as an issue in its own right.[7]

Ngāi Tahu also reminded the Crown about the changes they had accepted to their land-bank in 1992 in order to add the Wakatipu high-country stations and pointed out that these were now going to be retired to the conservation estate without the lessees' interests being taken into account. Ngāi Tahu's interests in the stations were commercial (tourism), farming and cultural, but at least they wanted their cultural interests protected. Ngāi Tahu, anxious to have something tangible before the election, favoured an interim settlement similar to the one offered in 1994 but with changes to specific redress for areas like Rarotoka Island and Whenua Hou.[8]

May 1996 had been a productive month, but there were still many differences between the Crown's and Ngāi Tahu's negotiating positions. These were evident in the minutes of a meeting held between Bolger and O'Regan and their respective advisers on 28 May. The Crown indicated in its version of the minutes that Ngāi Tahu and the Crown were in agreement on the 'comprehensiveness' of the settlement, the use of a right of first refusal and an amount of $170 million. Ngāi Tahu's version of the minutes revealed that although Ngāi Tahu had accepted the nominal figure of $170 million they still wanted it in 1994 dollars, as Waikato–Tainui had received its settlement. The Crown maintained that it would only provide Ngāi Tahu with a settlement in 1996 dollars. Ngāi Tahu also wished for an interim settlement as an expression of the Crown's goodwill but the government was uninterested in an interim settlement of any kind that would contradict the need for 'comprehensiveness'.[9] O'Regan directly lobbied the prime minister in late May 1996,[10] and only days later Graham returned to Cabinet to ask for, and receive, approval for a potential interim settlement. O'Regan noted that there was little risk for Ngāi Tahu in recommencing the negotiations and doing so would be best for the tribe.[11]

On 4 June 1996 O'Regan received a letter from the Office of Treaty Settlements to say that negotiations had officially restarted.[12] On 14 June an agreement on the interim settlement was officially reached. Ngāi Tahu would receive ownership of pounamu and Rarotoka Island (including its foreshore and seabed without a marginal strip), shared management of Tūtaepatu Lagoon and $10 million. Although the contents of the on-account settlement were reported in the media, there was still little public knowledge of what else the Crown might agree to. As the *Dominion* reported on 19 June, 'The best clue so far on the state of the negotiations is perhaps the face of Ngāi Tahu's chief negotiator. "I saw Tipene O'Regan on Lambton Quay today," a Government treaty official said last week. "I don't know how his talks are going, but he had a huge grin. I'd have to imagine they're going very well."'[13] With the negotiations headed towards a fruitful outcome, the negotiation over the historical account began in earnest.

Because Treaty of Waitangi settlement negotiations are intended to address and resolve historical claims by Māori against the Crown, they are infused with wide-ranging debate about colonisation in New Zealand. Early in the Waikato–Tainui negotiations it became clear that the Crown would need to go beyond purely monetary redress and even the return of land – also necessary were an apology and a historical account of the relations between the Crown and Waikato–Tainui.[14] As Doug Graham later commented, historical events had to be put in 'their proper place – not forgotten but accepted'.[15] State apologies in many parts of the world have increased in prominence, especially since the late twentieth century. Historians, political scientists, sociologists and lawyers have explored their development in North America, Europe, Japan, Australia and New Zealand,[16] but no one has analysed and described the specific process of producing a state apology and the players involved. Some of these accounts have also focused largely on apologies at state rather than iwi level.[17] In the New Zealand treaty settlement process the historical accounts, and the apologies they lead to, are meant to be as unbiased, unemotional and neutral as possible, and they rely on a great deal of discussion and debate. If, as one observer suggests, the writing of 'history is mostly about power', then in Ngāi Tahu's case these debates reflected the assertion of the iwi's rangatiratanga and the Crown's defence of its own sovereignty.[18]

Although both Ngāi Tahu and the Crown had concerns about the conclusions in the *Ngai Tahu Land Report*, they agreed to use it as the baseline for the negotiation. The quantification of loss was the focus of the first historical debate in Ngāi Tahu's negotiations with the National government in the early 1990s but it only lasted for approximately a year. As the negotiations slowly began to break down in 1993 and 1994, the historical debates ended, to resume only when the negotiations had restarted. There were widely differing views on the history of Ngāi Tahu's colonisation but a final compromise was reached. Ngāi Tahu's primary historical adviser was Te Maire Tau, aided by Nick Davidson. Office of Treaty Settlements and Crown Law representatives led the negotiation from the Crown side.

Historian Julie Bellingham has argued that the Crown has used historical accounts and apologies to liberate itself from past wrongs and blame, rather than as an accurate historical narrative. She has questioned the extent of Māori claimant input into the formulation of historical accounts, and noted the Crown's dominance of the process.[19] The negotiations over Ngāi Tahu's historical account reveal that many of Bellingham's observations were correct. Ngāi Tahu complained about the Crown's refusal to include historical details and the Crown's control of the overall process. Bellingham, however, overlooks the agency and role of Māori claimants. Ngāi Tahu had significant input into their apologies and historical accounts and obtained important concessions in the final versions. It has been said that historical accounts are 'inevitably lifeless, tedious to read and indeed to write'.[20] Although these aspects of treaty settlements tend to have the most neutral tone and to take uncontroversial positions, the debates that occur between the Crown and claimants are far from lifeless.

The debates regarding Ngāi Tahu's historical account and apology began soon after the interim settlement was signed in June 1996.

The Office of Treaty Settlements historian assigned to the Ngāi Tahu claim met Te Maire Tau in the middle of that month. The office's terms of reference included a strong reliance on the tribunal report for findings of breaches of treaty principles. Tau was largely content with these terms, but wanted to add an acknowledgement that the 'two parties would be approaching the statements from different cultural contexts and these contexts should be reflected in the statements'.[21] In that vein Tau wanted the preamble to have a specific structure beginning with a karakia followed by a poroporoaki, mihi and kaupapa, and to finish with a specially commissioned waiata. The apology was to be delivered orally as well as in written form. Many Ngāi Tahu members wanted the ceremony to be held on a marae, but Tau believed the occasion was of national significance and also wanted it in a public place; possibly there would be two ceremonies.[22]

Tau also advocated for royal involvement in the ceremony. Despite their history of antagonism to the Crown, Waikato–Tainui had received royal assent. Ngāi Tahu had always been strongly loyalist, raising funds for the military campaigns of the 1860s in Waikato and Taranaki and sending many soldiers to both world wars.[23] There was no opposition from the Crown for this recognition. The final version of the apology contained a section specifically addressing Ngāi Tahu's loyalty and military sacrifice for the nation.

As it had during the intense negotiations of 1992 and 1993 regarding the quantification of loss, the issue of tenths remained a point of difference between Crown and Ngāi Tahu representatives. Ngāi Tahu historians maintained that the principle of tenths mentioned in the 1991 tribunal report applied to all the Crown land purchases and therefore a large part of the value of Ngāi Tahu's loss lay within that grievance. The Crown Law historian questioned the validity of the Ngāi Tahu claim to tenths in the Otago Purchase, and opposed the notion of tenths for all the deeds. As we have seen, the tribunal found there was no evidence to support Ngāi Tahu's contention that the Crown had promised to retain for Ngāi Tahu a tenth of the land that had been sold at Otago. Nonetheless, the tribunal did state that had the Crown reserved a tenth of the purchased land, and done so for all the purchases, it would have been 'greatly to the advantage of Ngāi Tahu'.[24] The Crown Law historian noted that even those groups such as the Port Nicholson Trust that had tenths awarded in the mid-nineteenth century were not given private ownership of them; rather they were used for educational or whatever civilising purposes the government of the day desired. Not only, he claimed, would the tenths land have been used in that manner, but 'it may have been that, with the increasing genetic migration of Ngāi Tahu into the European population, the balance might have swung more towards public rather than purely native purposes'.[25] There is nothing controversial about recognising that the notion of tenths had not applied for each and every land purchase, especially considering the size of the Ngāi Tahu rohe compared with other groups around the country. Questionable, however, is rationalising tenths by making excuses for the way in which colonial governments formulated land trusts. Making guesses at the potential use of such lands because of alleged 'genetic migrations' is similarly unhelpful, even though the memorandum containing this point was not put directly to Ngāi Tahu.

The Crown's focus in Waikato–Tainui's preamble had been on a very general interpretation of the history with as little detail as possible.[26] In this case it was Ngāi Tahu who wanted to provide a more general view of tenths, while Crown historians wanted to restrict any mention strictly to the Otago Purchase. Crown Law sought to explain that although the Crown's obligations to Ngāi Tahu could have been achieved by using tenths, they could also have been achieved by other means. Ngāi Tahu historians rejected this approach, and in this they were supported by other Māori historians such as Ranginui Walker and by Ngāi Tahu's Pākehā historians, especially Ann Parsonson and Harry Evison.[27] The Crown Law historian was firm in his view of the alleged 'reality of the history' and pointed to the tribunal's findings. In his advice to his superiors he painted a rather stark picture of the way in which he believed Ngāi Tahu were using a subjective version of their claim history to their own benefit. In correspondence with Tau regarding tenths, the Office of Treaty Settlements historian also relied on the tribunal's findings.[28] Tenths would remain the most contentious historical issue. In the end it was included solely to describe the purchase of the Otago block, with the qualification that Crown may also have achieved its obligations in another way: 'The Tribunal considered that the Crown's obligation [to make further provision for Ngāi Tahu in the purchase of the Otago block] might have been satisfied by the creation of "Tenths", or by other adequate provision.'[29]

In 1849 Walter Mantell, on behalf of the Crown, had purchased Ngāi Tahu lands around Banks Peninsula. The tribunal found that Mantell had been unnecessarily high-handed in his negotiations with Ngāi Tahu for the Port Levy block, and had unfairly denied them reserves at Okains and Pigeon bays: 'It is plain that Ngāi Tahu did not wish to sell land at Okains Bay and at Pigeon Bay. But they were overborne by Mantell, in clear breach of article 2 which required the consent of Ngāi Tahu to the sale of their land.'[30] Ngāi Tahu had claimed that they had also requested reserves in another area within the Port Levy block, Kaituna Valley, but the tribunal did not comment on the validity of this. Tau wished to include in the historical account Mantell's denial of reserves requested by Ngāi Tahu at Okains Bay, Pigeon Bay and Kaituna Valley.[31]

The Office of Treaty Settlements official was concerned about the tribunal's lack of commentary on Kaituna Valley and was hesitant to include it in the historical account. Nonetheless, he recognised that the tribunal may have been mistaken in omitting the request to reserve Kaituna Valley from its finding. He told Tau that the office was 'quite prepared to accept that the Tribunal merely overlooked Kaituna Valley, provided that there is good contemporary evidence that, as with the other two sites, Ngāi Tahu requested this reserve and were unjustifiably turned down. You may be able to supply us with such a reference. In the meantime, we will try to pin the matter down.'[32] Ngāi Tahu maintained that the tribunal had merely overlooked Kaituna Valley and that Ngāi Tahu had requested its exclusion. The only reference Ngāi Tahu provided was the work of historian Harry Evison, whose primary source analysis of the Port Levy Purchase revealed that the valley was a culturally and economically significant fertile area and some members of Ngāi Tahu had specifically asked for its exclusion.[33] Evison's research was accepted;[34] the final wording in the deed read: 'Significant to the Tribunal's findings on the Port Levy purchase was the Crown's refusal to make reserves, as requested by Ngāi Tahu, at Okains Bay, Kaituna Valley and Pigeon Bay.'[35]

There were other areas of disagreement. Tau wanted the following phrases, italicised here for emphasis, incorporated into the apology:

The Crown recognises that it has failed in *every material aspect* to meet the obligations to Ngāi Tahu, its Treaty partner, which arose from the Deeds of Purchase whereby the Crown acquired Ngāi Tahu land in the South Island, and to act towards Ngāi Tahu with the utmost good faith in a manner consistent with the honour of the Crown. Indeed the Crown admits that its failure to act in good faith reduced several generations of Ngāi Tahu to a state of *landlessness and poverty* and failed to protect their rangatiratanga.[36]

This was too uncompromising for the Crown Law Office. Tau stressed that the Crown had caused Ngāi Tahu's complete landlessness; the Crown Law Office held that, although they were small, there were some reserves. As far as the failure in 'every material aspect', both historians considered that this was inaccurate. Although there was resounding failure on the Crown's part, it was not quite in 'every material aspect'. The Office of Treaty Settlements historian also alluded to the difficulties the term could present for parliamentary counsel when they were drafting the settlement legislation. (This comment could have been a reference to such problems during Waikato–Tainui's negotiations.)[37] Ngāi Tahu wanted the apology to describe the Crown as having acted 'unconscionably' in relation to the purchase of lands and apportioning of reserves for Ngāi Tahu. For the historians, the term 'unconscionably' was too strong, as it had not been specifically noted in the tribunal report.[38]

Despite this opposition, Tau's subsequent draft retained the terminology in both sections of the apology.[39] Although the reference to landlessness and the phrase 'every material aspect' would not remain, Tau was able to retain the use of the term 'unconscionably' to describe the Crown's conduct:

> The Crown acknowledges that it acted *unconscionably* and in repeated breach of the principles of the Treaty of Waitangi in its dealings with Ngāi Tahu in the purchases of Ngāi Tahu land. The Crown further acknowledges that in relation to the deeds of purchase it has failed in *most material respects* to honour its obligations to Ngāi Tahu as its Treaty partner, while it also failed to set aside adequate lands for Ngāi Tahu's use, and to provide adequate economic and social resources for Ngāi Tahu.[40]

The most controversial position put forward by the Crown Law Office was that the Crown had been responsible for keeping Ngāi Tahu in poverty, but that this was an improvement on their previous state.[41] This view of the 'primitive' state of Ngāi Tahu before European contact was not an isolated contemporary interpretation of indigenous peoples. In Canada, British Columbian Chief Justice Allan McEachern made similar comments in his 1991 judgement, in the Gitskan-Wet'suwet'en land claim case, where he infamously used the words from Thomas Hobbes' *Leviathan* to describe the lives of these First Nations people before the arrival of Europeans, as 'nasty, brutish and short'.[42] Although the Crown Law Office (and indeed McEachern) were endorsing the Eurocentric ideal of the 'noble savage', the significant point here was to call into question the Crown Law Office's very colonial rationales. The Crown Law Office historian's view gained no traction with the other historian. The reference to the Crown failing to act in good faith and subsequently reducing Ngāi Tahu to poverty would remain and was expanded in the final version of the apology.

The inclusion of a whakataukī or Māori proverb was another important aspect of the apology. The Waikato–Tainui apology had included wording that spoke of how kuia had felt like 'orphans' when their lands were confiscated by the Crown.[43] Tau included in the Ngāi Tahu preamble a whakataukī to recognise all those who had struggled for the resolution of Ngāi Tahu's claims since the middle of the nineteenth century.

By early August 1996 both groups of historians were in nearly complete agreement on all the aspects of the apology, the preamble, karakia and waiata. Then, on 5 August, Tau asked for another addition to the apology.[44] He recommended that a part of Matiaha Tiramorehu's petition to Queen Victoria in 1857 be included to represent the visions that had been conceived by Ngāi Tahu once the truly oppressive onslaught of British colonisation and settlement occurred: 'This was the command thy love laid upon these Governors ... that the law be made one, that the commandments be made one, that the white skin be made just equal with the dark skin, and to lay down the love of thy graciousness to the Maori that they dwell happily ... and remember the power of thy name.' The proposed addition was allowed.[45] Thereafter, the preamble and apology remained largely the same and there was little further contention regarding historical debates within Ngāi Tahu's negotiations with the

Crown. The attention of both sides was firmly on specific issues both on and off the negotiating table.

The negotiations regarding Ngāi Tahu's preamble and apology were negotiated relatively quickly within a three-month period, as the parties were able to use the Ngāi Tahu Tribunal Report to resolve any disagreements. In some cases Ngāi Tahu were unable to have the specific terminology they originally sought, but they did obtain many concessions.

The negotiations that took place following the passage of the Te Runanga o Ngai Tahu Act became dominated by detail as advisers from both sides worked to hammer out a deal. There were so many issues to address, from financial, legal and political angles, that it was a minor miracle that an agreement was signed when it was. Would the $170 million be adjusted for inflation? How many deferred selection properties would be available for inclusion? Were interest payments and the relativity clause still on the table? Would the Crown Tītī Islands be included? What about Whenua Hou or Rarotoka Island? The high-country stations also still remained to be addressed. The negotiations had well and truly recommenced but a successful negotiation was in no way guaranteed.

CHAPTER 10

A settlement at last

In October 1996, just before the election, a heads of agreement was signed. After five tough years of negotiation, all of a sudden within a few short months an agreement was in place. This was due to the patience of both the Crown and Ngāi Tahu, and the understanding from Ngāi Tahu's grassroots that the compromise that had been reached would be the best possible outcome in the circumstances. With some hard work and determination, by and large the major issues had been addressed by the time the heads of agreement was signed. The challenges were nowhere near concluded, though, as the pressure was on to complete a deed of settlement the following year. Before that could be done the approval of the Ngāi Tahu people was needed, and that was in no way guaranteed.

Following the agreement on the on-account settlement in June 1996 the two sides got back to the grind of the negotiations. Ngāi Tahu negotiators were still not quite convinced on the issue of whether the settlement would be paid in 1994 or 1996 dollars. They eventually backed down after receiving a panicked directive that Cabinet would not move on $170 million in 1996 dollars and that the alternative would be a breakdown of the negotiations. They correctly recognised that the shortfall could be made up by ensuring that interest would be paid on the delivery of the settlement and through the right of first refusal. Another outstanding issue was the ancillary claims, which Ngāi Tahu negotiators stressed they would not have the mandate to resolve as they were the specific claims of Ngāi Tahu individuals and whānau. They related to specific takings of land, often under various Public Works Act legislation, and families became personally involved in resolving them. Ultimately they would be settled without any financial cost as a part of the settlement.[1]

O'Regan was still concerned about the extinguishment of all future customary rights for Ngāi Tahu after the settlement and about the inclusion of mahinga kai and ancillary claims. The government was still not willing to provide SOE shares in airports and was sticking to the DOC report on the Wakatipu high-country stations, which had recommended that much of the land now be retired into the conservation estate. Furthermore, DOC was applying its position on the Wakatipu high-country stations of retiring lands to a whole range of ancillary claims, and business concessions on DOC land were off the negotiating table. O'Regan commented: '[Conservation Minister Bill] Mansfield is not behaving.'[2] There were clearly still a number of interrelated issues to work through.

The use of the right of first refusal was beginning to be portrayed as a key part of expanding the value of the settlement, but Ngāi Tahu negotiators stressed that it should apply to the amount of loss, not the size of settlement provided by the Crown. Ngāi Tahu wanted to ensure that the nominal value of money they received for purchasing lands and assets was not affected by the benefits resulting from the right of first refusal. Debate also continued over the scope of the right, as Ngāi Tahu sought what the Crown believed were 'illiquid assets', such as power stations. To protect Māori interests, the Treaty of Waitangi (State Enterprises) Act 1988 had placed special memorials on SOE lands before they were sold, but the Crown now wanted to ignore these properties that were now privately owned. It had probably been influenced by experiences during the Waikato–Tainui settlement when six Waikato farmers had their right to purchase back lands acquired through the Public Works Act extinguished because of the memorials placed on their land in the late 1980s. They created quite a furore in the media and were eventually awarded up to $20,000 compensation.[3]

There was significant pressure from within the government to arrange some type of agreement before the 1996 election and this pressure was passed onto Ngāi Tahu. Bolger was still very much the principal negotiator: he was being used as the Crown minister who broke deadlocks in meetings with O'Regan. For one such meeting in early August Bolger was advised to ensure that O'Regan did not try to separate mahinga kai from the negotiations to allow for future water rights. Ngāi Tahu had reduced the number of ancillary claims for which they were seeking redress from 117 to 36. That meant the right of first refusal was now open to slightly more interpretation, and a few more options were also on the negotiating table: variations in the options for future use of the Wakatipu high-country stations, the possible purchase of Highbank Power Station and Wigram airbase outside of the settlement process, the inclusion of The Power Company Limited (a Southland power company) properties and interests in airports. The high-country stations were a particularly prominent topic for discussion. Bolger expressed sympathy for Ngāi Tahu regarding the leases. In August 1996 he told iwi negotiators that if private interests had purchased the leases, the Crown would not have been able to obtain them for inclusion in the conservation estate.[4] This situation would change in the coming years following a wide-ranging national pastoral lease review, but at the time it served to affirm Ngāi Tahu's negative opinion of conservation interests. When the negotiations were approaching a heads of agreement, the conservation and sports recreation organisations resumed their heated opposition to using the high-country pastoral leases in the Ngāi Tahu settlement.[5]

As the Crown expected, Ngāi Tahu also sought a relativity clause because of their reservations about the full and final nature of such a fiscally limited settlement. The relativity clause was also necessary to appease the Ngāi Tahu constituency on the wider matter of finality.[6] There was, nonetheless, opposition from the Crown. A March Cabinet paper produced by the Office of Treaty Settlements and Treasury had stated that the risks of the relativity clause outweighed the benefits and advised against providing it.[7] The positions for each side largely remained firm throughout August 1996 and there was little movement in the negotiations.

In the vacuum other political voices filled the void. Labour MP Mike Moore raised the issue of the preferential land-banking procedures Ngāi Tahu received, although he later withdrew his accusations of preferential treatment. Graham had stated that taxpayers may have been ripped off by the Ngāi Tahu land-bank, while Denis Marshall, Minister of Lands, said otherwise. All of this was great fodder for arch-critic Mike Moore and left Ngāi Tahu somewhat stupefied. O'Regan wrote a letter to the *Timaru Herald* pointing out that they purchased the properties according to valuations set by the Public Works Act and the Land Act. The properties Moore had accused of being sold the same day were in fact sold anywhere from two to 11 months later. 'The way the point has been seized on by the commentators is more a reflection on their blundering indignation than on Ngāi Tahu.'[8] The election was now fast approaching and Moore was trying to score political points but his stance almost certainly bolstered Pākehā backlash.

Treasury favoured waiting until after the election, while the Office of Treaty Settlements wanted negotiations to continue.[9] Despite some disagreements, a considerable amount of momentum had been building to finalise the deal. Treasury's preferred option would, it was thought, present a series of risks, so the office's view prevailed. The Crown and Ngāi Tahu agreed to recommence negotiations with a view to attempt a heads of agreement before the election. If the principals did not meet to resolve outstanding issues there would be nothing to show after three months of negotiations. The Crown could be accused of not negotiating in good faith and Ngāi Tahu would be pressured by their constituency to return to litigation. The lead Office of Treaty Settlements official noted that Ngāi Tahu might even ask for more money after the election and proposed that a heads of agreement be signed by 30 September 1996.[10]

Perhaps the most important issue to be sorted in September was the purchase of Wigram airbase. In early September Ngāi Tahu negotiators were so concerned that O'Regan wrote a letter to Bolger requesting a meeting to discuss the matter. When this meeting was not arranged Ashton threatened that Ngāi Tahu negotiators would not meet with their Crown counterparts until the issue was resolved. They were quickly reassured that it would be dealt with. Ngāi Tahu wanted certainty on Wigram, but the Crown wished to extract some leverage from the base without impeding the negotiating process. O'Regan explained in a letter to Bill Birch that the transfer of Wigram airbase should be outside the negotiations because if it needed legislation then that could be halted 'when it is required to be strained through the Parliamentary sieve'. There was also still considerable cynicism about the Crown's integrity;

the transfer would go a long way towards reaffirming the relationship between the Crown and Ngāi Tahu. In return for the option to purchase Wigram airbase, Ngāi Tahu gave up any claims to The Power Company Limited assets and freehold title to Whenua Hou.[11] Ngāi Tahu still also wanted to hold back on mahinga kai and there were also some problems with the relativity clause. Treasury commented that Ngāi Tahu were 'going for something that they were not entitled [to]'.[12]

A 16 September briefing paper by Sid Ashton set out the negotiating team's frame of mind at the time. 'Ngāi Tahu is not in a supplicant position. Two Treaty Partners are attempting in an open frank manner to settle a long standing dispute. The CROWN is the Sinner not the Judge and Jury!' Ngāi Tahu were especially concerned about the transfer of the high-country station properties, which remained in the land-bank. It was looking increasingly likely that over 90 per cent of the properties would be retired into the conservation estate. The Crown continued to consult with third-party interests despite Ngāi Tahu's request to stop doing so.[13] Conservation interests also sought to have the scenic value of the Arahura River area recognised in addition to the historic reserve sought by Ngāi Tahu.[14] Ultimately, the Waitaiki Historic Reserve was vested in the Māwhera Incorporation, although Ngāi Tahu were unable to have the entire catchment vested as they had originally requested.[15]

On 25 September Graham sent O'Regan another Crown offer, asking for a response by the 27th. The $170 million would be supplemented by a deferred selection process, which Ngāi Tahu negotiators had sought in addition to the right of first refusal. This mechanism allowed the tribe to buy, with its own money, Crown assets from a defined 'pool' of assets, within 12 months of settlement legislation being passed. The Crown refused to include a relativity clause.[16] Originally Ngāi Tahu were given only an extra $5 million to spend on top of the $170 million cash settlement, but right before the heads of agreement was signed, Ngāi Tahu negotiators managed to have the amount increased to an extra $10 million. The specifics of the valuation procedures were left for the negotiations leading up to the final agreement. Most of the Wakatipu high-country stations would be leased at peppercorn rentals to DOC. Whenua Hou was to remain in the Crown's hands, but Rarotoka Island and the Crown Tītī Islands were to be transferred to Ngāi Tahu. Mahinga kai grievances would be addressed by the transfer of small, discrete sites, as well as a series of mechanisms enabling various forms of statutory recognition. The Crown agreed to settle 41 ancillary claims, including 33 that were upheld by the tribunal, but these would be negotiated after the heads of agreement was signed.

Rakiihia Tau Snr rejected Graham's offer because he claimed that there were 'too many denials' of Ngāi Tahu positions. In many ways O'Regan agreed with Tau but contended that it was still possible to shift the Crown's positions. This was confirmed by Anake Goodall, who spoke with the Office of Treaty Settlements the day after the offer was received.[17] He reported that he had 'received various signals from various Crown officials to the effect that "a reply by Sunday evening would be fine"; "if you've got a problem with the tight time-frame, just let us know"; "you'll have to counter-offer at least"; and "whatever you do, don't reject the offer outright, let's keep talking". There's obviously some Crown anxiety to keep the door open and the talks continuing.' The 'final' offer by the Crown was clearly far from final.[18] Goodall had a series of telephone conversations with the Office of Treaty Settlements to discuss the preliminary Ngāi Tahu reaction to the Crown's offer. The most pressing point was the Crown's stress on 'comprehensiveness', which extended to extinguishing even future aboriginal rights, that is all treaty rights, to which Ngāi Tahu were completely opposed.

Possible misunderstanding could be a problem. Reacting to a Department of Justice suggestion that extinguishment should essentially be possible by other means – in other words, specific historical claims could be extinguished rather than having a blanket extinguishment of all claims – a Te Puni Kōkiri official said he did not trust that ministers would even understand what aboriginal rights were or what the tribunal had said regarding them.

> After the section on Court of Appeal decisions you should add that jurisprudence does suggest that the Crown has a fiduciary duty to Maori to achieve its objectives, in this case finality and comprehensiveness, in a manner that is not intrusive or impinges as little as possible on their interests... Under section headed Aboriginal Rights I think we need to note many aboriginal rights are non-proprietal. Eg collecting shellfish, visiting waahi tapu, being tangata whenua, holding mana whenua. The Crown does not seek to extinguish these (or does it?).

The Crown's position would definitely soften and prove to be an important factor in encouraging the Ngāi Tahu negotiators towards signing the heads of agreement.

Goodall had further issues with the offer, such as the reserves boards related to Whenua Hou and the Arahura Valley, but the reply was that they had merely been accidentally omitted. On other points, such as the return of Te Waihora, the negotiation could be left for after the heads of agreement; as long as there was substantial agreement on most issues there should be no problem. A request from Goodall for a written record of some of the points made in their phone conversation prompted a defensive reaction: the official could not undermine the minister; the conversation was just a way of trying to advance the negotiations as best as they could.[19]

In late September 1996, Ngāi Tahu proposed that the fee simple title of Whenua Hou be transferred to Ngāi Tahu with immediate gift back to the Crown. When it was made clear that fee simple title would remain with the Crown, Ngāi Tahu sought an undertaking that if the island were no longer required for conservation purposes it would pass to Ngāi Tahu. This was in effect a right of first refusal to Whenua Hou. The Crown opposed this. Its final offer was that, instead of the establishment of a reserves board, a sub-committee of the Southland Conservation Board would be established with equal representation from Rakiura Ngāi Tahu and the Southland Conservation Board. The sub-committee would also prepare a policy setting out the conditions under which the conservation minister would grant permits for access to Whenua Hou. In exchange, Ngāi Tahu would receive the fee simple title to the Crown Tītī Islands and sole responsibility for their management.[20]

Ngāi Tahu remained adamant about the relativity clause. Ngāi Tahu advisers stated that it was 'essential', adding that it 'costs the Crown nothing if it sticks to the envelope (and if it doesn't intend to stick to the envelope, why is the quantum so low?)'.[21] Treasury believed that only Waikato–Tainui was entitled to the relativity clause because they were the first to settle. The Office of Treaty Settlements understood the importance of the clause to Ngāi Tahu and attempted to counter Treasury's rationales.[22] Ngāi Tahu sought a relativity clause that was identical to Waikato–Tainui's 17 per cent, but Crown officials countered that it should be proportionate to the size of the overall amount provided for all claims.[23] Since Ngāi Tahu did not receive the settlement in 1994 dollars it had wanted, the value of its settlement was only 16.1 per cent. Like Waikato–Tainui, Ngāi Tahu would not have settled without the relativity clause.

On 30 September 1996, against Treasury's advice, Cabinet authorised Graham to make another offer to Ngāi Tahu. This did not mean that the settlement was guaranteed. The same day O'Regan received notification from Finance Minister Bill Birch that the Crown approved of Ngāi Tahu purchasing Wigram airbase outside the settlement negotiations. This precondition for settlement had now been met. O'Regan seemed to be generally inclined towards settling, but Sid Ashton stressed caution, especially if Rakiihia Tau Snr had not given his approval. Ashton, though, supported signing the heads of agreement because of the huge costs of keeping up the negotiations (approximately $1.5–$2 million per year) and the potential uncertainty of a new government. Ashton felt there was no point in keeping the anti-Doug Graham line going and the longer the claim dragged on the more claims would be lodged within Ngāi Tahu's rohe.[24]

Between 1 and 5 October Ngāi Tahu managed to negotiate the inclusion of some major additions to the Crown offer. The Crown offered to pay interest on the unpaid sum from the deed of settlement until final payment, but Ngāi Tahu convinced it to pay interest from the date of the signing of the heads of agreement. The Crown also agreed to gift redress for the conservation aspects of the settlement and negotiations over specific sites of cultural significance such as the Crown Tītī Islands, Rarotoka Island, the Arahura Valley, access to mahinga kai sites and ancillary claims – that is, their monetary value would not be subtracted from the $170 million. Perhaps most significantly, Ngāi Tahu were able to arrange one dedicated seat on the New Zealand Conservation Authority; Waikato–Tainui had sought this but had received only a seat on the Waikato Conservation Board. Despite Treasury opposition Ngāi Tahu were successful and had the relativity clause included in the heads of agreement.[25]

When an agreement was finally reached on Whenua Hou and the Crown Tītī Islands just before the 1996 election, FMC and Forest & Bird continued to oppose any settlement involving conservation areas. Kevin Smith continued to express opposition to the transfer

of the Crown Tītī Islands,[26] and the Southland branch of Forest &
Bird expressed its concern about the allegedly 'speedy' negotiations.
Forest & Bird was against both the proposed handover of the Crown
Tītī Islands and the creation of a Whenua Hou sub-committee.
Barbara Marshall of FMC asked that neither the Crown Tītī Islands nor
Whenua Hou be used as redress, despite the clear recommendations of
the Waitangi Tribunal.[27]

Bryce Johnson of Fish and Game played a pivotal role in organising
consultation with conservation groups, which continued throughout
the negotiation to a final agreement. Forest & Bird and Public Access
New Zealand refused to attend nearly all of these consultations and
then released selective quotes about the settlement and its provisions.
They made no mention of the 30,350 hectares (75,000 acres) of land
Ngāi Tahu were being forced to contribute to the conservation estate
from the three high-country pastoral leases.[28] It was only in August 1996
that Forest & Bird had pleaded with the government to consult with
conservation groups.[29]

When, on 5 October 1996, a heads of agreement was finally signed
between Ngāi Tahu and the Crown, Graham commented to O'Regan,
'I want to thank you for allowing me to share your suffering.' He joked
that when negotiations began 'Tipene had a full head of hair and I
looked like Bill Birch.' He had started the Ngāi Tahu negotiations with a
reference to the innate 'fairness' of New Zealanders. 'This is the greatest
country in the world. We have everything going for us and it will only be
because of our own stupidity if we do not live in harmony, with respect
and dignity.' The *Dominion*'s Hugh Barlow commented that the Ngāi Tahu
negotiations were marked by more complex factors and influences than
those for Waikato–Tainui because of the opposition of conservationists
and the number of internal dissidents. The first point was correct,
because the claim to the river was excluded from the Waikato–Tainui
negotiations, but there certainly was substantial internal dissent from
academics such as Dr Pare Hopa, and Ngāti Wairere claimants camped
out on disputed land well into 1996. The difference in the case of Ngāi
Tahu was that dissidents Sandra Lee and Whetu Tirakatene-Sullivan
held very powerful positions in the machinery of government and were
able to more effectively influence the negotiation process.[30]

O'Regan's comment at the signing that while the settlement was acceptable it could hardly be called fair did not impress Graham. ACT leader Richard Prebble said to O'Regan, 'Well, you've out-negotiated the Crown again.' To O'Regan the question was no longer about justice, but about realistically achieving something for their grandchildren and the generations to come. TV1 News was particularly supportive. It chose to headline with a three-minute story, half of which was spent discussing the claim with Ngāi Tahu's own historian, Harry Evison. The news story detailed the historical nature of the grievances – the duplicity of Crown agents such as Kemp and Mantell – and was generally sympathetic to Ngāi Tahu's claims. News broadcasters noted that the approximately 255 hectares (630 acres) of DOC land planned to be returned was from a total of 4,856,280 hectares (12 million acres) of conservation land in the Ngāi Tahu region. On the *Holmes* show, Doug Graham spoke to host Susan Wood about the settlement. Although she questioned the political motivations with which the National government promoted the settlement, it could just as easily have hurt National, as *Dominion* columnist Adam Gifford pointed out.[31]

In early November 1996 Te Rūnanga o Ngāi Tahu met to discuss the ratification of the heads of agreement O'Regan had signed. Under considerable pressure, he had done this without Rakiihia Tau Snr being present, which caused some resentment. At the hui one of the representatives of the 18 papatipu rūnanga criticised O'Regan for signing without the rūnanga having a look. O'Regan emphasised, however, that it was a non-binding agreement and the measure was eventually passed. With such a democratic process disagreements within Ngāi Tahu were inevitable, but the vast majority backed the settlement. The large three-day hui-ā-tau held at the end of November also ratified the signing of the heads of agreement. The concern at this gathering centred mostly on the fear that customary rights would be extinguished. The Ngāi Tahu negotiators had to convince beneficiaries that that was not the case. Each papatipu rūnanga would have six weeks to submit concerns to Te Rūnanga o Ngāi Tahu and the negotiators would also conduct a settlement 'road-show' for each rūnanga.[32]

After New Zealand's first MMP election in October 1996 Winston Peters led his New Zealand First party into a coalition government with a former enemy for the first time, but certainly not the last.[33] It was important to keep the momentum of negotiations going. Had a Labour-led government been elected, rather than a National-led one, it would have had to ratify the heads of agreement. At best, it would only have extended the negotiating period; at worst, it would have halted it indefinitely, especially if it had been in coalition with the Sandra Lee-led Alliance Party.

With Graham's support assured, the Office of Treaty Settlements hoped to have a final agreement negotiated by March 1997. But the scope of this was not yet apparent to Crown officials and the negotiations would take another six months.[34] Because the negotiations with Waikato–Tainui specifically excluded any conservation issues, the Crown and Ngāi Tahu had no established precedents for the large number of new conservation redress decisions that had to be made. In global terms, the final negotiation between the heads of agreement and the deed was in fact completed in a very short time. As O'Regan had pointed out in 1993, negotiations in Canada generally took 10–15 years.[35]

The negotiations leading to the deed of settlement encompassed a series of different but complementary aspects. A process was required to value Crown properties purchased by Ngāi Tahu through the right of first refusal plus additional negotiation involving the deferred selection process. Ngāi Tahu advisers regarded the valuation arrangement agreed for Waikato–Tainui as unsuitable for Ngāi Tahu; they favoured an expansive process for as many Crown assets as possible. Treasury pressed the ministers of finance and justice to remain firm on the old process that would provide a very narrow approach.[36] The other major negotiation concerned the need for new precedents to resolve mahinga kai and ancillary claims grievances. Mahinga kai would require the transfer of discrete conservation sites and a series of legal instruments to recognise Ngāi Tahu's association with specific areas. Ancillary claims would also entail the transfer of small amounts of land. Each would require extended negotiations involving the Office of Treaty Settlements and DOC. The final negotiation, about the development of settlement legislation, involved large sections of the Crown Law Office. While these detailed negotiations went on, both the Crown and

Ngāi Tahu negotiators consulted with parliamentary personnel who would approve legislative support, the public and Ngāi Tahu beneficiaries.

A major aspect of the mahinga kai redress were nohoanga entitlements – 0.4-hectare (1-acre) conservation sites that would be available purely for Ngāi Tahu use. These sought to fulfil what the Fenton entitlements should have done in the mid-nineteenth century – give Ngāi Tahu places to collect kai. The Crown would eventually agree to significant concessions on the extension of nohoanga entitlements in both number and in duration – from one month to three months to seven months, so that all rūnanga could partake. It also agreed to provide legal backing for protocols with DOC that would improve consultation over deeds of recognition and redress intended to increase Ngāi Tahu participation in resource consent processes – statutory acknowledgements.[37] Under the latter, resource consent authorities such as Environment Canterbury must 'have regard' to the views of Ngāi Tahu when considering an application. This gives the iwi a marginally greater voice than the public. Gaining the support of local rūnanga was extremely important this late in the negotiations. In some ancillary claims cases Ngāi Tahu had been arguing for 100 per cent redress, which officials feared would create undesirable precedents.[38] Because of the importance of local Ngāi Tahu support for the negotiating team, the Crown increased the settlement fund for ancillary claims from $1 million to $2.5 million.[39]

The creation of nohoanga entitlements was one of many facets of the settlement that involved DOC and caused collisions with the Office of Treaty Settlements. Jockeying between the two had begun in 1994 when the interim settlement was so reduced by DOC recommendations that Ngāi Tahu's rejection of it was almost guaranteed. In May 1997, when a DOC official complained about a lack of consultation over the development of policy on the Ngāi Tahu settlement, the new chief Office of Treaty Settlements official working on the negotiations pointed to the incorporation of DOC's comments into Cabinet papers and frequent meetings with himself and other DOC officials and asked, 'What more do you want? I realise that much of what is involved in the N[gāi]T[ahu] settlement creates real challenges for your Department. That is not a reason for continually seeking to slow things down... I believe the problems are as much attitudinal as process.'[40]

Powerful DOC lobbying not only guaranteed public access to the high-country leases but ensured that it was markedly improved, so much so that some commentators worried that the 'wander at will' provisions would create unfortunate precedents for future settlements. At a meeting of the Select Committee on Māori Affairs on its final day of deliberations, MPs cross-examined Ngāi Tahu negotiators over fears that the provisions included in the high-country pastoral leases aspects of the settlement would be used by the government as a precedent in other treaty settlement negotiations. Anake Goodall said that Ngāi Tahu were not satisfied with the result, but that conservation politics had played a major part in Crown changes to the terms of the original agreement on high-country pastoral leases. New Zealand First Te Tai Tonga MP Tutekawa Wyllie understood the Ngāi Tahu position but asked, 'Where are we to go in terms of future settlements if the nature of the Ngāi Tahu settlement may be detrimental to the ability of other iwi to settle?' Goodall replied that he was painfully aware of their responsibilities and explained that they had tried to hold the land under the same terms as neighbouring private landowners. 'It is a dark irony that the access requirement was imposed as part of the settlement of a grievance over Māori being treated differently because of their race.'[41] In the end, a large majority of the three high-country stations were added to the conservation estate and Ngāi Tahu farms the remaining area. While most Treaty settlements represent situations in which land is transferred from the Crown to Māori claimants, the retirement of over 30,350 hectares (75,000 acres) of previously private high-country pastoral leases resulted in the Crown acquiring land from Ngāi Tahu's treaty settlement.

Ngāi Tahu's desire to have title to Aoraki/Mount Cook was a particularly pressing matter for the negotiators, who regarded it as a symbol of the enhancement of the iwi's rangatiratanga. Against Crown opposition, Ngāi Tahu were able to achieve recognition of the mountain's original name – it officially became Aoraki/Mount Cook – and the return of the peak. After seven days, Ngāi Tahu would gift it back to the nation, though it would continue to manage the mountain.[42] The gifting back has yet to happen.

Goodall was also concerned about the Crown unilaterally including separate individual claims in the South Island in Ngāi Tahu's tribunal claim (Wai 27). The iwi was not prepared to allow any claim lodged by independent third parties to be voided by the proposed settlement of Ngāi Tahu's claim. Ngāi Tahu wanted only to extinguish their own very specific claims as set out in the tribunal report, not all claims made by individuals of Ngāi Tahu descent and even those in Te Tau Ihu who were not Ngāi Tahu. As Anake Goodall noted, 'This is an exact mirror of the Crown's own position that independent third party rights will not be detrimentally affected by this settlement and that no [Pākehā] person or persons will lose their Article III rights as a result of this claims resolution process.'[43] By attempting to include those claims in Ngāi Tahu's settlement, the Crown would only fuel the animosity that many other Māori groups had already begun exhibiting against Ngāi Tahu.

In mid-June 1997 Graham and O'Regan met to break the deadlock over mainly minute right of first refusal and deferred selection process matters. Ngāi Tahu had sought to increase the total amount from the previously agreed $200 million to $415 million. They also sought shares in the Dunedin and Invercargill airports. Cabinet had authorised Graham to offer Ngāi Tahu the opportunity to purchase $250 million worth of assets for the deferred selection process. Although the meeting was not very contentious there was still substantial disagreement on many issues. At a July 1997 meeting of the principals, O'Regan and Graham, officials and advisers from both sides wanted to ratchet down the hostility.[44]

An important part of the final negotiations was related to South Island Landless Natives Act (SILNA) claimants, who had been given what in 1906 was largely unusable land usually situated in remote forested areas of Southland. Intended as a form of redress for the grievances that Ngāi Tahu brought to the Crown's attention, it served only to create another grievance. By the 1990s this land and the forestry assets it contained were valuable because advances in technology had made milling viable. However, conservationists' concerns had led to a ban on export wood chips from beech trees and other indigenous species. These claimants filed a claim with the Waitangi Tribunal (WAI 158) but their grievance was in fact more modern than historical as a result of the loss of income from the wood chip ban. The compensation negotiated by the claimants (who were not represented by the Ngāi Tahu negotiators) was therefore not tied to historical grievances, but the Crown wished that amount to be part of Ngāi Tahu's overall financial settlement. After lengthy negotiations, the Crown conceded that WAI 158 would apply only to the Ngāi Tahu settlement for losses incurred before 21 September 1992, the Crown's cut-off date for historical claims.[45]

After the painstaking negotiations to the deed of settlement led by Anake Goodall, there was opposition to the settlement from within Ngāi Tahu. Rakiihia Tau Snr, the original claimant, attempted to place an injunction on the signing of the settlement. His concern was primarily on behalf of his own hapū, which believed it should receive its share of the settlement, rather than the entire settlement being controlled by the iwi. The lawsuit was fairly quickly dropped but still remaining was the litigation led by the Waitaha opponents, who disputed the mandate of the Ngāi Tahu negotiating team and the inclusion of Waitaha in the Te Runanga o Ngai Tahu Act. Ngāti Apa, Rangitāne and other Te Tau Ihu groups in the northern South Island wished to reopen a decision of the 1990 Maori Appellate Court regarding Ngāi Tahu's northern boundaries, but their claims, like Waitaha's, were ultimately rejected.[46] After what Graham has described as 'physically and emotionally draining' negotiations, a final deed of settlement was agreed and signed in an emotional ceremony at Takahanga Marae in Kaikōura on 21 November 1997.[47]

It would take another year for the settlement legislation to go through the parliamentary process and in August 1998 the Ngāi Tahu Claims Settlement Act passed its third and final reading.[48] There were criticisms that, despite the Māori Affairs Select Committee hearing a number of critical submissions, no changes were made to the settlement and the legislation. But changing one aspect could cause the entire delicately balanced agreement to unravel. A deed of settlement had been agreed between the Crown and Ngāi Tahu and the legislation was intended to give effect to the agreement. The legislation could not change the deed itself.

The legislation was widely debated in Parliament, particularly by its opponents, such as Ken Shirley of the ACT Party, Jim Anderton and Sandra Lee of the Alliance Party and Labour's Dover Samuels and

Jim Sutton. Shirley took every direction in his opposition to the bill, focusing on the minority rights of Waitaha and boundary issues with iwi in Te Tau Ihu. He also argued that the settlement was negotiated by the executive branch of the Crown but that Parliament had to be the ultimate sovereign. This has not been the pattern through most of New Zealand's political history, as the executive had widespread powers, especially before the introduction of MMP. Lee echoed Shirley's comments about Waitaha and Rangitāne who, she alleged, would have their rights to redress removed. Her opposition to the Ngāi Tahu leadership was well known; in a select committee hearing for the bill she had quoted Rakiihia Tau Snr to great effect. She claimed that the settlement was far from final and that future generations of Ngāi Tahu would be back to press the claim again. Samuels criticised Tutekawa Wyllie and Graham for their role in progressing the bill through Parliament. He criticised the lack of transparency in treaty settlement negotiations, claiming that agreements reached behind closed doors could never be lasting. Sutton was particularly scathing about the select committee process, describing it as a 'sham'. Nonetheless, in a sign of cross-party cooperation, the Leader of the Labour Party, Helen Clark, provided her support for the legislation. She stated plainly that the hard work done by Ngāi Tahu and the Crown should not be sacrificed for the price of a minor political advantage. Sutton grudgingly agreed.[49]

Labour MP John Delamere had a much different view from Sutton about the mandate and especially about the inclusion of Waitaha in the settlement. He pointed out the apparent need for decisions in the Māori world to have 100 per cent backing when the same standard would never be used in any Pākehā decision-making. Delamere's uncle, Sir Monita Delamere, who had Waitaha, Ngāti Māmoe and Ngāi Tahu whakapapa, was a member of the Waitangi Tribunal panel that heard the Ngāi Tahu claim. He had always held that all three descent lines were represented by the Ngai Tahu Maori Trust Board and later by Te Rūnanga o Ngāi Tahu, and that was the reality of tribal governance in the late twentieth century. 'So I say to everyone in this House, for me personally it is not a matter of supporting the Government position, it is a matter of supporting the position of my family.'[50] Wyllie's support for the bill in many ways reflected Delamere's position. National MP Arthur Anae was effusive in his praise of all parties involved, mentioning the Office of Treaty Settlements twice during the debate. National MP Georgina Te Heuheu was the final chair of the Māori Affairs Select Committee that was charged with shepherding the Ngāi Tahu Claims Settlement Bill through Parliament in 1997 and 1998. She saluted the work of Doug Graham in bringing the Ngāi Tahu claim to its conclusion. Te Heuheu was uniquely placed to understand the gravity of the issues to be settled, since she was a member of the Waitangi Tribunal panel that heard the claim. It was fitting that she should have such an important role in bringing the resolution of the claim through its final stages.

After the settlement legislation passed its final reading in Parliament, the next step was the Crown apology. Waikato–Tainui had received an apology directly from Queen Elizabeth II, as they had requested, and Ngāi Tahu expected the same treatment. They were disappointed in this but their apology was delivered by Prime Minister Jenny Shipley. Nearly all the settling groups that have followed Ngāi Tahu's agreement have had their apology delivered by the minister of treaty negotiations.

Surrounded by pictures and paintings of their tūpuna, hundreds of Ngāi Tahu members were in attendance when the apology was delivered at Ōnuku Marae in Akaroa on 29 November 1998:

> The Crown recognises the protracted labours of the Ngāi Tahu ancestors in pursuit of their claims for redress and compensation against the Crown for nearly 150 years, as alluded to in the Ngāi Tahu proverb 'He mahi kai takata, he mahi kai hoaka' ('It is work that consumes people, as greenstone consumes sandstone'). The Ngāi Tahu understanding of the Crown's responsibilities conveyed to Queen Victoria by Matiaha Tiramōrehu in a petition in 1857, guided the Ngāi Tahu ancestors. Tiramōrehu wrote: 'This was the command thy love laid upon these Governors ... that the law be made one, that the commandments be made one, that the nation be made one, that the white skin be made just equal with the dark skin, and to lay down the love of thy graciousness to the Māori that they dwell happily ... and remember the power of thy name.' The Crown hereby acknowledges the work of the Ngāi Tahu ancestors and makes this apology to them and to their descendants.
>
> The Crown acknowledges that it acted unconscionably and in repeated breach of the principles of the Treaty of Waitangi in

its dealings with Ngāi Tahu in the purchases of Ngāi Tahu land. The Crown further acknowledges that in relation to the deeds of purchase it has failed in most material respects to honour its obligations to Ngāi Tahu as its Treaty partner, while it also failed to set aside adequate lands for Ngāi Tahu use, and to provide adequate economic and social resources for Ngāi Tahu.

The Crown acknowledges that, in breach of Article Two of the Treaty, it failed to preserve and protect Ngāi Tahu use and ownership of such of their land and valued possessions as they wished to retain.

The Crown recognises that it has failed to act towards Ngāi Tahu reasonably and with the utmost good faith in a manner consistent with the honour of the Crown. That failure is referred to in the Ngāi Tahu saying 'Te Hapa o Niu Tireni!' ('The unfulfilled promise of New Zealand'). The Crown further recognises that its failure always to act with good faith deprived Ngāi Tahu of the opportunity to develop and kept the tribe for several generations in a state of poverty, a state referred to in the proverb 'Te mate o te iwi' ('The malaise of the tribe').

The Crown recognises that Ngāi Tahu has been consistently loyal to the Crown, and that the tribe has honoured its obligations and responsibilities under the Treaty of Waitangi and duties as citizens of the nation, especially, but not exclusively, in their active service in all of the major conflicts up to the present time to which New Zealand has sent troops. The Crown pays tribute to Ngāi Tahu loyalty and to the contribution made by the tribe to the nation.

The Crown expresses its profound regret and apologises unreservedly to all members of Ngāi Tahu Whānui for the suffering and hardship caused to Ngāi Tahu, and for the harmful effects which resulted to the welfare, economy and development of Ngāi Tahu as a tribe. The Crown acknowledges that such suffering, hardship and harmful effects resulted from its failures to honour its obligations to Ngāi Tahu under the deeds of purchase whereby it acquired Ngāi Tahu lands, to set aside adequate lands for the tribe's use, to allow reasonable access to traditional sources of food, to protect Ngāi Tahu rights to pounamu and such other valued possessions as the tribe wished to retain, or to remedy effectually Ngāi Tahu grievances.

> The Crown apologises to Ngāi Tahu for its past failures to acknowledge Ngāi Tahu rangatiratanga and mana over the South Island lands within its boundaries, and, in fulfillment of its Treaty obligations, the Crown recognises Ngāi Tahu as the tangata whenua of, and as holding rangatiratanga within, the Takiwā of Ngāi Tahu Whānui.
>
> Accordingly, the Crown seeks on behalf of all New Zealanders to atone for these acknowledged injustices, so far as that is now possible, and, with the historical grievances finally settled as to matters set out in the Deed of Settlement signed on 21 November 1997, to begin the process of healing and to enter a new age of co-operation with Ngāi Tahu.[51]

Once negotiations had officially recommenced and the two sides worked towards the signing of the heads of agreement, it became easy to forget how much animosity had separated Ngāi Tahu and the Crown only months before. But that acrimonious recent history and the enormous amount of legal and political detail were successfully managed. There were disagreements and compromises on both sides, whether in relation to practical conservation issues, such as return of the islands, or to such high-level matters as the potential extinguishment of customary rights. The pressure of the imminent election may ultimately have been for the best: potential issues would have continued to arise and a hard deadline can sometimes help to solve impasses.

The need to finalise the deed of settlement may have pressed more heavily on the Crown, since every day that the negotiations dragged on interest payments increased on the unpaid settlement. Despite that, the Crown's estimate of a six-month period between the heads of agreement and the signing of the deed of settlement stretched to 13 months. Less than a year later, legislation was passed as Ngāi Tahu kaumātua, kuia and rangatahi packed Parliament's visitors' gallery. As the sound of haka resounded through the chamber, there was finally some relief for those who had championed Ngāi Tahu's claim, Te Kerēme, for generations.

Ngāi Tahu settlement contents

Crown apology redress
- Historical account
- Crown acknowledgements
- Crown apology

Cultural redress
- Return of pounamu (Ngai Tahu (Pounamu Vesting) Act 1997)
- Return of Crown Tītī Islands without a marginal strip
- Return of Rarotoka Island with blue water title
- Return of Tūtaepatu Lagoon
- Co-management of Whenua Hou (Codfish Island)
- Waitaiki Historic Reserve in the Arahura Valley vested in the Māwhera Incorporation
- Return of Aoraki (Mount Cook) with gifting back to the nation seven days later
- Elfin Bay, Greenstone and Routeburn high-country stations (90 per cent of the total area leased back to DOC)
- Statutory acknowledgments and deeds of recognition over 64 areas taking up the majority of the rivers and lakes of the Ngāi Tahu rohe
- Tōpuni over 14 areas of land of significance to Ngāi Tahu
- Provision of 72 nohoanga sites to support mahinga kai activities
- 88 dual place names
- Dedicated seats on statutory bodies: New Zealand Conservation Authority (1), each Conservation Board in the Ngāi Tahu rohe (2), each Northern South Island Conservation Board (1), New Zealand Geographic Board (1)
- Vesting of the lakebeds of Te Waihora, Lake Mahināpua and Muriwai (Coopers Lagoon)

Financial redress
- $170 million (October 1996 dollar value) paid over five years
- Interest payments on unpaid sum ($20–25 million)
- 16.1 per cent relativity clause
- Right of first refusal over the purchase of Crown lands for 150 years
- Deferred selection process (allowed to purchase $250 million of Crown lands and then lease back to the Crown)

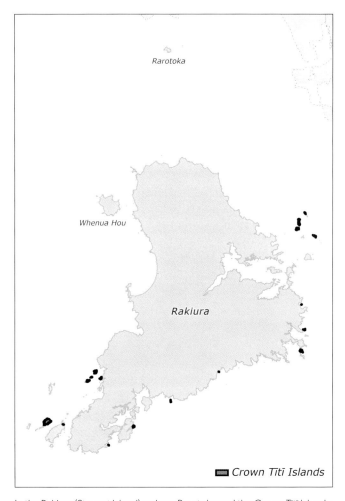

In the Rakiura (Stewart Island) redress Rarotoka and the Crown Tītī Islands were returned in the settlement. A co-management arrangement was established for Whenua Hou (Codfish Island).

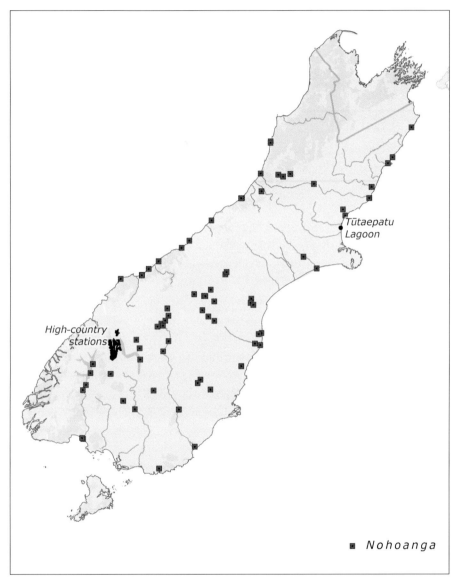

The locations of the 72 nohoanga or camping sites in Te Wai Pounamu, Tūtaepatu Lagoon and the three high-country stations: Greenstone, Elfin Bay and Routeburn.

CHAPTER 11

The post-settlement journey

After spending over a century seeking a resolution of long-standing claims, one of the greatest challenges, inevitably, was moving from grievance mode to growth and expansion. Ngāi Tahu's experiences provide a template for the experiences of later settling iwi and hapū throughout New Zealand.

The pressure from the grassroots membership was heightened following settlement, as the pūtea (sum) had to be spent in a way that benefited tribal members in the short term but also maintained continued growth – and that this was completed with a Ngāi Tahu-centred view of tikanga. The number of post-settlement successes achieved by Ngāi Tahu are significant, and far outstrip the failures, but many hopes and aspirations still remain.

As Te Maire Tau has commented, Ngāi Tahu went from being better off 'dead and out of the way' in the late nineteenth century to being seen 'to belong' in its own rohe in the early twenty-first. As the largest private landowner, and one of the biggest businesses in the South Island, Ngāi Tahu now holds increased political influence and power regionally. This manifested itself especially in the aftermath of the Christchurch earthquakes in 2010–11. When the Canterbury Earthquake Recovery Authority was established, Te Rūnanga o Ngāi Tahu were included as partners in the organisation, along with the Christchurch City Council and central government. This progression from interested party to equal partner reflected Ngāi Tahu's new profile. Under the deferred selection process, Ngāi Tahu purchased the land under the Central Police Station in Christchurch shortly after settlement and owned a number of other properties in the CBD, which increased their clout. In addition to holding tangata whenua status in the region, Ngāi Tahu were also now something that wider New Zealand always respected – a significant and powerful fee-simple landowner.

One of the first direct fruits of the negotiations was the establishment, in 1996, of Te Rūnanga o Ngāi Tahu. The Ngai Tahu Maori Trust Board had consisted of representatives of seven constituencies and a secretary. Six of the constituencies were based in the South Island: Kaikōura, Maahunui–Canterbury/West Coast, Arowhenua–South Canterbury/ North Otago, Akaroa–Banks Peninsula, Araiteuru–Otago and Murihiku–Southland. The last constituency, Te Ika a Māui, represented tribal members living in the North Island. Under Te Rūnanga o Ngāi Tahu the constituencies increased in number to 18 and became known as papatipu rūnanga, focused on marae. All were based within the Ngāi Tahu rohe. Moving south from the top of the east coast across the southern end, then north up the west coast, the new papatipu rūnanga were Te Rūnanga o Kaikōura, Te Ngāi Tūāhuriri Rūnanga, Te Hapū o Ngāti Wheke, Te Rūnanga o Koukourarata, Wairewa Rūnanga, Ōnuku Rūnanga, Te Taumutu Rūnanga, Te Rūnanga o Arowhenua, Te Rūnanga o Waihao, Te Rūnanga o Moeraki, Kāti Huirapa Rūnaka ki Puketeraki, Te Rūnanga o Ōtākou, Hokonui Rūnanga, Waihōpai Rūnaka, Awarua Rūnanga, Ōraka–Aparima Rūnaka, Te Rūnanga o Makaawhio and Te Rūnanga o Ngāti Waewae.

As we have seen, the trust board had been financially limited, and could only distribute a minimal amount of funding, mainly for educational scholarships. A completely fresh structure was developed under the new system. Te Rūnanga o Ngāi Tahu is split into two major sections. The first, the office, is governed through the 18-seat rūnanga, which represent each of the papatipu rūnanga. They provide oversight and control over how funds are distributed. The office creates initiatives that benefit and enhance Ngāi Tahu whānau through a focus on Oranga (wellbeing), Mātauranga (knowledge), Ngāi Tahutanga (culture and identity) and Te Ao Tūroa (environment). The second section is

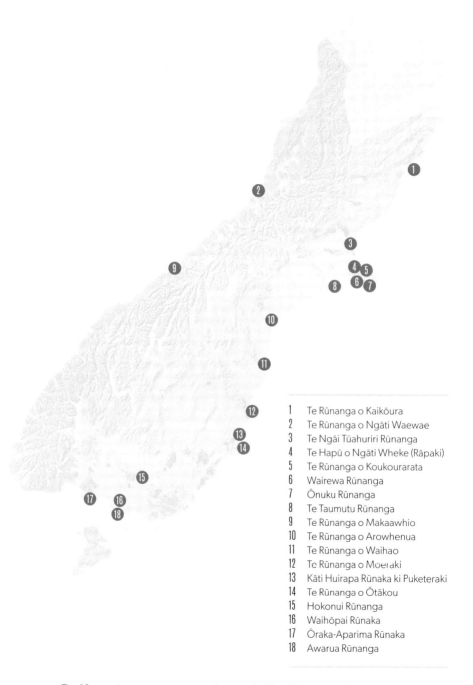

1   Te Rūnanga o Kaikōura
2   Te Rūnanga o Ngāti Waewae
3   Te Ngāi Tūahuriri Rūnanga
4   Te Hapū o Ngāti Wheke (Rāpaki)
5   Te Rūnanga o Koukourarata
6   Wairewa Rūnanga
7   Ōnuku Rūnanga
8   Te Taumutu Rūnanga
9   Te Rūnanga o Makaawhio
10   Te Rūnanga o Arowhenua
11   Te Rūnanga o Waihao
12   Te Rūnanga o Moeraki
13   Kāti Huirapa Rūnaka ki Puketeraki
14   Te Rūnanga o Ōtākou
15   Hokonui Rūnanga
16   Waihōpai Rūnaka
17   Ōraka-Aparima Rūnaka
18   Awarua Rūnanga

The 18 papatipu rūnanga are spread across the Ngāi Tahu region. Each elects a representative to sit on the central body, Te Rūnanga o Ngāi Tahu.

Ngāi Tahu Holdings, which is the money-making arm of the tribal organisation. It generates revenue to support tribal aspirations and provides for future generations through business investment, owning and operating businesses, utilising iwi assets strategically and working within the Ngāi Tahu values framework. One of the biggest challenges is managing the way that Ngāi Tahu Holdings conducts its business. Although ostensibly it is monitored by the office, its financial clout means that it can wield power beyond its prescribed limits.

The operations of the office are split into five sections: Te Uru Kahikatea, Strategy and Influence, Te Taumatua, Te Ao Tūroa and Oranga. Te Uru Kahikatea provides legal and administrative support as well as communications, including the Tahu FM radio station. Strategy and Influence concentrates on the political influence necessary to maintain Ngāi Tahu's newly established position and power within both central and local government. Te Taumatua protects and manages the revitalisation of history, te reo Māori and marae. Te Ao Tūroa is concerned with the environment, especially mahinga kai, and Oranga with economic, physical and social wellbeing.

Holdings is split into five sections representing the different parts of Ngāi Tahu's businesses: capital, farming, property, seafood and tourism. Ngāi Tahu Capital focuses on owning and investing in business, investments in the stock market and general financial management. Ngāi Tahu Farming and Property are responsible for all farming and property developments and investments. Ngāi Tahu Seafood manages the fisheries business and quota that emerged from the fisheries settlement. Ngāi Tahu Tourism operates tourist experiences across the country, many of them in the iwi's rohe. The steady economic growth since settlement has provided opportunities for the development of innovative methods to not only distribute funding but also empower tribal members.

Following settlement, some of the first projects for Ngāi Tahu concerned core issues for tribal members: education, health, te reo and Ngāi Tahutanga. One of the first initiatives, established in 1998, was Te Tapuae o Rehua, a collaborative partnership between Te Rūnanga o Ngāi Tahu and education providers throughout the South Island that is committed to increasing Māori participation in tertiary institutions and offering opportunities for whānau members in higher education, trades and agriculture. In 2000, with Te Rūnanga o Ngāi Tahu support, He Oranga Pounamu Charitable Trust was established to help organise and integrate health and social services for Māori in the Ngāi Tahu rohe. In 2015 it was disestablished in favour of empowering papatipu rūnanga to deliver the same services within their own takiwā. This followed the devolutionary trend within Te Rūnanga o Ngāi Tahu over the last decade.

In order to reinvigorate the use of te reo Māori in Ngāi Tahu homes in New Zealand and abroad, Kotahi Mano Kāika was created in 2003. This 25-year strategy, which aims to have at least 1000 Ngāi Tahu households speaking te reo Māori by the year 2025, is supported by a wide range of language programmes and resources. By 2017 more than 1500 whānau had registered. In 2006 Ngāi Tahu Funds and Aoraki Bound were launched to strengthen Ngāi Tahutanga. The funds help whānau build cultural knowledge and revive traditional practices such as weaving, carving and mahinga kai. Individuals or whānau groups can acquire funding for projects that assist them in connecting with their cultural identity. Aoraki Bound, developed in partnership with Outward Bound, allows participants to be immersed in the landscapes and histories of the South Island over 20 days, learning about their Ngāi Tahu identity. Perhaps one of the most significant achievements of Te Rūnanga o Ngāi Tahu has been the Marae Development Fund, which allows papatipu rūnanga to develop or even rebuild their marae, creating new structures that attempt to 'uphold the mana and traditions of [Ngāi Tahu] tipuna, while supporting the daily functions of modern life'.[1] By 2019 nearly every single Ngāi Tahu marae had used some of the fund to produce some outstanding buildings of varied styles that provide areas to nurture the grassroots of Ngāi Tahu communities and offer welcoming spaces for the multitudes of Ngāi Tahu from outside the rohe whenever they return home.

Through sound investment policies, the initial $170 million, plus the provisions contained in the right of first refusal, the deferred selection process and interest payments, which amounted to around $200 million, had grown to over $1.5 billion in total assets by 2019. By then, too, over $573 million for tribal development had been distributed to papatipu rūnanga and individuals to support mātauranga (through scholarships and other educational initiatives), employment, health and wellbeing, papatipu rūnanga development and Ngāi Tahutanga. In 2013 Ngāi Tahu received $68.5 million from its relativity clause and in 2017 a further $198.9 million was paid out. In February 2020 the Crown announced the results of four arbitration processes related to disagreements between Ngāi Tahu and the Crown about what should be included in the calculations of the total value of treaty settlements. The arbitration is confidential, but the total amount paid to Ngāi Tahu was $59 million on top of a total of $326.4 million so far (not adjusted for inflation).[2] The clause expires in 2047.

A desire for the iwi to build up their financial knowledge and economic independence led to the establishment of the Whai Rawa scheme in 2006. This hybrid between a superannuation scheme and a unit trust delivers a range of benefits to its members through a flexible savings structure for retirement, home ownership or tertiary education. Te Rūnanga o Ngāi Tahu matches contributions at the rate of 4:1 for child members and 1:1 for adult members and covers all the operating costs of the scheme.[3]

The return of pounamu in the June 1996 interim agreement was one of the key aspects of the Ngāi Tahu settlement. This signified the importance of pounamu to the wider iwi and especially hapū on the West Coast, including Ngāti Waewae and Ngāti Māhaki ki Makaawhio. A very successful business has grown up since the 1997 transfer of all naturally occurring pounamu within the Ngāi Tahu takiwā from the Crown to Te Rūnanga o Ngāi Tahu. In the 12 years following the transfer, Ngāi Tahu established a decentralised ownership and management structure, Ngāi Tahu Pounamu, which reflected the customary ownership already in place thanks to the active guardianship of the resource by West Coast hapū. The ownership of pounamu was placed with Te Rūnanga o Ngāi Tahu, but the hapū, such as Ngāti Waewae, regained their customary right to establish and enforce rules for the sustainable management of the resource. They were also able to re-establish their right to commercially harvest and process pounamu. Under the rules of ownership established under Ngāi Tahu Pounamu, the iwi invested in an online tracing, marketing and sales portal for the sale of authentic pounamu jewellery. The central structure provided the resources to market Ngāi Tahu pounamu, but the hapū controlled the carving process with multiple individual and whānau carvers supplying physical and online shops. Some carvers have not approved of the new scheme and have bristled at central control of the resource, but they are in the minority.[4] Overall, the business has been a resounding success, with distribution increasing from one to 50 outlets within two years of its establishment. Both hapū and individual carvers involved in the business contribute a portion of their turnover, which is then invested in social and cultural initiatives that benefit the iwi as a whole. Individuals, families, hapū and iwi are working together to support each other in their endeavours, sharing ownership and benefits.[5]

The property rights regime developed for pounamu has, however, been challenging for the iwi. Working in concert with the New Zealand Police and Ministry of Justice, Te Rūnanga o Ngāi Tahu has endeavoured to punish those accused of stealing pounamu. The most significant cases have included tonnes of pounamu valued at hundreds of thousands of dollars. Harvey Hutton and Dougal Peter Innes were charged with stealing pounamu valued at up to $1.6 million between 1997 and 2004. The charges against Innes were dropped but Hutton was found guilty in 2005 and sentenced to 18 months' imprisonment, though he spent only two months in jail. Hutton was also ordered to pay $300,000 to Te Rūnanga o Ngāi Tahu and relinquish his cache of pounamu. After being charged with stealing pounamu worth up to $800,000 between 1995 and 2004, in 2007 David and Morgan Saxton were ordered to pay $300,000 to Te Rūnanga o Ngāi Tahu. No money was ever paid, however, and they served very little of their short sentences, both of which were reduced to home detention on appeal. Morgan Saxton died in a helicopter accident in 2008. Although there have been some prosecutions, the relatively light sentences handed out to guilty parties in the first 10 years after settlement suggest that the new collectively owned Māori property rights developed for pounamu have some way to go before they enjoy the same protection afforded private property generally.[6]

In considering gains made by Ngāi Tahu in the over two decades since settlement, in 2017 Sir Tipene O'Regan identified some of the iwi's greatest challenges. With over 60,000 tribal members 'who are distant from [their] tribal communion', there was some urgency to ensure that they believed that their views and aspirations still matter. Progress had certainly been made in increasing the ability to vote in papatipu rūnanga elections. One of the most pressing concerns for O'Regan was that commercial success should proceed on the basis of an intergenerational Ngāi Tahu whānau-focused basis, not that of 'a Pakeha traders' market'. For O'Regan this was embodied in the 'constantly-eroding territorial footprint' that had resulted from tribal investment strategies. After all, the central plank of the main claim had been the reserves not awarded in the Ngāi Tahu purchases. As O'Regan put it:

> That we recovered huge areas of profitable land 20 years ago and we today hold only a modest fraction of that territory is a huge regret to me. 'No hea koe?' [Where are you from?] is at the very heart of the query, 'Ko wai koe?' [Who are you?]. To be rich and landless is a reasonable aim for a Pakeha investment trust. It can never be a sufficient ambition for an indigenous people seeking to recover their mana in their ancestral territory.

A considerable amount of grassroots opinion within Ngāi Tahu was pushing back against this divestment from land.[7]

To some outsiders, Ngāi Tahu's achievements in the period since settlement have occasionally seemed contradictory, but they merely reflect the diversity of opinion across the iwi. Thanks to Te Rūnanga o Ngāi Tahu's increased influence, the iwi has attempted to change public perceptions about the use of water, especially in agriculture. In 2009–10 Te Rūnanga o Ngāi Tahu was concerned by the scale and intensity of proposals for irrigation and intensive dairying in the Mackenzie Basin and Upper Waitaki – millions of cubic metres of water and nearly 27,115 hectares (67,000 acres) of land. Ngāi Tahu individuals expressed their concern about the effect that such a project could have on mahinga kai in the Upper Waitaki. The first application to farm 17,850 dairy cows on just over 8500 hectares (21,000 acres) of land in the Mackenzie Basin was heard in March 2010. Minister for the Environment Nick Smith established a specialist board of inquiry (which included former Te Rūnanga o Ngāi Tahu deputy kaiwhakahaere (director), the New Zealand Conservation Authority member and sheep farmer Edward Ellison) to consider the application and in November 2011 the application was declined. Ngāi Tahu's concerns were influential in the decision.[8]

In 2000, as a part of its settlement under the deferred settlement process, Te Rūnanga o Ngāi Tahu purchased the Crown forest of Eyrewell, near Oxford in North Canterbury. As the forestry licences had expired, Holdings pushed to convert the lands from forestry to pasture in 2011 and announced plans to establish three dairy farms, which would each have 1000 cows and be based on nearly 1214 hectares (3000 acres) of land. This would be a first stage in a project that could ultimately lead to the development of almost 16,200 hectares (40,000 acres) of dairy operations. A Manawhenua Working Party was formed to provide input into the farming model and there was consultation with Lincoln University to develop best-practice farming and minimise environmental concerns. Local hapū Ngāi Tūāhuriri have been vocal about the detrimental effects of extensive dairy farming on the freshwater resources of their rohe, but some within the rūnanga still think a balance can be struck and sustainable dairy farming can exist. Outside commentators criticised the Eyrewell development when Te Rūnanga o Ngāi Tahu had recently helped to defeat the Mackenzie Basin dairying scheme. Ngāi Tahu Holdings, however, was very different from the opposition related to the the Mackenzie Basin scheme; there were diverse views within Ngāi Tahu.[9]

Although Ngāi Tahu's treaty settlement provided many opportunities for associated hapū, rūnanga, whānau and individuals, many hopes and aspirations have yet to be fulfilled. At the forefront of these lies the achievement of a greater balance between the centralised structure of Te Rūnanga o Ngāi Tahu and the papatipu rūnanga and whānau. Currently the central structure gradually increases the pūtea and distributes benefits through grants and other mechanisms such as Whai Rawa. This structure is largely based on a passive recipient model, under which Ngāi Tahu individuals are effectively equal shareholders rather than active participants. Ngāi Tahu Pounamu is an excellent example of a balanced central structure that can still function within a devolutionary model. If it could be replicated for other economic opportunities managed and controlled by flaxroots Ngāi Tahu at marae and whānau level, it would further empower the iwi. Grants and financial support for small-scale Ngāi Tahu businesses are the next step in cementing Ngāi Tahu tino rangatiratanga at all organisational levels. This has begun under the Tribal Economies unit established in 2015.

A major hope of Ngāi Tahu communities is the ability to regulate and control their lands in the same manner as local government. This would also mean controlling resource consent processes in Ngāi Tahu-owned areas. Although, under section 33 of the Resource Management Act, local authorities can transfer their functions, powers or duties to public bodies, including iwi authorities, regional and district councils have been unwilling to relinquish their powers. Ngāi Tahu communities have, however, made their desire to take on resource consent capabilities clear to local authorities. In the Canterbury region, the dysfunction of Environment Canterbury led to the institution of statutory management from 2010 to 2018. In the vacuum this created, Ngāi Tahu communities were ready, willing and able to make resource consent decisions on their own.

After many decades of intergenerational negotiation, the Waimakariri District Council consented to regulations that allowed Ngāi Tahu at Tuahiwi to once again build on their ancestral lands nearly 60 years after the Town and Country Planning Act 1953 restricted landowners from building more than one house on every 10 acres (4 hectares) of rural zoned land. This prevented Māori landowners, often in the hundreds if not thousands, from building houses on their own whenua for their own people. In 2015 the Tuahiwi community managed to have their lands rezoned under the Land Use Recovery Act of the 2011 Canterbury earthquake legislation which, among other things, required local councils to take into account Ngāi Tahu values and the underlying principles of the 1848 Canterbury Purchase and the 1862 Crown Grants Act (No. 2).[10] These new powers are now being sought to extend to Ngāi Tahu properties in Christchurch and across Ngāi Tahu land throughout the South Island. This rezoning could allow communities to re-establish their pā and re-energise their local communities by building multiple affordable homes.

Another major hope for Ngāi Tahu centres on control of water allocation on iwi land and the regeneration of major waterways and lakes such as Te Waihora and Wairewa. Large-scale irrigation projects in the Ngāi Tahu rohe have wreaked havoc on the availability of freshwater and many rivers continue to run dry throughout the summer months. Te Waihora, the nation's fifth-largest lake (by area), has been of great concern to Ngāi Tahu, as it is the most polluted in New Zealand. In August 2011 the minister for the environment announced an $11.6 million package to clean up Te Waihora, but the amount was woefully inadequate: tens of millions of dollars were needed. The restoration plan was for only two years, whereas a 25-year plan was required. Canterbury has over 70 per cent of New Zealand's irrigated lands, and the reliance on and expansion of dairy is increasing. Local communities remain concerned about the erosion of Ngāi Tahu's freshwater resources long after their treaty settlement.

A final word

There is a burgeoning interest in treaty settlements, though people seem to be more interested in what is being done with the settlement pūtea than in how the negotiators arrived at that outcome. Unfortunately, this is probably due to a negative opinion of the settlements: 'What are those bloody Maoris doing with the millions we gave them that they didn't deserve?' Focusing on the negotiation process might show those who hold such views that the amount provided was a mere fraction of what was lost and that the pain and grievances could never be adequately remedied solely through economic means. With that kind of lens it would be easy to see how much Ngāi Tahu have done with their limited settlement. More can always be achieved, and in better ways, but the path since settlement has been marked by a huge number of successes. The failures have always been used as lessons. In light of Ngāi Tahu's growth and empowerment, the Canterbury region and the South Island can no longer ignore the iwi as they once did.

Ultimately, Ngāi Tahu rangatiratanga and the Crown's kāwanatanga were simultaneously challenged and enhanced by the negotiations. While Ngāi Tahu's settlement and negotiations were far from perfect from any participant's perspective, as a process of reconciliation they have changed New Zealand forever.

NOTES

Introduction

1   Andrew Sharp, *Justice and the Māori: The Philosophy and Practice of Māori Claims in New Zealand since the 1970s*, Auckland: Oxford University Press, 1997, 1–12.

2   Joan Metge and Patricia Kinloch, *Talking Past Each Other*, Wellington: Victoria University Press, 1978.

3   Alexandra Emma-Jane Highman, 'Te Iwi o Ngāi Tahu: An Examination of Ngāi Tahu's Approach to, and Internal Expression of, Tino Rangatiratanga', Masters thesis, University of Canterbury, 1997.

4   Robert Joseph, 'Unsettling Treaty Settlements: Contemporary Māori Identity and Representation Challenge', in Nicola R. Wheen and Janine Hayward (eds), *Treaty of Waitangi Settlements*, Wellington: Bridget Williams Books, 2012, 151–65.

5   *Final Agreement: Between the Minister of Justice on Behalf of the Crown and the Trustees of Ngāti Rangiteaorere for and on Behalf of the People of Ngāti Rangiteaorere in Relation to Claim WAI 32, 1993; Agreement: Between the Minister of Justice on Behalf of the Crown, Pukeroa-Oruawhata Trustees and the Proprietors of Ngāti Whakaue Tribal Lands Inc. for and on behalf of the People of Ngāti Whakaue in Relation to Claim WAI 94, 1993; Deed of Agreement: In the Matter of the Treaty of Waitangi Act 1975 Between Her Majesty the Queen ('The Crown') Represented by the Honourable Douglas Graham, Her Majesty's Minister of Justice and the Claimants, George Hakaraia of Russell and Matutaera Clendon of Manurewa Acting on Behalf of Themselves and the Other Trustees of the Hauai Trust (the 'Claimants'), Wellington, 1993; Deed of Agreement: This Deed is made this 20th Day of December Between Her Majesty the Queen ('The Crown') Acting by the Minister in Charge of Treaty of Waitangi Negotiations and the Waimakuku Whanau Trust Board Incorporated (the Trust) on Behalf of all Beneficiaries Thereof, Wellington, 1995; Deed of Agreement: This Deed is made this 6th Day of October 1996 Between Her Majesty the Queen ('The Crown') acting by the Minister in Charge of Treaty of Waitangi Negotiations and the Proprietors of Rotoma No. 1 Block Incorporated (the Incorporation) on Behalf of all Beneficiaries Thereof, Wellington, 1996; Deed of Agreement: This Deed is Made on this 2nd Day of October 1996 Between Her Majesty the Queen ('The Crown') acting by the Minister in Charge of Treaty of Waitangi Negotiations and the Representatives of the Te Maunga Railways Land Claim (WAI315) On Behalf Of The Wai 315 Claimants*, Wellington, 1996.

Chapter 1: The history of Te Kerēme: the Ngāi Tahu claim

1   4 South Island Appellate Court Minute Book 673 Folio 6/3. Many of these iwi who had lost their case in the Maori Appellate Court were somewhat vindicated by the Waitangi Tribunal's *Report on the Te Tau Ihu Claims* in 2007, which found that they shared interests with Ngāi Tahu in the western and eastern northern border.

2   Tipene O'Regan, 'Ka korero o Kai Tahu Whanui', Waitangi Tribunal Wai-27, Document A-27, Macmillan Brown Library, University of Canterbury.

3   Throughout this book 'the Crown' will refer to the executive branch of government: ministers, government departments and agencies and officials. For an excellent discussion of the difficulty of defining the Crown as a treaty partner see Janine Alyth Deaker Hayward, 'In Search of a Treaty Partner: Who, or What, is the Crown?', PhD thesis, Victoria University of Wellington, 1995.

4   Te Maire Tau, 'Ngāi Tahu – Spreading South and West', http://www.TeAra.govt.nz/en/Ngāi-tahu/page-3, accessed 30 July 2019.

5   Alan Ward, *An Unsettled History: Treaty Claims in New Zealand Today*, Wellington: Bridget Williams Books, 1999, 13–18; Claudia Orange, *An Illustrated History of the Treaty of Waitangi*, Wellington: Bridget Williams Books, 2004, 39–41.

6   Ruth Ross, 'Te Tiriti o Waitangi: Texts and Translations', *New Zealand Journal of History* 6, no. 2 (1972): 129–57.

7   Michael Belgrave, 'Pre-emption, the Treaty of Waitangi and the Politics of Crown Purchase', *New Zealand Journal of History* 37, no. 1, issue 5 (1997): 23–37; Rose Daamen, *The Crown's Right of Pre-emption and Fitzroy's Waiver Purchases*, Wellington: Waitangi Tribunal Rangahaua Whānui Series, 1998.

8   Waitangi Tribunal, *Ngāi Tahu Land Report*, Wellington: Waitangi Tribunal, 1991, 3 vols, 30–50, 281–386; Harry Evison, *The Long Dispute: Māori Land Rights and European Colonisation in Southern New Zealand*. Christchurch: Canterbury University Press, 1997, 139–57.

9   Waitangi Tribunal, *Ngāi Tahu Land Report*, 51–82, 387–524; Evison, *The Long Dispute*, 177–213.

10   Waitangi Tribunal, *Ngāi Tahu Land Report*, 527–43; D. Moore, B. Rigby, M. Russell, *Old Land Claims – Rangahaua Whānui National Theme A*, Wellington: Waitangi Tribunal, 1997.

11   Waitangi Tribunal, *Ngāi Tahu Land Report*, 83–98, 544–86; Evison, *The Long Dispute*, 214–34.

12   James Mackay to Donald McLean, quoted in Evison, *The Long Dispute*, 264.

13   Waitangi Tribunal, *Ngāi Tahu Land Report*, 99–120, 587–688; Evison, *The Long Dispute*, 235–37, 241, 257–60, 279, 310.

14   *Ngai Tahu Land Report*, 121–41, 689–796; Evison, *The Long Dispute*, 266, 268, 279, 310.

15   *Ngai Tahu Land Report*, 142–48, 797–820; Evison, *The Long Dispute*, 279.

16   Waitangi Tribunal, *Ngāi Tahu Land Report*, 175–214, 821–920.

17   Waitangi Tribunal, *Ngāi Tahu Land Report*, 149–64, 841–920.

18   https://ngaitahu.iwi.nz/ngai-tahu/te-whakataunga-celebrating-te-kereme-the-ngai-tahu-claim/, accessed 28 April 2020; Evison, *The Long Dispute*, 297.

19   Waitangi Tribunal, *Ngāi Tahu Land Report*, 503–24; Evison, *The Long Dispute*, 298.

20   Evison, *The Long Dispute*, 322.

21   Waitangi Tribunal, *Ngāi Tahu Land Report*, 1003–32; Te Maire Tau, 'Ngāi Tahu – From "Better Be Dead and Out of the Way" to "To Be Seen to Belong", in John Cookson and Graeme Dunstall (eds), *Southern Capital, Christchurch: Towards a City Biography 1850–2000*, Christchurch: Canterbury University Press, 222–31.

22   Tau, 'Ngāi Tahu – From "Better Be Dead"...', 228.

23   https://www.ngaitahuholdings.co.nz/manawa-ngai-tahu/the-history-of-ngai-tahu-tribal-investment/, accessed 28 April 2020.

24   Tau, 'Ngāi Tahu – From "Better Be Dead"...', 229–34.

25   Stephanie Kelly, 'The Ngāi Tahu Māori Trust Board', Masters thesis, University of Canterbury, 1991, 36.

Chapter 2: Ngāi Tahu takes action

1   E. S. Poata-Smith, 'He pokeke uenuku i tu ai: The Evolution of Contemporary Māori Protest' in Paul Spoonley, David G. Pearson and Cluny MacPherson (eds), *Nga Patai: Racism and Ethnic Relations in Aotearoa New Zealand*, Palmerston North: Dunmore Publishing, 1996, 97–116; Aroha Harris, *Hīkoi: Forty Years of Māori Protest*. Wellington: Huia Publishers, 2004, 70.

2   M. P. K. Sorrenson, *Ko te Whenua te Utu/Land is the Price: Essays on Maori History, Land and Politics*, Auckland: Auckland University Press, 2014, 257–59.

3   Janine Hayward, 'Flowing from the Treaty's Words', in *The Waitangi Tribunal*, Janine Hayward and Nicola R. Wheen (eds), Wellington: Bridget Williams Books, 2004, 30–32; Paul Hamer, 'A Quarter-century of the Waitangi Tribunal', in Hayward and Wheen (eds), *The Waitangi Tribunal*, 3–5; Mason Durie, *Te Mana, Te Kawanatanga: The Politics of Māori Self-determination*, Auckland: Oxford University Press, 1998, 184; Jane Kelsey, 'From Lame Duck to Toothless Tiger', *Mana Magazine* 3 (1993): 41.

4   Jane Kelsey, *A Question of Honour? Labour and the Treaty, 1984–1989*. Wellington: Allen & Unwin, 1990, 3.

5   Claudia Orange, *An Illustrated History of the Treaty of Waitangi*, Wellington: Bridget Williams Books, 2004, 162–63; Alan Ward, *An Unsettled History: Treaty Claims in New Zealand Today*, Wellington: Bridget Williams Books, 1999, 34–37.

6   Ward, *An Unsettled History*, 34–37.

7   Kelsey, *A Question of Honour?*, 140–61; Orange, *Illustrated History*, 164–66; Ward, *An Unsettled History*, 37–38; Michael King, *The Penguin History of New Zealand*, Auckland: Penguin, 2003, 501.

8   Waitangi Tribunal, *Ngāi Tahu Land Report*, 1991, 3 vols, 3–10.

9   Ann Parsonson, 'Ngāi Tahu – The Whale That Awoke: From Claim to Settlement (1960–1998)', in John Cookson and Graeme Dunstall (eds), *Southern Capital, Christchurch: Towards a City Biography 1850–2000*, Christchurch: Canterbury University Press, 2000, 257.

10   Waitangi Tribunal, *Ngāi Tahu Land Report*, 1991, 3 vols, 1.6.5.

11   *Te Karaka*, no. 75 (2017): 12.
12   Waitangi Tribunal, Te Roroa Report, Wellington: Department of Justice, 1992; Treaty of Waitangi Amendment Act 1993.
13   *Te Karaka*, no. 75 (2017): 15.
14   Parsonson, 'Ngāi Tahu – The Whale that Awoke', 261.
15   *Te Karaka*, no. 75 (2017): 12.
16   There was no funding from the Crown Forestry Rental Trust as there was in later settlement processes, although there was some after settlement.
17   Judge Ashley McHugh, 'Concluding Remarks', 10 October 1989; David Palmer to Minister of Lands Peter Tapsell: C-27-4-02 Vol. 1, Office of Treaty Settlements [OTS] archives.
18   Public Works Act 1981, Section 40.
19   Department of Survey and Land Information [DoSLI] official 3 to David Palmer, 14 December 1989; O'Regan to Tapsell, 15 December 1989; Tapsell to O'Regan, 20 December 1989; Tapsell to Geoffrey Palmer, 20 September 1989: C-27-4-02 Vol. 1, OTS archives.
20   Department of Prime Minister and Cabinet [DPMC] official 1 to Prime Minister's Private Secretary, 3 November 1989; Commissioner of Crown Lands, 'The Ngāi Tahu Consultative Process', December 1989; STA (91) M 19/5; ECC (91) M 38/1; CAB (91) M 27/10: all C-27-4-02 Vol. 1, OTS archives.
21   O'Regan to Geoffrey Palmer, 4 May 1990, C-27-4-01 Vol. 1, OTS archives.
22   Ward, *An Unsettled History*, 30.
23   Richard Hill, *Māori and the State: Crown–Māori Relations in New Zealand/Aotearoa, 1950–2000*. Wellington: Victoria University Press, 2009, 229.

Chapter 3: The negotiating principles
1   Jack Vowles and and Peter Aimes (eds), *Voters' Vengeance: The 1990 Election in New Zealand and the Fate of the Fourth Labour Government*, Auckland: Auckland University Press, 1993, 1–2.
2   David McCan, *Whatiwhatihoe: The Waikato Raupatu Claim*, Wellington: Huia, 2001, 284; Ward, *An Unsettled History*, 34; Jim Bolger, *A View from the Top*, Auckland: Viking Press, 1998, 175.
3   Tom Brooking, *The History of New Zealand*, Westport: Greenwood Press, 2004, xxxii; Richard Hill, *Māori and the State: Crown–Māori Relations in New Zealand/Aotearoa, 1950–2000*, Wellington: Victoria University Press, 2009, 251–53.
4   Interview with Douglas Graham, 22 May 2011; Graham noted that he lunched nearly every week through the 1980s and 1990s with Paul Temm, a prominent lawyer who specialised in treaty matters; Ward, *An Unsettled History*, 34.
5   Minutes of a meeting between Ngāi Tahu and Crown Negotiators, 18 September 1991, C-27-8-01 Vol. 4, OTS archives; Framework Agreement between Ngāi Tahu and the Crown, 27 November 1991, C-27-2-02 Vol. 3, OTS archives.

6   Treasury official 6 to Treaty of Waitangi Policy Unity [ToWPU] official
        5, 'Proposed Plan of Action for Dealing with Waitangi Tribunal's
        Ngāi Tahu Report', 17 April 1991; Treasury official 3 to ToWPU official 5,
        'Ngāi Tahu – Action Plan', 24 April 1991; Treasury official 3 to ToWPU
        official 5, 'Ngāi Tahu – Proposed Plan of Action', 26 April 1991; CAB (91)
        M 19/22; ToWPU official 6, 'Ngāi Tahu Negotiations – Interim Synthesis
        Report', 2 September 1991: all C-27-8-01 Vol. 4, OTS archives.
7   Ngai Tahu Maori Trust Board [NTMTB] report, 22 November 1991,
        NT140 C5 Box 54, Macmillan Brown Library [MB].
8   CAB (91) M 19/22, OTS archives.
9   ToWPU official 6 to ToWPU official 1, 11 September 1991, C-27-4-01
        Vol. 1, OTS archives.
10   Multiple agencies' Interim report on the Waitangi Tribunal's *Ngai Tahu
        Land Report*, 15 August 1991, C-27-3-01 Vol. 1, OTS archives.
11   'Comments on Draft Report on Tribunal report', 20 March 1991,
        C-27-8-01 Vol. 4, OTS archives.
12   Treasury official 6 and Treasury official 3 to ToWPU official 5,
        17 April 1991, C-27-8-01 Vol. 4, OTS archives.
13   CAB (91) M 28/10, 15 July 1991, C-27-2-02 Vol. 3, OTS archives;
        Commissioner of Crown Lands memorandum, 24 July 1991,
        C-27-4-01 Vol. 1, OTS archives.
14   Ngāi Tahu negotiations Cabinet Paper, 2 September 1991, C-27-8-01
        Vol. 4, OTS archives.
15   Manatū Māori official 1, Cabinet report on Ngāi Tahu negotiations,
        4 September 1991, C-27-8-01 Vol. 5.
16   Manatū Māori official 2 to ToWPU official 7, 11 September 1991,
        C-27-8-01 Vol. 5.
17   File note on meeting between Department of Conservation [DOC],
        ToWPU and Ngāi Tahu, 1 October 1991, C-27-2-03 Vol. 1, OTS archives.
18   'Comments on Draft Report on Tribunal report', 20 March 1991,
        C-27-8-01 Vol. 4, OTS archives.
19   DOC official 3 to ToWPU official 7, 21 November 1991, C-27-7-04 Vol. 1,
        OTS archives.
20   Marshall to Graham, 5 December 1991, C-27-04 Vol. 1, OTS archives.
21   Meeting of NTMTB, 20–22 November 1991, NT140, A38, Box 11A, MB.
22   DOC official 1 to ToWPU official 7, 21 November 1991, C-27-7-04 Vol. 1,
        OTS archives.
23   March–April 1994, 'Dr Henrik Moller and the kereru files', NT140 Q22,
        MB.
24   'Ngāi Tahu: External Communications, Liaison NGOs', C-27-7-04 Vol. 1,
        OTS archives.
25   Barbara Marshall (Federated Mountain Clubs) to Doug Graham,
        16 March 1992, C-27-7-04 Vol. 1, OTS archives.
26   Hugh Barr (Federated Mountain Clubs) to Graham, 21 May 1992,
        C-27-7-04 Vol. 1, OTS archives.
27   Bruce McFadgen, *Hostile Shores*, Auckland: Auckland University Press,
        2008, 128.
28   Hugh Barr (Federated Mountain Clubs) to Graham, 21 May 1992,
        C-27-7-04 Vol. 1, OTS archives.
29   Various to Graham, November 1993, AAKW W5105 7812 5,
        Archives New Zealand [ANZ].

30   Joanna Reid 'The Grassland Debates: Conservationists, Ranchers, First Nations, and the Landscape of the Middle Fraser', *BC Studies* 160 (Winter 2008/09): 93–118; Eve Vincent and Timothy Neale (eds), *Unstable Relations: Indigenous People and Environmentalism in Contemporary Australia*, Perth: UWA Publishing, 2016.

31   O'Regan, 'Chairman's Report', *Ngāi Tahu Annual Report 1993*, NT140 C4, Box 54, MB, 7–9.

32   Tom Metcalfe, 'Board Backs Return of Lake to Maoris', *Press*, 23 April 1991.

33   Letter to Doug Graham, 8 October 1992, C-27-7-04 Vol. 1, OTS archives.

34   Email from former Maruia Society member, 11 May 2018.

Chapter 4: The negotiations begin

1   Finlayson was a very successful minister of treaty negotiations in the National governments of 2008–17, signing dozens of agreements and continuing the work of Doug Graham, whom he greatly admired.

2   'Ngāi Tahu Annual Hui, 22–24 November 1991', NT140 M14 (c), MB.

3   Te Rūnanga o Ngāi Tahu, 'The Negotiators', https://ngaitahu.iwi.nz/ ngai-tahu/the settlement/the-negotiators/, accessed 24 May 2020.

4   'Crown Negotiating Team for the Ngāi Tahu Claim', 11 September 1991, NE-12-027-00-02 Vol. 1, OTS archives.

5   Davidson, 'Lunch with [TPK official 1]', 13 February 1996, Vhi 48 (j), Te Rūnanga o Ngāi Tahu [TRoNT] archive.

6   Minutes of a meeting between Ngāi Tahu and Crown Negotiators, 18 September 1991, C-27-8-01 Vol. 4, OTS archives.

7   Minutes of a meeting between Ngāi Tahu and Crown Negotiators, 17 October 1991, C-27-8-01 Vol. 4, 1-2, OTS archives.

8   Treasury official 11, 11 October 1991, C-27-4-01 Vol. 1, OTS archives.

9   ToWPU official 3, 'Ngāi Tahu Forestry meeting', 22–23 January 1992, C-27-4-01 Vol. 2, OTS archives.

10   ToWPU official 3, 'Ngāi Tahu Forestry meeting', 22–23 January 1992, C-27-4-01 Vol. 2, OTS archives.

11   Treasury official 7/David Oughton memorandum for Graham, 27 January 1992, C-27-4-01 Vol. 2, OTS archives.

12   Matt Nippert, 'A Tsar is Born', *Listener*, 11 August 2007; Jane Clifton, 'The Kiwi Oligarch', *Listener*, 25 April 2009.

13   Treasury official 1, Memorandum on Ngai Tahu, 11 October 1991; O'Regan to Graham and Treasury official 7, 17 October 1991; Graham to O'Regan, 23 October 1991; Stephen Jennings to Treasury official 7, 24 December 1991; Treasury official 7 to Jennings, 6 January 1992; O'Regan to Treasury official 7; ToWPU official 3, 'Ngāi Tahu Forestry meeting', 22–23 January 1992: all C-27-4-01 Vol. 2, OTS archives.

14   O'Regan to Graham, 5 February 1992, C-27-4-01 Vol. 2, OTS archives.

15   O'Regan to Sid Ashton, 28 May 1991; O'Regan to Doug Kidd, 13 June 1991: both NT140 F(x)4 Box 158, MB.

16   CAB (91) M 27/5; Commissioner of Crown Lands to Doug Graham, 'Ngāi Tahu Negotiations – Milford Sound Aerodrome', 24 July 1991; ToWPU official 7 to Ministry of Transport official 1, 25 July 1991; CEG (91) 137; ToWPU official 6 to ToWPU official 1, 11 September 1991; CEG (91) 171; ToWPU official 3, 'Ngāi Tahu and Electricorp', 19 September 1991: all C-27-4-01 Vol. 1.

17   Framework Agreement between Ngāi Tahu and the Crown,
        27 November 1991, C-27-2-02 Vol. 3, OTS archives.
18   Minutes of a meeting between Ngāi Tahu and Crown Negotiators,
        27 November 1991, C-27-2-03 Vol. 1, OTS archives.

Chapter 5: Establishing Te Rūnanga o Ngāi Tahu and rangatiratanga
1   Charles Crofts, 'Kaiwhakahaere Report', *Ngai Tahu Maori Trust Board
        Annual Report*, 1996, 26–27, TRoNT archive.
2   Richard Hill, *Māori and the State: Crown–Māori Relations in New Zealand/
        Aotearoa, 1950–2000*, Wellington: Victoria University Press, 2009,
        241–43; Tipene O'Regan, 'Submission to the Repeal of the Runanga
        Iwi Act 1990', C-27-2-04 Vol. 1, OTS archives; Waitangi Tribunal,
        The Ngai Tahu Claim: Supplementary Report on Legal Personality,
        Wellington: Waitangi Tribunal, 1991.
3   Tipene O'Regan, 'The Ngāi Tahu Claim', in Hugh Kawharu (ed.),
        Waitangi, Auckland: Oxford University Press, 1989, 259; Gabrielle Huria,
        'The Bill: Ngāi Tahu Putting a Stamp on our Identity and Tribal Rights',
        Te Karaka, Raumati/Summer 1996, 6.
4   David McCan, *Whatiwhatihoe: The Waikato Raupatu Claim*, Wellington:
        Huia, 2001, 297–316.
5   O'Regan to Graham, 30 June 1991, C-27-2-04 Vol. 1, OTS archives.
6   Winston Peters to Graham, 2 August 1991 and Nick Davidson to Manatū
        Māori official 1, 13 November 1991: both C-27-2-04 Vol. 1, OTS archives.
7   Nick Davidson to David Oughton and Crown Law office [CLO]
        official 1, 20 November 1991, C-27-2-04 Vol. 1, OTS archives; Graham
        to Manatū Māori official 2, 21 November 1991, C-27-2-04 Vol. 1,
        OTS archives.
8   CLO official 2 to Graham, 25 November 1991, C-27-2-04 Vol. 1,
        OTS archives.
9   CLO official 3 to ToWPU official 7, 25 November 1991, C-27-2-04 Vol. 1,
        OTS archives; Meeting between Crown and Ngāi Tahu Negotiators,
        27 November 1991, C-27-2-03 Vol. 1, OTS archives.
10   J. J. McGrath to Graham, 6 December 1991; ToWPU official 7 to
        David Oughton, 9 December 1991: both C-27-2-04 Vol. 1, OTS archive, 1.
11   O'Regan to Graham, 11 December 1991 and Graham to O'Regan
        17 December 1991: C-27-2-04 Vol. 1, OTS archives; Minutes of
        4 February 1992 meeting between Ngāi Tahu and the Crown,
        C-27-8-01 Vol. 1, OTS archives.
12   One of Ngāi Tahu's advisers mused: 'How do these people live with
        themselves?' The officials were acting in the role of public servant,
        so perhaps that advice was expected of them. Nick Davidson, 'Vogel
        House Meeting', 10 February 1992, Vh 12 (c) Box 150, TRoNT archive.
13   Minutes of 1 March 1992 meeting between Ngāi Tahu and the Crown,
        C-27-8-01 Vol. 1, OTS archives.
14   'Draft Legal Personality Bill', 25 February 1992, C-27-2-04 Vol. 2,
        OTS archives; Davidson to O'Regan, 28 February 1992, Vhi 12 (g)
        Box 150, TRoNT archive.

Chapter 6: The economics of Ngāi Tahu's settlement

1   Damian Stone, 'Financial and Commercial Dimensions of Settlement',
        in Nicola R. Wheen and Janine Hayward (eds), *Treaty of Waitangi*
        Settlements, Wellington: Bridget Williams Books, 2012, 145.
2   Working party on reserves not awarded report, 18 October 1991,
        C-27-3-01 Vol. 1, OTS archives.
3   Waitangi Tribunal, *Ngāi Tahu Land Report*, Wellington:
        Waitangi Tribunal, 1991, 3 vols, 828–29. 'Given that Ngai Tahu
        undoubtedly owned the land, the vesting in them of an area which
        amounted to about 1133 acres per person, particularly when compared
        with the much more extensive runs thought appropriate to the
        needs of European settlers, could scarcely be regarded as generous.
        The tribunal cites this merely by way of example and not because we
        see it as the appropriate measure of the land which should have been
        left with Ngai Tahu. Ngai Tahu clearly had a need of land which would
        have been suitable for pastoral or other forms of farming. But Ngai
        Tahu also had a strong affinity, in some cases of a spiritual nature, to
        other notable features of the landscape. Prominent is Aoraki (Mount
        Cook). Their trails throughout their extensive domain, including those
        over the great mountain range, their lakes and rivers, were all taonga,
        all greatly prized. Instead, these people, the tangata whenua, whose
        homeland it was, were against their will reduced to subsist on a mere
        12 acres per person. Their rangatiratanga denied; their future both
        tribally and individually bleak; their Treaty rights ignored. All this with
        the knowledge or connivance of successive governors acting on behalf
        of the Crown.'
4   O'Regan to Ashton, 16 October 1991, Vhi 10 (a) Box 149, TRoNT
        archive, 1–2; Davidson, 'Establishing Principles for the Negotiations
        on Reserves Not Awarded', 14 October 1991, Vhi 10 (a) Box 149,
        TRoNT archive; Malcolm Hanna, 'Report to the Ngāi Tahu Negotiating
        Team Concerning Principles & Procedures for the Assessment of
        Compensation for Land Claims, December 1991', Vhi 14 (e) Box 150,
        TRoNT archive.
5   Malcolm Hanna, 'Public Works Act', 18 December 1991, Vhi 14 (e)
        Box 150, TRoNT archive.
6   Malcolm McKinnon, *Treasury: The New Zealand Treasury 1840-2000*,
        Auckland: Auckland University Press, 2003, 1–11.
7   Commissioner of Crown Lands, 'Reserves Not Awarded Working Party',
        C-27-3-01 Vol. 1, OTS archives.
8   O'Regan to Treasury official 7, 23 December 1991, C-27-3-01,
        OTS archive, 2.
9   Cybele Locke, *Workers in the Margins: Union Radicals in Post-War*
        New Zealand, Wellington: Bridget Williams Books, 2012, 13.
10   Michael Belgrave, *Historical Frictions: Māori Claims and Reinvented*
        Histories, Auckland: Auckland University Press, 2005, 320, 325–26.
11   O'Regan to Treasury official 7, 27 December 1991, C-27-3-01 Vol. 1,
        OTS archive, 3; O'Regan to Treasury official 7, 30 December 1991,
        Vhi 10 (d) Box 149, TRoNT archive.
12   'Framework Agreement between Crown and Ngāi Tahu Negotiators',
        27 November 1991, C27/2/02 Vol 1.

13   (Graph) 'Sequencing Work Required to Settle Ngāi Tahu Claim',
        4 November 1991, C27/2/02 Vol. 1, 2–3; Dangerfield to O'Regan, 20 and
        24 December 1991, C-27-3-01 Vol. 1, OTS archives; O'Regan to Treasury
        official 7, 27 December 1991, C-27-4-01 Vol. 1, OTS archives.

14   Memorandum for Cabinet, 'Proposed Objectives and Approaches
        to Redress for the Ngāi Tahu Negotiations', 13 September 1991,
        C27-2-02 Vol. 1, OTS archive, 2–3; Lord Normanby to Captain Hobson,
        14 August 1839, Great Britain Parliamentary Papers 1840 in Vincent
        O'Malley, Bruce Stirling and Wally Penetito (eds), *The Treaty of
        Waitangi Companion: Māori and Pākehā from Tasman to Today*,
        Auckland: Auckland University Press, 2010, 35–36; Claudia Orange,
        The Treaty of Waitangi, Wellington: Allen & Unwin, 1987, 29–31.

15   Treasury official 6, 'Principles for Ngāi Tahu Negotiations',
        November 1991, C27/2/02 Vol. 1, 1–2.

16   Jennings to Dangerfield, 4 December 1991, C-27-3-01 Vol. 1,
        OTS archives.

17   O'Regan to Ashton, 16 October 1991, Vhi 10 (a) Box 149,
        TRoNT archive, 1–2.

18   Meeting between Crown and Ngāi Tahu Negotiators, 4 February 1992,
        C-27-8-01 Vol. 1, OTS archive, 5.

19   Meeting between Crown and Ngāi Tahu Negotiators, 4 February 1992,
        C-27-8-01 Vol. 1, OTS archive, 5, 7.

20   Stephen Jennings to Ngāi Tahu Negotiators, 3 February 1992, VH i 10 (g)
        Box 149, TRoNT archive, 3.

21   O'Regan to Graham, 7 February 1992, C-27-3-01 Vol. 1, OTS archive, 2;
        Meeting between Crown and Ngāi Tahu Negotiators, 29 April 1992,
        C-27-2-02 Vol. 2, OTS archive.

22   Secretary of Justice, 'Ngai Tahu', 11 February 1992, C-27-3-01 Vol. 1,
        OTS archives.

23   Meeting of Ngai Tahu and Crown Negotiators, 11 February 1992,
        C-27-2-03 Vol. 1, OTS archive, 2.

24   O'Regan to Graham, 12 February 1992, C-27-3-01 Vol. 1, OTS archive,
        1–2; during after-meeting drinks with Graham and a few other Crown
        officials Ngāi Tahu legal adviser Nick Davidson was able to have
        some candid conversations regarding Ngāi Tahu's recent proposal for
        settlement sent to the Crown. 'There was no specific mention of the
        letter we tabled on Friday other than one brief comment from the
        Minister not directed at me specifically but to the effect that perhaps
        we had got the decimal point in the wrong place. I apologised for the
        fact that laser printers sometimes throw fullstops too far to the left.'

25   Nick Davidson, 26 June 1992, Vhi 10 (gg) Box 149, TRoNT archive.

26   Nick Davidson, 'Note of a Meeting at Vogel House', 9 February 1992,
        Vh 12 c Box 150, TRoNT archive, 5.

27   O'Regan to Graham, 27 February 1992, C-27-3-01 Vol. 1, OTS archive, 1–3.

28   James Belich, *Paradise Reforged: A History of the New Zealanders from
        the 1880s to the Year 2000*, Auckland: Penguin, 2001, 394–413; Cybele
        Locke, *Workers in the Margins: Union Radicals in Post-War New Zealand*,
        Wellington: Bridget Williams Books, 2012, 12–13.

29   O'Regan to Graham, 27 February 1992, C-27-3-01 Vol. 1, OTS archive, 1–3.

30   Interview with Sir Tipene O'Regan, 5 May 2011.

31   Treasury official 6 to Treasury official 7, 17 February 1992, C-27-3-01
        Vol. 2, OTS archives.

32   VNZ official 1 to Treasury Secretary and Treasury official 6,
      17 February 1992, C-27-3-01 Vol. 2, OTS archives.
33   VNZ official 2 to Stephen Jennings, 3 and 9 March 1992, Vhi 14,
      TRoNT archive.
34   Valuation report to Ngāi Tahu negotiators, 28 April 1992, Vhi 14,
      TRoNT archive.
35   Graham to O'Regan, 15 April 1992 C-27-02 Vol. 2.
36   O'Regan to Graham, 29 April 1992, C-27-4-01 Vol. 2, OTS archives.
37   Ngāi Tahu's argument was not accepted by the Crown, which cited
      the support of Southern Māori MP Eruera Tirikatene and a number
      of Ngāi Tahu marae in 1944.
38   ToWPU official 3 and ToWPU official 6 to Graham, 16 June 1992;
      CSC (92) 89; Minister of Justice to Chairperson Cabinet Strategy
      Committee, 'Ngāi Tahu Negotiations', 12 June 1992: all C-27-1-02 Vol. 2,
      OTS archives.
39   CAB (92) M38/11, para C viii, C-27-1-02 Vol. 2, OTS archives.
40   *Fisheries Deed of Settlement*, 23 September 1992, Clause 4.6.
41   Denese Henare to Mahuta, 4 March 1993; Mahuta file note, 18 May 1993:
      both RC Vol. 30 1993, Box 11, W-T.
42   Treasury official 4 to Paul Baines, 28 July 1992, Vhi 10 (ii) Box 149,
      TRoNT archive; 'Ngāi Tahu Position Paper', 1 August 1992, NT140,
      F(i)3, MB, 2.
43   J. J. McGrath to Graham, 6 August 1992, 3; Rahui Katene to Graham,
      11 August 1992, 2: both C-27-4-01 Vol. 2, OTS archives.
44   CLO official 4 to Treasury, 16 July 1992, C-27-4-01 Vol. 2, OTS archives;
      Interview with ToWPU official 2.
45   Graham comments on 28 October 1992 Meeting, C-27-2-03 Vol. 2,
      OTS archives; Gavin Muirhead, *Footprints to the Future: The Story
      of Landcorp's First 20 Years*, Wellington: Landcorp, 2009.

Chapter 7: The gradual breakdown of 1992–94

1   CLO official 2 to Treasury, 16 July 1992, C-27-4-01 Vol. 2, OTS archives;
      'Hotel de Vin meetings', 4 August 1992, NT140, F(i)3; Interview with
      ToWPU official 3, 18 April 2011.
2   Meeting between Ngāi Tahu and Crown negotiators, 5 March 1993;
      Meeting between Ngāi Tahu and Crown negotiators, 31 March 1993;
      Meeting between Ngāi Tahu and Crown negotiators, 28 April 1993:
      all C-27-2-02 Vol. 2, OTS archives; Nick Davidson, 3 February 1993,
      VB268 (j), TRoNT archive.
3   Waitangi Tribunal, *Ngāi Tahu Land Report*. Wellington: Waitangi
      Tribunal, 1991, 3 vols, 347–790; Harry Evison, *New Zealand Racism in
      the Making: The Life & Times of Walter Mantell*, Lower Hutt: Panuitia
      Press, 2010.
4   O'Regan to Graham, 1 February 1993, C-27-2-02 Vol. 2, OTS archives;
      ToWPU official 3, 'Analysis of *Ngai Tahu Land Report* of the Negotiation
      Process and Position', 4 March 1993, C-27-2-02 Vol. 2, OTS archives.
5   Adella Ferguson, 'Treaty Package Claimed', *New Zealand Herald*,
      18 May 1993.
6   Meeting between Ngāi Tahu and Crown Negotiators, 31 March 1993,
      C-27-2-02 Vol. 2, OTS archives.

7   Meeting between Ngāi Tahu and Crown negotiators, 1 July 1993,
         C-27-2-02 Vol. 2, OTS archives; Meeting between Ngāi Tahu and Crown
         negotiators, 28 July 1993, C-27-2-02 Vol. 2, OTS archives; O'Regan
         to David Filer, 1 October 1993, C-27-2-02 Vol. 2, OTS archives;
         Meeting between Ngāi Tahu and Crown negotiators, 6 October 1993,
         C-27-2-02 Vol. 2, OTS archives; O'Regan to Graham, 8 October 1993,
         C-27-2-02 Vol. 2, OTS archives.
8   O'Regan, 'Chairman's Report', *Ngāi Tahu Annual Report 1993*, NT140 C4,
         Box 54, MB, 7–9.
9   Sid Ashton, 'Pan-Maori Forestry Hui', 12 February 1994, Vhi 15 (n),
         TRoNT archive; Shane Solomon, 'CFRT hui', RC Vol. 33, Box 13, W-T.
10   Graham to Chairman Cabinet Committee on Treaty of Waitangi Issues,
         'Settlement of the Ngāi Tahu Maori Trust Board Claim to the Waitangi
         Tribunal', 20 May 1992, C-27-4-07 Vol. 1, OTS archives.
11   Manager Crown Forest Lands to David Oughton, 19 June 1992; ToWPU
         official 4 to Graham, 19 June 1992: both C-27-4-07 Vol. 1, OTS archives;
         Meeting between Ngāi Tahu and Crown negotiators, 24 June 1992,
         C-27-4-02 Vol. 4, OTS archives.
12   Minister of Conservation to Chairman Cabinet Committee on Treaty of
         Waitangi Issues, 'Greenstone Pastoral Lease: Exclusion from Area to go
         in the Crown Land Bank', 19 June 1992, C-27-4-07 Vol. 1, OTS archives;
         O'Regan to Graham, 6 August 1992, C-27-4-07 Vol. 1, OTS archives.
13   Les Cleveland to Graham, 30 July 1992, C-27-4-07 Vol. 1, OTS archives.
14   Kerry O'Donohue to Graham, 29 July 1992, C-27-4-07 Vol. 1,
         OTS archives.
15   Niall Watson to Graham, 9 July 1992; M. A. Rodway to Graham,
         28 July 1992: both C-27-4-07 Vol. 1, OTS archives.
16   Graham to O'Regan, undated but most likely July 1992; Meeting
         between Ngāi Tahu and Crown negotiators, 24 July 1992: both
         C-27-4-02, Vol. 4, OTS archives; CSC (92) 387, C-27-4-07 Vol. 1,
         OTS archives.
17   CAB (92) 643; ToWPU official 4 to Graham, 'Ngāi Tahu Negotiations:
         Advance on Settlement', 31 July 1992: both C-27-4-07 Vol. 1,
         OTS archives.
18   O'Regan to Manager Crown Forest Lands, 13 August 1992, C-27-4-07
         Vol. 1, OTS archives.
19   CAB (92) M23/10a, C-27-4-02 Vol. 4, OTS archives. In July 1993 Ngāi
         Tahu sought another high-country pastoral lease, at Glenmore Station,
         but the Crown was very hesitant and in the end the station was taken
         off the market before it was ever sold. Graham, 'Purchase of Glenmore
         Station for Part Settlement of the Ngāi Tahu Claim', 8 July 1993;
         ToWPU official 10 to Treasury official 8, 'Re Glenmore Station',
         12 July 1993: both C-27-8-01 Vol. 6, OTS archives.
20   ToWPU official 4, 'Meeting with Fish & Game Council and Federated
         Mountain Clubs', 20 October 1992, C-27-7-04 Vol. 1, OTS archives.
21   Barbara Marshall (FMC) to Graham, 21 October 1992; Bryce Johnson
         to Graham, 21 October 1992: all C-27-7-04 Vol. 1, OTS archives.
22   Johnson to Graham, 28 October 1992, C-27-7-04 Vol. 1, OTS archives.
23   ToWPU official 11 to Graham, 15 June 1993, AAKW W5105 7812 5, ANZ, 1.
24   Meeting between Crown and Ngāi Tahu Negotiators, 1 July 1993,
         C-27-2-02 Vol. 2, OTS archives.

25   Graham to O'Regan, 21 September 1993, NT140, F(i)1 Box 129, MB.
26   Graham to Forest & Bird, Environmental and Conservation Groups,
      Fish & Game, Maruia Society, FMC, New Zealand Deerstalkers Association
      and the New Zealand Conservation Authority, 16 December 1991;
      Catherine Wallace to Graham, 4 April 1992; ToWPU official 2, 'Meeting
      with Fish & Game Council and FMC', 20 October 1992; Denis Marshall
      to Graham, 7 December 1992: all C-27-7-04 Vol. 1; Denis Marshall,
      'Speech to the Federated Mountain Clubs', 12 June 1993, NT140 G20b,
      MB; B. F. Webb to Sid Ashton, 21 March 1994, NT140 M4 (g), MB;
      DOC official 1, 'Consultations for Ngāi Tahu', 11 May 1994, C-27-7-04
      Vol. 1; Graham, 'Speech to Public Access NZ', June 1994, C-27-7-04
      Vol. 1; Graham, 'Ngāi Tahu Negotiations: Preliminary Crown Position
      on Sites of Recreational and Conservation Interest, 17–18 September
      1996 in Christchurch and Dunedin', Vhi 52c (r), TRoNT archive.
27   Bruce Mason to Graham, 12 November 1991; Graham to Mason,
      3 December 1991; Mason to Graham, 24 November 1992; Graham to
      Mason, 19 February 1993: all C-27-7-04 Vol. 1, OTS archives; Mason to
      Graham, 2 May 1994; Graham to Mason, 25 May 1994; C-27-7-03 Vol. 1,
      OTS archives.
28   Meeting between Crown and Ngāi Tahu Negotiators, 18 July 1994,
      C-27-2-02 Vol. 3, OTS archives.
29   Catherine Wallace to Graham, 4 April 1992, C-27-7-04 Vol. 1,
      OTS archives.
30   O'Regan to Graham, 8 March 1994 and 3 June 1994; Minutes of a
      meeting between Crown and Ngāi Tahu negotiators, 16 March 1994,
      C-27-2-03 Vol. 3; Minutes of Public Consultation Process Hui by the
      Ngai Tahu Maori Trust Board, 22 April 1994; C-27-7-04 Vol. 1.
31   Edward Ellison to Ashton, 2 June 1994, Vhi 16 (t), TRoNT archive.
32   DOC official 2 to ToWPU official 11, 18 January 1994, AAKW W5105
      7812 5, ANZ; Minutes of a meeting between Crown and Ngāi Tahu
      negotiators, 8 June 1994, C-27-2-02 Vol. 3, OTS archives, 2.
      Hostile consultation processes regarding treaty settlements and
      indigenous rights have also been explored by Canadian authors –
      by anthropologist Elisabeth Furniss in the British Columbian context
      during the same time period in the Cariboo–Chicotlin area and by
      journalist Alex Rose in his history of the Nisga'a claim: Elisabeth
      Furniss, *Burden of History: Colonialism and the Frontier Myth in a Rural
      Community*, Vancouver: UBC Press, 1999; Alex Rose, *Spirit Dance
      at Meziadin: Chief Joseph Gosnell and the Nisga'a Treaty*, Vancouver:
      Harbour Publishing, 2000.
33   Ngāi Tahu Negotiating Team to Crown 'A' Team Negotiators, 'Options
      for Dealing with Crown Asset Sales', 10 December 1991, C-27-4-02
      Vol. 1, OTS archives; O'Regan to Treasury, 24 January 1992, 'Landcorp
      South Island Assets', and O'Regan to Justice Secretary, 4 February 1992,
      'Information on Crown Assets': both C-27-4-02 Vol. 2, OTS archives;
      Alan Ward, *An Unsettled History: Treaty Claims in New Zealand Today*,
      Wellington: Bridget Williams Books, 1999, 36.
34   O'Regan to ToWPU, 'Crown Asset Disposal', 11 December 1991,
      C-27-4-02 Vol. 1, OTS archives.
35   O'Regan to Graham, 27 August 1993, C-27-4-02 Vol. 4, OTS archives.
36   Graham to O'Regan, 27 September 1993, C-27-4-02 Vol. 4, OTS archives.

37   Waitangi Tribunal, *Ngāi Tahu Land Report*, 725, 1061.

38   Maika Mason and Russell Beck, *Pounamu Treasures: Ngā Taonga Pounamu*, Auckland: Penguin, 2012. The Crown continued to provide consent to private companies to mine pounamu in the Arahura Valley: O'Regan to Graham, 24 January 1992, Vhi 9a(c), TRoNT archive.

39   Meeting of Crown and Ngāi Tahu negotiators, 4 February 1992, C-27-8-01 Vol. 1, OTS archives.

40   In the Ngāi Tahu dialect of the Māori language, the 'ng' is often replaced with a 'k'. Hence taonga, or treasured possession, is taoka.

41   The meaning of mana is many and varied but in this case signifies the Crown's honour.

42   Minutes of a meeting between Crown and Ngāi Tahu negotiators, 30 September 1992, C-27-2-02 Vol. 2, OTS archives.

43   O'Regan to Graham, 25 March 1993, C-27-2-02 Vol. 2; Minutes of a meeting between Crown and Ngāi Tahu negotiators, 31 March 1993; O'Regan to ToWPU official 11, 6 April 1993; ToWPU official 11 to O'Regan, 8 April 1993; ToWPU official 10 to Graham, 29 June 1993; Graham to O'Regan, 18 October 1993: all C-27-2-02 Vol. 2, OTS archives; Minutes of a meeting between Crown and Ngāi Tahu negotiators, 4 May 1994, C-27-2-02 Vol. 3, OTS archives.

44   Minutes of a meeting between Crown and Ngāi Tahu negotiators, 26 January 1994, C-27-2-02 Vol. 3, OTS archives.

45   Michael Stevens, 'Settlements and "Taonga": A Ngāi Tahu Commentary', in Nicola R. Wheen and Janine Hayward (eds), *Treaty of Waitangi Settlements*, Wellington: Bridget Williams Books, 2012, 135; Michael Stevens, 'Muttonbirds and Modernity in Murihiku: Continuity and Change in Kai Tahu Knowledge', PhD thesis, University of Otago, 2009.

46   Waitangi Tribunal, *Ngāi Tahu Land Report*, 1064.

47   Harold Ashwell to Waitangi Tribunal, 17 August 1991, Vhi 9b(f), TRoNT archive; Meeting between Ngāi Tahu, DOC and ToWPU officials, 1 October 1991, C-27-2-03 Vol. 1, OTS archives.

48   Minutes of meeting between Ngāi Tahu and Crown Negotiators, 30 October 1991, C-27-2-03 Vol. 1, OTS archives.

49   Ibid.

50   Minutes of meeting between Ngāi Tahu and Crown Negotiators, 4 February 1992, C-27-8-01 Vol. 1, OTS archives; minutes of meeting between Ngāi Tahu and Crown Negotiators, 6 October 1993, C-27-2-02 Vol. 2, OTS archives.

51   DOC official 2 to O'Regan, 23 June 1992, Vhi 13 (k) Box 150, TRoNT archive.

52   O'Regan to Graham, 25 March 1993, C-27-2-02 Vol. 2, OTS archives.

53   In 1985 Ayers Rock or Uluru was returned as freehold title to the local Aboriginal community and leased back to the Australian government. Uluru is co-managed by a park board with an Aboriginal majority: David Lawrence, 'Managing Parks/Managing "Country": Joint Management of Aboriginal Owned Protected Areas in Australia', Research Paper 2, 1996–97, Canberra: Parliament of Australia.

54   Minutes of meeting between Ngāi Tahu and Crown Negotiators, 31 March 1993; ToWPU official 11 to Graham, 27 April 1993; Minutes of meeting between Ngāi Tahu and Crown Negotiators, 28 April 1993; ToWPU official 10 to Graham, 29 June 1993: C-27-2-02 Vol. 2, OTS archives.

55   Minutes of meeting between Ngāi Tahu and Crown Negotiators,
      1 March 1992, C-27-8-01 Vol. 1, OTS archives.

56   CSC (92) 89, C-27-2-02 Vol. 2, OTS archives.

57   O'Regan to Graham, 25 March 1992, C-27-2-02 Vol. 2, OTS archives.

58   Minutes of meeting between Ngāi Tahu and Crown Negotiators,
      31 March 1993, C-27-2-02 Vol. 2, OTS archives.

59   Rakiura Ngāi Tahu were also intimately involved in the negotiations
      regarding Whenua Hou and the Crown Tītī Islands. Rakiura Ngāi
      Tahu were disappointed with the proposal for the former and believed
      that the proposals should have allowed for greater Rakiura Ngāi
      Tahu control of the island. The Rakiura Tītī Committee was the
      coordinating group regarding the Tītī Islands and O'Regan and the
      NTMTB consulted with it during the negotiation. The committee gave
      its interim approval for the draft management structure deed for the
      Crown Tītī Islands in mid-1993, but it was split on the vesting of the
      Tītī Islands. Some committee members believed that the islands should
      be vested locally rather than into TRoNT. Eventually it was agreed that
      the islands would be vested in TRoNT with local direct management:
      Minutes of meeting between Ngāi Tahu and Crown negotiators,
      1 July 1993; Minutes of meeting between Ngāi Tahu and Crown
      Negotiators, 28 July 1993: both C-27-2-02 Vol. 2, OTS archives.
      O'Regan to Graham, 18 January 1994; Minutes of meeting between
      Ngāi Tahu and Crown Negotiators, 26 January 1994: both C-27-2-02
      Vol. 3, OTS archives.

60   Forest & Bird's immediate response to the draft deed is unclear,
      but in line with their opposition to all other aspects of the Ngāi Tahu
      settlement it was most likely negative. Minutes of meeting between
      Ngāi Tahu and Crown Negotiators, 1 July 1993; Minutes of meeting
      between Ngāi Tahu and Crown Negotiators, 28 July 1993; Minutes of
      meeting between Ngāi Tahu and Crown Negotiators, 6 October 1993:
      all C-27-2-02 Vol. 2, OTS archives.

61   Minutes of meeting between Ngāi Tahu and Crown Negotiators,
      8 June 1994, C-27-2-02 Vol. 3, OTS archives.

62   O'Regan to ToWPU official 8, 8 August 1994; Graham to Cabinet
      Strategy Committee, 'Ngāi Tahu On-account Settlement',
      24 August 1994; CAB (94) M 40/10, all C-27-2-02 Vol. 3, OTS archives.

63   ToWPU official 4 to ToWPU official 6 file notes, February and March
      1992, C-27-2-04 Vol. 2, OTS archives. Tuhuru and Waitaha were also
      challenging the allocation of the fisheries quota. See Tipene O'Regan,
      'Old Myths and New Politics: Some Contemporary Uses of Traditional
      History', *New Zealand Journal of History* 26, no. 1 (April 1992): 5–27.

64   O'Regan to Negotiating Team, 27 January 1992, MB; O'Regan to
      Negotiating Team, 17 January 1992, Vhi 9B (k), TRoNT archive.

65   Malcolm Birdling, 'Healing the Past or Harming the Future?
      Large Natural Groupings and the Waitangi Settlement Process',
      New Zealand Journal of Public and International Law 2, no. 2 (2004):
      259–84; Therese Crocker, 'Mandating Matters: Maori Representation
      and Crown Policy in the Early Treaty Settlements Processes,
      1988–1998', Wellington: Treaty Research Series, 2013.

66   Eli Weepu to Graham and ToWPU official 3, 9 March 1992,
      C-27-2-01 Vol. 2, OTS archives.

67   Te Rūnanga o Tuhuru to Doug Kidd [Minister of Māori Affairs], 22 May 1992; ToWPU official 7 to O'Regan, 27 July 1992: C-27-2-01 Vol. 2, OTS archives.

68   Meeting of Te Rūnanganui o Tahu, 25–26 April 1992, NT140 Mi (u), MB.

69   Mohammed Shabadet to Charles Crofts, 25 August 1992, NT140 Mi (u), MB.

70   Edward Taihakerei Durie to Tuhuru, 22 December 1992, C-27-2-01 Vol. 2, OTS archives. Tuhuru attempted to submit a claim for urgency again in mid-1994: ToWPU official 8 to Graham, 8 June 1994, C-27-2-02 Vol. 3, OTS archives.

71   Meeting of the Ngai Tahu Maori Trust Board, 6 and 9 November 1992, NT 140 A39 Box 11A, MB.

72   Ngai Tahu Maori Trust Board to Māori Affairs Select Committee, 29 September 1993, NT140 M4 (g) Box 298, MB.

73   'Hui a tau o Ngāi Tahu', 5–7 November 1993, MB; *New Zealand Parliamentary Debates* [*NZPD*], Vol. 554, 11947.

74   ToWPU official 8 to CLO official 3, 26 May 1994, C-27-2-01 Vol. 2, OTS archives. Tuhuru were supported by the National Māori Congress: Charles Crofts to Api Mahuika, 11 February 1993, MB.

75   Cabinet Memorandum Treaty of Waitangi Issues (92) 37, C-27-2-04 Vol. 2, OTS archives.

76   Sandra Lee to Graham, 20 March 1992; Lee to Sid Ashton (NTMTB Secretary), 26 March 1992: NT140 Mi (u), MB.

77   O'Regan to Whetu Tirikatene-Sullivan, 1 April 1992, MB.

78   O'Regan to Graham, 1 February 1993; Minutes of meeting between Ngāi Tahu and Crown Negotiators, 5 March 1993, C-27-2-02 Vol. 2, OTS archives.

79   *NZPD*, Vol. 536, 16890–92.

80   *NZPD*, Vol. 536, 16892–93.

81   *NZPD*, Vol. 536, 16894–95.

82   *NZPD*, Vol. 536, 16895–900.

83   *NZPD*, Vol. 536, 16900–02.

84   Minutes of meeting between Ngai Tahu and Crown Negotiators, 28 July 1993, C-27-2-02 Vol. 2, OTS archives.

85   Memorandum to file claim by Sandra Te Hakamatua Lee for Tuhuru on the processing of Te Runanga o Ngai Tahu Bill, 13 September 1993, MA 2/1/1, Archives NZ.

86   Minutes of meeting between Ngai Tahu and Crown Negotiators, 26 January 1994, C-27-2-02 Vol. 3, OTS archives.

87   'Maori Bill Questioned', *New Zealand Herald*, 5 March 1994.

88   'Ngai Tahu Maori Trust Board *In Committee Minutes*', 8–10 April 1994, NT140 M14 (c), MB.

89   Graham to O'Regan, 3 June 1994, C-27-4-01 Vol. 3, OTS archives.

90   'Ngāi Tahu hui-a-tau', 21–22 January 1994, MB140, B(x)6 Box 53, MB; Davidson to Harry Evison, 31 January 1994, Vhi 15 (k), TRoNT archive; Davidson to O'Regan, 9 March 1994, Vhi 15 (x), TRoNT archive.

91   Garry Moore and Michael Knowles, 'Ngāi Tahu negotiations', 30 June 1994, C-27-2-02 Vol. 3, OTS archives; Graham to O'Regan, 10 August 1994, C-27-2-02 Vol. 3, OTS archives.

92   Waitangi Tribunal, *Motonui-Waitara Report*, Wellington: Department of Justice, 1983; *Kaituna River Report*, Wellington: Department of Justice, 1984; *Report of the Waitangi Tribunal on the Manukau Claim* (*Wai-8*), Wellington: Waitangi Tribunal, 1985.

Chapter 8: Collapse, late 1994–early 1996

1   O'Regan to Ngāi Tahu Negotiating Group, 17 January 1994, NT140 Q13, TRoNT archive, 1.

2   Meeting between Ngāi Tahu and Crown Negotiators, 26 January 1994, C-27-2-02 Vol. 3, OTS archives; Martin Fisher, 'Balancing Rangatiratanga and Kawanatanga: Waikato-Tainui and Ngāi Tahu's Treaty Settlement Negotiations with the Crown', PhD thesis, Victoria University of Wellington, 2015, 119–45.

3   Sid Ashton, 'Pan-Maori Forestry Hui', 12 February 1994, Vhi 15 (n), TRoNT archive; Sid Ashton, 'Meeting of Maori Trust Boards', 2 June 1994, Vhi 16 (q), TRoNT archive.

4   Meeting between Ngāi Tahu and Crown Negotiators, 8 June 1994, C-27-2-02 Vol. 3, OTS archives.

5   Meeting between Ngāi Tahu and Crown Negotiators, 4 May 1994, C-27-2-02 Vol. 3, OTS archives; O'Regan to Graham, 18 May 1994, C-27-2-02 Vol. 3, OTS archives.

6   Meeting between Ngāi Tahu and Crown Negotiators, 18 July 1994, C-27-2-02 Vol. 3, OTS archives.

7   A marginal strip is an area of land, usually 20 metres wide, which extends along and abuts the landward margins of parts of the foreshore and the beds of other water bodies that meet certain minimum size requirements. The strips are created when the Crown disposes of land, http://www.linz.govt.nz/survey-titles/cadastral-surveying/publications/marginal-strips.

8   For all other iwi with land-banks, the properties contained in the land-bank would have to be used in any treaty settlement. Ngāi Tahu could purchase lands in the land-bank with their own funds and on-sell them for a profit. They were then allowed to add additional lands to the bank. This was tenable only in the large rohe of Ngāi Tahu that consists of most of the South Island.

9   Pete Barnao, 'Ngāi Tahu settlement "far away"', *Otago Daily Times*, 26 October 1994; Graham to O'Regan, 2 November 1994, C-27-2-02 Vol. 3, OTS archives; O'Regan to Graham, 20 December 1994, C-27-2-02 Vol. 3, OTS archives.

10   Ngāi Tahu negotiations work strategy and programme Cabinet Select Committee Memorandum, 25 October 1994, C27-1-02 Vol. 2, OTS archives.

11   O'Regan to Graham, 20 December 1994, C-27-2-02 Vol. 3, OTS archives.

12   O'Regan to Graham, 20 February 1995; Graham to O'Regan, 17 March 1995; O'Regan to Graham, 20 March 1995: all NE-18-027-00-01, OTS archives.

13   Office of Treaty Settlements, *Crown Proposals for the Settlement of Treaty of Waitangi Claims: Detailed Proposals; Summary*, Wellington: Office of Treaty Settlements, 1994.

14   Richard Price, *The Politics of Modern History-making: The 1990s Negotiations of the Ngāi Tahu Tribe with the Crown to Achieve a Treaty of Waitangi Claims Settlement*, Christchurch: Macmillan Brown Research Series, 1994, 79–84.

15   O'Regan to Graham, 10 February 1995, Vhi 17(f) TRoNT archive; Steve Evans, 'Crown forced Ngāi Tahu to take legal steps', *Independent*, 23 June 1995.

16   Andrew Stone, 'Cool Welcome for "Fiscal Envelope"', *New Zealand Herald*, 9 December 1994; 'Govt Land Claim Offer an "Insult"', *Waikato Times*, 9 December 1994; 'Flexing the Envelope', *New Zealand Herald*, 9 December 1994; 'National Māori Vice-president [Cliff Bidwell] Criticises Cap', *Waikato Times*, 10 December 1994; Andrew Stone, 'Debate on Treaty Plans Constructive, Moderate', *New Zealand Herald*, 10 December 1994; Michael Laws, 'Arrogant Land Proposal Doomed', *New Zealand Herald*, 11 December 1994; 'Settlement starter', *Sunday Star Times*, 11 December 1994; Alan Duff, 'Brave Move, but $1b too Low', *Waikato Times*, 13 December 1994; David Lange, 'Government Ignores Responsibilities', *Waikato Times*, 19 December 1994.

17   Solomon to Te Maru, 11 January 1995; Solomon, 'File Note', 24 January 1995, RC1, Correspondence Vol. 37, December 1994, Box 15, W-T; 'Fiscally Fair and Timely', *National Business Review* 25, No. 43, Issue 1906; Gareth Morgan, 'Want to Know Why the Fiscal Envelope is so Thick?', *National Business Review*, 10 February 1995.

18   Winston Peters to Graham, 17 January 1995, VB51 (j), TRoNT archive; Moana Jackson, 'Return to Sender – An Analysis of the Fiscal Envelope: Proposals for Settlement of Treaty Grievances', January 1995, TRoNT archive.

19   Solomon, 'Turangi Hui', RC1, Correspondence Vol. 38, Jan–Feb 1995, Box 16, W-T, 6–7.

20   Wira Gardiner, *Return to Sender: What Really Happened at the Fiscal Envelope Hui*, Auckland: Reed Books, 1996.

21   Margaret Mutu, *The State of Māori Rights*, Wellington: Huia, 2011, 21–25; Aroha Harris, *Hīkoi: Forty Years of Māori Protest*, Wellington: Huia Publishers, 2004, 124–33; Belgrave, *Historical Frictions: Māori Claims and Reinvented Histories*, Auckland: Auckland University Press, 2005, 330–31; Ranginui Walker, *Ka whawhai tonu matou: Struggle Without End*, Auckland: Penguin, 2004, 301–4; Alan Ward, *An Unsettled History: Treaty Claims in New Zealand Today*, Wellington: Bridget Williams Books, 1999, 52–53.

22   Douglas Graham, *Trick or Treaty?* Wellington: Institute for Policy Studies, 1997, 55–67; Douglas Graham, 'The Treaty and Treaty Negotiations', in Margaret Clark (ed.), *The Bolger Years: 1990–1997*, Wellington: Dunmore Publishing, 2008, 166–69; Interview with ToWPU official 4, 24 May 2011; Interview with ToWPU official 1, 27 July 2011; Richard Hill, *Māori and the State: Crown–Māori Relations in New Zealand/ Aotearoa, 1950–2000*, Wellington: Victoria University Press, 2009, 262.

23   Chris Finlayson, 'Ngāi Tahu Negotiations', in Margaret Clark (ed.), *The Bolger Years: 1990–1997*, Wellington: Dunmore Publishing, 2008, 181–95; OTS Director to Graham, 30 March 1995, NE-10-027-00-02 Pt. 1, OTS archives.

24   Meeting of Te Rūnanganui o Tahu, 29 January 1994, NT140 M14 (c), MB; Minister of Justice to Cabinet Strategy Committee, 19 July 1995, 'Ngāi Tahu: Overview of Ngāi Tahu Claims and Legal/Redress Proceedings', NE-12-027-00-2 Vol. 1, OTS archives.

25   Minister of Justice to Cabinet Strategy Committee, 19 July 1995, 'Ngāi Tahu: Overview of Ngāi Tahu Claims and Legal/Redress Proceedings', NE-12-027-00-2 Vol. 1, OTS archives.

26   Under the Treaty of Waitangi (State Enterprises) Act 1988 SOEs'
      properties were marked with a protection memorial that ensured that if
      a claim were well founded then the tribunal could make a binding order
      for the mandatory resumption of the property for transferral to the
      settling Māori group.
27   Steve Evans, 'Ngai Tahu to File in High Court over South Island
      Forestry Claim', *Independent*, 31 March 1995; Durie files, Vols 1–3,
      TP-02-027-00-01, OTS archives.
28   'Ngāi Tahu hui-a-tau', 2–3 November 1994, NT 140 B(x)9, Box 53.
29   Graham to O'Regan, 18 January 1995, AAKW W5105 7812 Box 34, ANZ;
      C. F. Finlayson to the Editor of the *Otago Daily* Times and Graham,
      27 January 1995, AAKW W5105 7812 Box 34, ANZ; O'Regan to Graham
      and Graham to O'Regan, 10 and 12 February 1995, NE-10-027-00-01
      pt. 1, OTS archives.
30   *Waikato–Tainui Raupatu Deed of Settlement*, 22 May 1995, 2.
31   Davidson to Ngāi Tahu Negotiating Group, 23 February 1995,
      NT140 M4 e, MB, 4.
32   Interview with Sir Tipene O'Regan, 5 May 2011.
33   'Good Morning NZ with Geoff Robinson', 4 August 1995, NT140 M4 (c),
      MB; O'Regan to Simon Murdoch, 3 August 1995, NT140 M4 (d), MB, 2.
34   Davidson to Ngāi Tahu Negotiating Group, 15 September 1995,
      Vhi 51 (f), TRoNT archive.
35   Richard Parata to Davidson and Parata to O'Regan,
      6 and 17 October 1995, Vhi 51 (f), TRoNT archive, 3; Rakiihia Tau Senior
      to Parata, 21 October 1995, Vhi 51 (f), TRoNT archive, 2.
36   Richard Meade to Sid Ashton, Charles Crofts, Anake Goodall,
      15 December 1995, Vhi 51 (g), TRoNT archive, 1.
37   Report of Maori Affairs Committee on Te Runanga o Ngai Tahu Bill,
      13 December 1995, MA 2/1/1, ABGX W5189 16127 Box 18, ANZ.
38   Report of Maori Affairs Committee on Te Runanga o Ngai Tahu Bill,
      13 December 1995, MA 2/1/1, ABGX W5189 16127 Box 18, ANZ.
39   Report of Maori Affairs Committee on Te Runanga o Ngai Tahu Bill,
      13 December 1995, MA 2/1/1, ABGX W5189 16127 Box 18, ANZNZ.
40   Davidson, 'Lunch with [OTS Director 1]', 13 February 1996, Vhi 48 (j),
      TRoNT archive; O'Regan to DPMC official 1, 13 February 1996,
      NE-12-027-00-02 Vol. 4, OTS archives.
41   Tipene O'Regan to DPMC official 1, 16 February 1996; Nick Davidson,
      'Note of a Telephone Conservation with ... [DPMC Official 2]',
      27 February 1996, TRoNT archive.
42   Draft Paper for Cabinet with written notes by DPMC official 2,
      28 February 1996, NE-12-027-00-02 Vol. 2, OTS archives.
43   Bolger to O'Regan, 7 March 1996, NE-12-027-00-02 Vol. 2, OTS archive, 1;
      O'Regan, 'Meeting with Bolger', 7 March 1996, Vhi48 (u),
      TRoNT archive.
44   Tipene O'Regan, 'TOR MTG. WITH PM', 17 March 1996,
      TRoNT archive.
45   Impending Principals' meeting(s), 9 June 1997, TRoNT archive.
      This would, unfairly, make Bolger the equivalent of Nixon.
46   Anake Goodall, 'Te Waihora and DoC-Proposed Asset Alienations',
      8 March 1996, TRoNT archive; Nick Davidson, 'Note of a Telephone
      Conversation with ... Office of Treaty Settlements [Official]',
      15 March 1996, TRoNT archive.

47   TPK official 3 to OTS official 3, 20 March 1996 and Minister of Treaty
      Negotiations to Cabinet Strategy Committee, 'Ngāi Tahu: Specific
      Assets with Conservation Implications', 31 March 1996, both
      NE-12-027-00-02 Vol. 3, OTS archives; CSC (96) M 10/3a, b&c,
      NE-12-027-00-02 Vol. 4, OTS archives.
48   Crown Pastoral Land Act 1998.
49   R. Haworth to O'Regan, 4 October 1997, VB 256 (l), TRoNT archive;
      South Island High Country Committee of Federated Farmers of NZ,
      'Farmers Stand by Defence of Ngāi Tahu', 23 March 1995, MB; Waitangi
      Tribunal, *Ngāi Tahu Land Report*, Wellington: Waitangi Tribunal, 1991,
      3 vols, 1040–42; Michele D. Dominy, 'White Settler Assertions of Native
      Status', *American Ethnologist* 22, no. 2 (May 1995): 358–74; H. A. P. Barker
      to Graham, 23 September 1996, Vhi 54j, TRoNT archive.
50   DPMC official 3 to Bolger, 28 February 1996, NE-12-027-00-02 Vol. 2.
51   DOC official 2 to OTS official 3, 20 March 1996, NE-12-027-00-02 Vol. 3.
52   TPK official 3 to OTS official 3, 20 March 1996 & Graham to Cabinet
      Strategy Committee, 'Ngāi Tahu: Specific Assets with Conservation
      Implications', 31 March 1996: both NE-12-027-00-02 Vol. 3.
53   CSC (96) M 10/3a, b&c, NE-12-027-00-02 Vol. 4, OTS archives.
54   OTS official 3 to DPMC, CLO, Treasury and DOC officials,
      18 March 1996; Graham to Cabinet Strategy Committee Chair,
      'Ngāi Tahu: Specific Assets with Conservation Implications',
      31 March 1996, NE-12-027-00-02 Vol. 3, OTS archives; Bolger to
      O'Regan, 22 April 1996, NE-12-027-00-02 Vol. 5, OTS archives.
55   O'Regan to Jim Bolger, 31 March 1996, NE-12-027-00-02 Vol. 3, 1-3;
      Sid Ashton, 'Future Negotiations', March or April 1996, TRoNT archive.
      Handwritten notes by Ashton under the above heading began with
      'We must always remember the CROWN is the enemy!'
56   *NZPD*, Vol. 554, 11943–61.
57   Te Runanga o Ngai Tahu Act 1996.

Chapter 9: Negotiations recommence
1   OTS official 6 to DPMC official 4, 30 April 1996, NE-12-027-00-02
      Vol. 5, OTS archives.
2   Richard Meade, 2 May 1995, TRoNT archive.
3   Ashton, May 1996, TRoNT archive, Vhi 51a (k).
4   Ashton to O'Regan, 'Claim Negotiations', 7 May 1996, Vhi 49 (l),
      TRoNT archive.
5   DPMC official 1 to O'Regan, 8 May 1996, TRoNT archive; O'Regan
      to DPMC official 1, 9 May 1996, TRoNT archive.
6   CLO officials, 15 May 1996, Chapman Tripp Materials no. 6,
      OTS archives.
7   Summary of week's meetings, 17 May 1996, Chapman Tripp Materials
      no. 9, OTS archives, 1-2.
8   Summary of week's meetings, 17 May 1996, Chapman Tripp Materials
      no. 9, OTS archives, 2–3.
9   Crown account of meeting, 28 May 1996, Chapman Tripp Materials
      no. 14, OTS archives; Ashton, 'Crown – Ngāi Tahu Meeting of Principals
      Tuesday 28 May 1996', Vhi 51b (k), TRoNT archive; Anake Goodall,
      'Note of a Meeting held in the Prime Minister's Office', 28 May 1996,
      Vhi 51b (k), TRoNT archive.

10   O'Regan, 'Negotiating with Politicians', in Margaret Clark (ed.),
      The Bolger Years: 1990–1997. Wellington: Dunmore Publishing, 2008,
      179–80.

11   O'Regan, 'Recommencing Negotiations', 30 May 1996, Vhi 51b,
      TRoNT archive.

12   OTS official 2 to O'Regan, 4 June 1996, Chapman Tripp Materials no. 16,
      OTS archives.

13   'The Ngāi Tahu [sic] Wait in the Wings', *Dominion*, 19 June 1996.

14   Maureen Hickey, 'Apologies in Settlements', in Nicola R. Wheen and
      Janine Hayward (eds), *Treaty of Waitangi Settlements*, Wellington:
      Bridget Williams Books, 2012, 82.

15   Douglas Graham, *Trick or Treaty?* Wellington: Institute for Policy
      Studies, 1997, 74.

16   Roy L. Brooks (ed.), *When Sorry Isn't Enough: The Controversy Over
      Apologies and Reparations for Human Injustice*, New York: New York
      University, 1999; Charles S. Maier, 'Overcoming the Past? Narrative
      and Negotiation, Remembering and Reparation: Issues at the Interface
      of History and the Law', in John Torpey (ed.), *Politics and the Past:
      On Repairing Historical Injustices*, Lanham, Maryland: Rowman &
      Littlefield, 2003, 295–304; Nicholas Tavuchis, *Mea Culpa: A Sociology of
      Apology and Reconciliation*, Stanford: Stanford University Press, 1991.

17   Melissa Nobles, *The Politics of Official Apologies*, New York: Cambridge
      University Press, 2008; Robert R. Weyeneth, 'The Power of Apology
      and the Process of Historical Reconciliation', *The Public Historian* 23,
      no. 3 (2001): 9–38; Michael Cunningham, 'Prisoners of the Japanese
      and the Politics of Apology: A Battle Over History and Memory', *Journal
      of Contemporary History* 39, no. 4 (2004): 561–74; Kenneth Minogue,
      'Aborigines and Australian Apologetics', *Quadrant* (September 1998):
      11–20; Elazar Barkan, *The Guilt of Nations: Restitution and Negotiating
      Historical Injustices*, New York: W.W. Norton & Co., 2000.

18   Linda Tuhiwai Smith, *Decolonizing Methodologies*, Dunedin:
      University of Otago Press, 1999, 34.

19   Julie Bellingham, 'The Office of Treaty Settlements and Treaty
      History: An Historiographical Study of the Historical Accounts,
      Acknowledgements and Apologies Written by the Crown, 1992 to 2003',
      Masters thesis, Victoria University of Wellington, 2006, 63–131.

20   Richard Boast, *The Native Land Court: A Historical Study, Cases and
      Commentary, 1862–1887*, Auckland: Thomson Reuters, 2013, 13.

21   This kind of thinking would be reflected in Tau's later work.
      In 'Matauranga Māori as an Epistemology', Tau argued that traditional
      Māori knowledge was a separate form of knowing that had to be
      preserved from the methods of Western epistemology. Te Maire Tau,
      'Matauranga Māori as an Epistemology', in Andrew Sharp and Paul
      McHugh (eds), *Histories, Power and Loss: Uses of the Past: A New Zealand
      Commentary*, Wellington: Bridget Williams Books, 2001, 61–73.

22   OTS official 5 to CLO contractor, 19 June 1996, Chapman Tripp
      Materials, OTS archives.

23   OTS official 5 to CLO official 5 & CLO official 6, 30 July 1996,
      NE-12-027-00-04 Pt. 2, OTS archives; OTS official 5 to CLO contractor,
      19 June 1996, Chapman Tripp Materials, OTS archive, 1.

24   Waitangi Tribunal, *Ngāi Tahu Land Report*, Wellington:
      Waitangi Tribunal, 1991, 3 vols, 828–29.

25   CLO official 6, 'Extract from My Memo on the 15 July Version of the Recitals', 24 July 1996, NE-12-027-00-04 Pt. 2, OTS archive, 1.

26   Martin Fisher, 'The Politics of History and Waikato-Tainui's Raupatu Treaty Settlement', *New Zealand Journal of History* 50, no. 2 (2016): 68–89.

27   Ranginui Walker, *Ka whawhai tonu matou: Struggle Without End*, Auckland: Penguin, 2004, 105–10; Harry Evison, *The Long Dispute: Māori Land Rights and European Colonisation in Southern New Zealand*, Christchurch: Canterbury University Press, 1997, 139–57; Ann Parsonson, 'Evidence of Dr Ann R. Parsonson on the Otakou Tenths', Report for Ngāi Tahu claimants in the Ngāi Tahu Waitangi Tribunal inquiry, C1, 1987.

28   OTS official 5 to Te Maire Tau and Nick Davidson, 24 July 1996, NE-12-027-00-04 Pt. 2, OTS archives.

29   *Ngāi Tahu Deed of Settlement*, 22 November 1997, 14.

30   Waitangi Tribunal, *Ngāi Tahu Land Report*, Wellington: Waitangi Tribunal, 1991, 3 vols, 561.

31   Te Maire Tau to OTS official 5, 29 July 1996, NE-12-027-00-04 Pt. 2, OTS archives.

32   Te Maire Tau to OTS official 5 to Te Maire Tau & Nick Davidson, 24 July 1996, NE-12-027-00-04 Pt. 2, OTS archives.

33   Evison, *The Long Dispute*, 218–19.

34   OTS official 5, 'Ngāi Tahu History', 29 August 1996; CLO official 5 to OTS official 5, 29 August 1996; OTS official 5 to CLO official 5, 5 September 1996; OTS official 5 to Te Maire Tau, 5 September 1996, all NE-12-027-00-04 Pt. 2, OTS archives.

35   *Ngāi Tahu Deed of Settlement*, 22 November 1997, 15.

36   Te Maire Tau to OTS official 5, 29 July 1996, NE-12-027-00-04 Pt. 2, OTS archives.

37   Te Maire Tau to OTS official 5, 29 July 1996, NE-12-027-00-04 Pt. 2, OTS archive, 2; CLO official 5 and CLO official 6 to OTS official 5, 30 July 1996, NE-12-027-00-04 Pt. 2, OTS archives; Martin Fisher, 'The Politics of History and Waikato-Tainui's Raupatu Treaty Settlement', *New Zealand Journal of History* 50, no. 2 (2016): 68–89.

38   OTS official 5 to CLO official 5 and CLO official 6, 23 July 1996, NE-12-027-00-04 Pt. 2, OTS archives; OTS official 5 to Te Maire Tau and Nick Davidson, 24 July 1996, NE-12-027-00-04 Pt. 2, OTS archives; OTS official 5 to OTS official 2, 28 August 1996, NE-12-027-00-04 Pt. 2, OTS archives.

39   OTS official 5 to Te Maire Tau, 2 August 1996, NE-12-027-00-04 Pt. 2, OTS archives; Te Maire Tau to OTS official 5, 12 August 1996, NE-12-027-00-04 Pt. 2, OTS archives.

40   *Ngāi Tahu Deed of Settlement*, 22 November 1997, 3.

41   CLO official 5 and CLO official 6 to OTS official 5, 30 July 1996, NE-12-027-00-04 Pt. 2, OTS archives.

42   The Honourable Chief Justice Allan McEachern, *Delgamuukw et al. v The Queen*, 'Reasons for Judgement', Smithers Registry No. 0843, 8 March 1991, 13.

43   Alex Frame, 'Raupatu Settlement – Legal Finality and Political Reality', in Richard Hill and Richard Boast (eds), *Raupatu: The Confiscation of Māori Land*, Wellington: Victoria University Press, 2009, 258.

44   Te Maire Tau stated that Gabrielle Huria had given him the idea:
      Interview with Te Maire Tau, 5 May 2011.
45   OTS official 5 to Tau, 8 August 1996, NE-12-027-00-04 Pt. 2,
      OTS archive, 3.

Chapter 10: A settlement at last

1   O'Regan and Ashton, handwritten notes, 20–21 June 1996, Vhi 51b,
      TRoNT archive.
2   Davidson to Ashton, 2 August 1996, Vhi 52e, TRoNT archive.
3   DPMC official 2 to Bolger, 23 July 1996, NE-10-027-00-02 Pt. 1,
      OTS archives; 'Coleridge and Highbank Hydro Stations: Treaty
      Consultation Meeting', 23 July 1996, Vhi 55a (c), TRoNT archive;
      Davidson to Ashton, 2 August 1996, Vhi52 (e), TRoNT archive; Martin
      Fisher, 'I riro whenua atu me hoki whenua mai: The Return of Land
      and the Waikato-Tainui Raupatu Settlement', *Journal of New Zealand
      Studies* 23 (2016): 19–36.
4   Ashton, 'Wakatipu Titles', 19 August 1996, Vhi 52 (g), TRoNT archive.
5   Barbara Marshall to Bolger, 12 September 1996, NE-18-027-00-01,
      OTS archives; 'Fears Land Deal Could Exclude Public Access',
      Otago Daily Times, 3 October 1996.
6   OTS official 2 to Graham, 22 September 1996, NE-10-027-00-02 Pt. 1,
      OTS archives.
7   'Ngāi Tahu: Redress Package', 31 March 1996, NE-12-027-00-02 Vol. 3,
      OTS archives.
8   *Timaru Herald*, 27 August 1996.
9   Treasury to ToWPU, 30 August 1996 and CAB (96) M 37/15:
      NE-10-027-00-02 Pt. 1, OTS archives; ToWPU Memorandum to
      Graham, 3 September 1996 and Graham to O'Regan, 25 September 1996:
      Chapman Tripp Materials, OTS archives.
10   Treasury official 7 to OTS official 2, 30 August 1996,
      NE-10-027-00-02 Pt. 1, OTS archives; OTS official 2 to Graham,
      2 September 1996, Chapman Tripp Materials no. 28, OTS archives.
11   OTS official 2 to DPMC official 2, 4 September 1996, NE-10-027-00-02
      Pt. 1, OTS archives; O'Regan to DPMC official 2, 10 September 1996,
      Vhi 52b (j), TRoNT archive; Ashton, handwritten notes, 10 September
      1996, Vhi 52c (a), TRoNT archive; O'Regan to Birch, 17 September 1996,
      Vhi 52c (p), TRoNT archive, 1.
12   'Outstanding Issues Requiring Resolution by Principals',
      4 September 1996, NE-10-027-00-02 Pt. 1, OTS archives.
13   Ashton, Memo, 16 September 1996, TRoNT archive, 2; Goodall to
      Doug Kidd, 19 September 1996, Vhi 52c (u), TRoNT archive.
14   Goodall, 'File Note of Telephone Conversation with [OTS official 2]',
      27 September 1996, Vhi 52b (d), TRoNT archive; Reserves Act 1977,
      Sections 18 and 19.
15   *Ngāi Tahu Deed of Settlement*, 21 November 1997, Section 13.3.2.
16   Graham to O'Regan, 25 September 1996, Chapman Tripp Materials,
      OTS archives.
17   Rakiihia Tau Senior to Anake Goodall, 27 September 1996 and
      O'Regan to Goodall, 27 September 1996, Vhi 52b (b), TRoNT archive.

18   Graham to O'Regan, 25 September 1996, Chapman Tripp Materials (25),
      OTS archives; Rakiihia Tau Senior to Goodall, 27 September 1996,
      Vhi 52b (b), TRoNT archive; O'Regan to Goodall, 27 September 1996,
      Vhi 52b (b), TRoNT archive; Goodall to Ngāi Tahu Negotiating Group,
      27 September 1996, Vhi 52b (b), TRoNT archive.
19   Goodall to Ngāi Tahu Negotiating Group, 27 and 29 September 1996;
      Goodall to OTS official 2, 27 and 29 September 1996; OTS official 2
      to Goodall, 29 September 1996: all Vhi 52b (d), TRoNT archive.
20   Goodall to Ngāi Tahu Negotiating Team, 19 September 1996, Vhi 52c (u),
      TRoNT archive.
21   Meade to Ashton and Davidson, 11 September 1996, Vhi 52c (r),
      TRoNT archive.
22   'Outstanding Issues Requiring Resolution by Principals',
      4 September 1996, NE-10-027-00-02 Pt. 1, OTS archives.
23   Meade to Ashton and Davidson, 11 September 1996, Vhi 52c (r),
      TRoNT archive; ToWPU official 5 to Graham, 22 September 1996,
      NE-10-027-00-02 Pt. 1, OTS archives.
24   Bill Birch to O'Regan, 30 September 1996, Vhi 53b (g), TRoNT archive;
      Ashton, handwritten notes, 30 September and 2 October 1996,
      Vhi 52b (j), TRoNT archive; Goodall to OTS official 2, 1 October 1996,
      Vhi 53b (k), TRoNT archive; Graham, 'Ngāi Tahu: Heads of Agreement',
      5 October 1996, NE-10-027-00-01 Pt. 1, OTS archives. The specific
      aspects were the right of first refusal over SOEs and DOC concessions,
      that the methodology would be based on the Public Works Act 1981
      section 40 offer-back process and that the deferred selection process
      would include Landcorp financial instruments.
25   OTS, 'Heads of Agreement between Ngāi Tahu and the Crown for a
      Settlement of all of Ngāi Tahu's Historical Claims', 7 October 1996,
      Chapman Tripp File, OTS archives.
26   Kevin Smith to Doug Kidd, 3 October 1996, Vhi 54 (f), TRoNT archive.
27   Owen Cox to Graham, 27 August 1996, NE-18-027-00-01, OTS archives;
      C. E. Henderson to Graham, 4 September 1996, NE-18-027-00-01,
      OTS archives; Forest & Bird, 'Postpone Ngāi Tahu Settlement, Forest
      & Bird Plea', 1 October 1996, Vhi 53b (l), TRoNT archive; Kevin Smith
      to Doug Kidd, 3 October 1996, Vhi 54 (f), TRoNT archive. In a similar
      vein, PANZ claimed that access to climbing Aoraki would be completely
      banned under Ngāi Tahu control, while Forest & Bird argued that the
      government would be giving away the entire conservation estate in the
      South Island: PANZ, 'Climbing Mt Cook Could be Banned under Secret
      Deals with Ngāi Tahu', 1 October 1996, Vhi 53b (l), TRoNT archive.
28   OTS official 2 to Bolger, 5 August 1996, NE-10-027-00-02 Pt. 1, OTS
      archives; Anake Goodall, 'File Note of Meeting with Prime Minister',
      6 August 1996, TRoNT archive; Ashton, handwritten notes,
      13, 15, 19, 20 August 1996, Vhi 52 (g), TRoNT archive.
29   Valerie Campbell to Graham, 4 August 1996, NE-18-027-00-01,
      OTS archives.
30   Hugh Barlow, 'Freeing the Future from Grievance', *Dominion*,
      6 October 1996; Martin Fisher, 'Balancing Rangatiratanga and
      Kawanatanga: Waikato-Tainui and Ngāi Tahu's Treaty Settlement
      Negotiations with the Crown', PhD thesis, Victoria University of
      Wellington, 2015, 119–45.

31   Adam Gifford, 'Rush to Settle Claims Unlikely to Help Nats', *Dominion*,
      1 October 1996; *TV1 News*, 5 October 1996 and *Holmes*, 6 October 1996,
      both TVNZ archives, Avalon, Lower Hutt; Interview with Sir Douglas
      Graham, 22 May 2011.

32   'Notes from Extraordinary Meeting 2–3 November 1996', Vhi 55c (a),
      TRoNT archive; Tina Nixon, 'Tribal Hui Backs $170m Deal',
      Southland Times, 25 November 1996.

33   Martin Hames, *Winston First: The Unauthorised Account of Winston
      Peters' Career*, Auckland: Random House, 1995; Ian Wishart, *Winston:
      The Story of a Political Phenomenon*, Auckland: Howling at the Moon
      Publishing, 2014.

34   OTS official 3 to David Chisnall, 25 November 1996, Vhi 55c (i),
      TRoNT archive.

35   Chairman's Report, 21 October 1993, NT140 C4, Box 54, MB.

36   Treasury official 11 to Bill Birch, 7 March 1997, NE-10-027-00-02 Pt. 1,
      OTS archives.

37   OTS official 6 to Goodall, 19 March 1997, Vhi 56 (b), TRoNT archive.

38   OTS Director to Graham, 14 April 1997, NE-10-027-00-02 Pt. 2,
      OTS archives.

39   OTS official 6 to Graham, 4 June 1997, NE-10-027-00-02 Pt. 2,
      OTS archives.

40   OTS official 6 to DOC official 3, 19 May 1997, NE-10-027-00-01 Pt. 1,
      OTS archives.

41   Tina Nixon, 'Fear Precedent Set with Ngāi Tahu Deal', *Southland Times*,
      19 June 1998; Interview with Anake Goodall, 7 May 2011.

42   CLO contractor to OTS Director, 23 April 1997, NE-10-027-00-02 Pt. 2,
      OTS archives.

43   Anake Goodall to CLO contractor, 29 April 1997, Vhi 56 (aa),
      TRoNT archive.

44   Meade to Ngai Tahu Negotiating Team, 14 August 1997, TRoNT archive.

45   OTS official 11 to Minister of Conservation, 'Ngāi Tahu Settlement:
      SILNA Claims', 3 July 1997, NE-10-027-00-02 Pt. 2, OTS archives;
      'Ngāi Tahu-Crown Meeting', 17 June 1997, NE-10-027-00-01 Pt. 1,
      OTS archives; Neal Campbell, 'Landowners Urge Rejection of
      Ngāi Tahu Settlement', *Otago Daily Times*, 5 November 1997.

46   Andrew Sharp, 'Recent Juridical and Constitutional Histories of Māori',
      in Andrew Sharp and Paul McHugh (eds), *Histories, Power and Loss*,
      Wellington: Bridget Williams Books, 2001, 48–56.

47   Douglas Graham, 'The Treaty and Treaty Negotiations', in Margaret
      Clark (ed.), *The Bolger Years: 1990–1997*, Wellington: Dunmore
      Publishing, 2008, 172–73.

48   Ngāi Tahu Claims Settlement Act 1998.

49   *NZPD*, Vol. 571, 11666–86.

50   Ibid.

51   *Ngāi Tahu Deed of Settlement*, 21 November 1997, Section 2.1.

Chapter 11: The post-settlement journey

1   *Te Karaka*, no. 75 (2017): 22–25.
2   *TRoNT Annual Report 2018*, Te Whakaariki section; Te Kahui Whakatau, 'Ngāi Tahu: Relativity Mechanism Payments', February 2020.
3   'Whai Rawa', http://www.whairawa.com/.
4   'Ngāi Tahu Wants its Stolen Tahutahi or Snowflake Pounamu Returned', *Marae TV*, 23 July 2012.
5   John Reid and Matthew Rout, 'Māori Tribal Economy: Rethinking the Original Economic Institutions' in Terry Anderson (ed.), *Unlocking the Wealth of Indian Nations*, Lanham: Lexington Books, 2016, 98–99.
6   Michael Stevens, 'Settlements and "Taonga": A Ngāi Tahu Commentary', in Nicola R. Wheen and Janine Hayward (eds), *Treaty of Waitangi Settlements*, Wellington: Bridget Williams Books, 2012, 129.
7   *Te Karaka*, no. 75 (2017): 30–31.
8   Michael Stevens, 'Ngāi Tahu and the "Nature" of Māori Modernity', in Eric Pawson and Tom Brooking (eds), *Making a New Land: Environmental Histories of New Zealand*, Dunedin: Otago University Press, 2013, 298–99.
9   Stevens, 'Ngāi Tahu and the "Nature" of Māori Modernity', 302–04.
10   Appendix 2 to the Waimakariri Council's District Plan sets out a change that includes: 'Recognising and providing for the relationship of Ngāi Tūāhuriri with the land and associated resources in Māori Reserve 873 to enable the land to be used as intended by Kemps Deed of 1848 and the Crown Grants Act (No. 2) 1862, for places of residence and living activities for the original grantees and their descendants.' Waimakariri District Council, *Land Use Recovery Plan – Appendix 2: Maori Reserve 873*, Kaiapoi: Waimakariri District Council, 2015.

GLOSSARY

haka	vigorous dance with actions and rhythmically shouted words
hapū	tribe/sub-tribe
hīkoi	march/land march
hui	gathering/meeting/assembly
hui-ā-iwi	meeting of iwi/tribe
hui-ā-tau	annual meeting
iwi	tribal federation/tribe
kāinga	village/settlement
kaiwhakahaere	leader/director
kanohi ki te kanohi	face to face
karakia	chant/incantation
kaumātua	male elder/person of status
kaupapa	topic/issue/matter for discussion
kāwanatanga	right to govern
koha	gift/offering/donation
kōrero	speech/narrative
kuia	female elder
mahinga kai	garden/food-gathering place
mana	status/prestige/spiritual power
manuhiri	visitor/guest
marae	refers to the open area in front of the wharenui/meeting house, but often used to refer to the entire complex of a Māori meeting house and adjoining buildings
mātauranga	knowledge
mihi	greeting
Ngāi Tahutanga	Ngāi Tahu culture and identity
nohoanga	seasonal campsites/conservation reservations
oranga	wellbeing

pā	fortified village/fort
paepae	orator's bench
Pākehā	non-Māori
papatipu	ancestral land
poroporoaki	a farewell/eulogy
pounamu	greenstone/jade
pōwhiri	welcome ceremony onto a marae
pūtea	funds/sum of money
rangatahi	young people
rangatira	chief/person of high rank
rangatiratanga	sovereignty
rohe	territory/boundary
rūnanga	council
takiwā	district/region/territory
tangata whenua	Māori/the indigenous people of a country/people of the land
te ao tūroa	environment
te reo Māori	the Māori language
tikanga	protocol/customs/correct procedure
tino rangatiratanga	self-determination/absolute sovereignty
tīpuna	ancestors
tītī	muttonbird/sooty shearwater
tōpuni	provides an overlay of Ngāi Tahu values on DOC land which ensures that Ngāi Tahu values are recognised, acknowledged and provided for
tūpuna	ancestors
upoko	head
wāhi tapu	sacred place
waiata	song
whakapapa	genealogy/descent
whakataukī	proverb
whānau	family/extended family
whānui	community
wharekai	dining hall
wharenui	meeting house
whenua	land

A NOTE ON SOURCES

The research for this book was enabled by the Office for Treaty Settlements, which provided access to its archives. These sources were supplemented by the collections held by Te Rūnanga o Ngāi Tahu and the Macmillan Brown Library at the University of Canterbury. In addition, Sir Douglas Graham, who was minister of treaty negotiations for most of the 1990s, provided unrestricted access to his own personal files held at Archives New Zealand, Wellington.

Throughout this book nearly all Crown officials are unidentified, because the advice they gave reflected an institutional, not a personal, view. Ministers, secretaries of ministries, principal negotiators and Ngāi Tahu advisers are named, where they agreed to this.

The primary sources of memoranda, briefing and Cabinet papers, correspondence and minutes of meetings were supplemented by contemporary newspapers such as the *Evening Post*, *Waikato Times*, *New Zealand Herald*, the *Dominion* and the *Press* and magazines such as the *New Zealand Listener* and *North and South*. The TVNZ Archives, formerly held at Avalon Studios, Lower Hutt, and the New Zealand Film Archive (now Ngā Taonga Sound & Vision) in Wellington also contained much of relevance.

Also vital was a series of interviews I held with Crown and Māori negotiators and advisers: Sir Douglas Graham (principal Crown negotiator), Sir Tipene O'Regan (principal Ngāi Tahu negotiator), Te Maire Tau (Historical Adviser Ngāi Tahu), Sid Ashton (Ngai Tahu Maori Trust Board secretary and Te Rūnanga o Ngāi Tahu CEO), Richard Meade (Financial Adviser Ngāi Tahu), Anake Goodall (Adviser and Claims Manager Ngāi Tahu) and Alex Frame (Treaty of Waitangi Policy Unit Director). I also talked with four Treaty of Waitangi Policy Unit officials, a Treasury official, a Te Puni Kōkiri official/Office of Treaty Settlements Director and a Crown Law Office official.

For the official monthly meetings, both the Crown and the respective claimant negotiating group took minutes. These were subject to revision from both sides and then an agreed set of minutes became the Crown's official record of the meeting. Ngāi Tahu also produced their own minutes, which were not subject to Crown revision and were often not shared with the Crown unless there was a substantial disagreement over a negotiation issue or over the accuracy of the Crown's version of the meeting. The Crown's minutes of meetings were always shorter than Ngāi Tahu's, sometimes just one page compared with 10.

Graham's archive was a much more official collection containing hardly any file notes. O'Regan, on the other hand, kept copious notes of phone calls and meetings. The extensive files of Sid Ashton, in the Ngāi Tahu Archive, provide a singular view of certain meetings when there was no evidence of the meeting in the Crown archive.

In general, larger meetings had more sources of information and could be better corroborated. Sometimes there would be numerous different accounts; often, at best, there would be only one version from the Crown and one from Ngāi Tahu. Much bigger meetings that involved public consultation would also engender newspaper accounts and television coverage.

It is understandable that the Crown would sometimes want to provide as little detail as possible in its minutes, because these could be subject to Official Information Act requests. It might wish to preserve its negotiating position and tactics for future negotiations. Ngāi Tahu, by contrast, provided an almost intimate level of detail, which was also understandable. The accuracy of the minutes was important not only for future historians but also for the negotiations themselves. Precision was necessary for the sake of the Crown's institutional knowledge, as staff turnover is inevitable in any workplace and was heightened during the change from the Treaty of Waitangi Policy Unit to the Office of Treaty Settlements. Ngāi Tahu had a deep and wide archive of institutional knowledge, which they found extremely beneficial. They excelled at documenting their negotiating experience. For a settlement to endure, the journey that led to it must remain etched in the memory of those who negotiated it and those who follow.

SELECT BIBLIOGRAPHY

PRIMARY SOURCES

Archives
Douglas Graham Collection, AAKW W5105 7812 Series, Archives New Zealand
    (Wellington)
Treaty of Waitangi Policy Unit (ToWPU, 1989–94), C-27 series, Wellington
Office of Treaty Settlements (1995–), Negotiations (NE), Settlement
    Legislation (SL) series, Wellington
Macmillan Brown Ngāi Tahu Archives (1988–98), NT140, MB140 series,
    Christchurch
Te Rūnanga o Ngāi Tahu archives (1991–98), Vh series, Christchurch

Deeds of settlement
Fisheries Deed of Settlement, 23 September 1992
Waikato–Tainui Deed of Settlement, 1995
Ngāi Tahu Deed of Settlement, 1997
Ngāti Turangitukua Deed of Settlement, 1998

Interviews

Crown
Alex Frame
Sir Douglas Graham
Treaty of Waitangi Policy Unit, officials 1, 3, 4, 6; Crown Law Office, official 6
Te Puni Kōkiri official/Office of Treaty Settlements Director
Treasury official 10

Ngāi Tahu
Sid Ashton
Anake Goodall
Richard Meade
Sir Tipene O'Regan
Te Maire Tau

Newspapers and magazines
Dominion
Evening Post
Forest & Bird
Independent
Mana Magazine
National Business Review
New Zealand Herald
New Zealand Listener
North and South

Otago Daily Times
Press
Southland Times
Sunday Star Times
Te Karaka
Waikato Times

Official documents
New Zealand Parliamentary Debates

Unofficial documents

Department of Justice. *Principles for Crown Action on the Treaty of Waitangi.* Wellington: Department of Justice, 1989.
————. *Settlements of Major Māori Claims in the 1940s: A Preliminary Historical Investigation.* Wellington: Treaty of Waitangi Policy Unit, Department of Justice, 1989.
Office of Treaty Settlements. *Crown Proposals for the Settlement of Treaty of Waitangi Claims: Detailed Proposals; Summary.* Wellington: Office of Treaty Settlements, 1994.
————. *Healing the Past, Building a Future: A Guide to Treaty of Waitangi Claims and Negotiations.* Wellington: Department of Justice, 2015.
Te Puni Kōkiri. *Crown Proposals for the Settlement of Treaty of Waitangi Claims: Consultation with Māori.* Wellington: Te Puni Kōkiri, 1994.
Waimakariri District Council. *Land Use Recovery Plan – Appendix 2: Maori Reserve 873.* Kaiapoi: Waimakariri District Council, 2015.

SECONDARY SOURCES

Articles, books, theses

Anderson, Atholl. *Te Puoho's Last Raid.* Dunedin: Otago Heritage Books, 1986.
————. *The Welcome of Strangers: The Ethnohistory of Southern Maori, 1650–1850.* Dunedin: Otago University Press, 1998.
Anderson, Terry (ed.). *Unlocking the Wealth of Indian Nations.* Lanham: Lexington Books, 2016.
Archie, Carol (ed.). *Māori Sovereignty: The Pākehā Perspective.* Auckland: Hodder Moa Beckett, 1995.
————. *Skin to Skin: Intimate, True Stories of Māori–Pākehā Relationships.* Auckland: Penguin, 2005.
Barkan, Elazar. *The Guilt of Nations: Restitution and Negotiating Historical Injustices.* New York: W.W. Norton & Co., 2000.
Belgrave, Michael. 'Pre-emption, the Treaty of Waitangi and the Politics of Crown Purchase', *New Zealand Journal of History* 37, no. 1, issue 5 (1997): 23–37.
————. *Historical Frictions: Māori Claims and Reinvented Histories.* Auckland: Auckland University Press, 2005.
Belgrave, Michael et al. (eds). *Waitangi Revisited: Perspectives on the Treaty of Waitangi.* Auckland: Oxford University Press, 2005.
Belich, James. *The New Zealand Wars and the Victorian Interpretation of Racial Conflict.* Auckland: Penguin, 1988.
————. *Paradise Reforged: A History of the New Zealanders from the 1880s to the Year 2000.* Auckland: Penguin, 2001.

————. *Making Peoples: A History of the New Zealanders from Polynesian Settlement to the end of the Nineteenth Century*. Auckland: Penguin, 2007.

Bell, Rachael. '"Texts and Translations", Ruth Ross and the Treaty of Waitangi', *New Zealand Journal of History* 43, no. 1 (2009): 39–58.

Bellingham, Julie. 'The Office of Treaty Settlements and Treaty History: An Historiographical Study of the Historical Accounts, Acknowledgements and Apologies Written by the Crown, 1992 to 2003'. Masters thesis, Victoria University of Wellington, 2006.

Binney, Judith. *The Legacy of Guilt: A Life of Thomas Kendall*. Auckland: Oxford University Press, 1968.

Binney, Judith, Gillian Chaplin and Craig Wallace. *Mihaia: The Prophet Rua Kenana and his Community at Maungapohatu*. Auckland: Oxford University Press, 1979.

Birdling, Malcolm. 'Healing the Past or Harming the Future? Large Natural Groupings and the Waitangi Settlement Process', *New Zealand Journal of Public and International Law* 2, no. 2 (2004): 259–84.

Blackburn Carole. 'Producing Legitimacy: Reconciliation and the Negotiation of Aboriginal Rights in Canada', *Journal of the Royal Anthropological Institute* no. 13 (2007): 621–38.

————. 'Searching for Guarantees in the Midst of Uncertainty: Negotiating Aboriginal Rights and Title in British Columbia', *American Anthropologist* 107, no. 4 (2005): 586–96.

Boast, Richard. *The Native Land Court: A Historical Study, Cases and Commentary, 1862–1887*. Auckland: Thomson Reuters, 2013.

Bolger, Jim. *A View from the Top*. Auckland: Viking Press, 1998.

Brookfield, Jock. *Waitangi & Indigenous Rights: Revolution, Law & Legitimation*. Auckland: Auckland University Press, 1999.

Brooking, Tom. '"Busting Up" the Greatest Estate of All: Liberal Māori Land Policy, 1891–1911', *New Zealand Journal of History* 26, no. 1 (1992): 78–98.

————. *The History of New Zealand*. Westport: Greenwood Press, 2004.

Brooks, Roy L. (ed.). *When Sorry Isn't Enough: The Controversy Over Apologies and Reparations for Human Injustice*. New York: New York University, 1999.

Clark, Margaret (ed.). *The Bolger Years: 1990–1997*. Wellington: Dunmore Publishing, 2008.

Coates, Ken S. and Paul G. McHugh (eds). *Living Relationships = Kōkiri Ngatahi: The Treaty of Waitangi in the New Millenium*. Wellington: Victoria University Press, 1998.

Cookson, John and Graeme Dunstall (eds). *Southern Capital, Christchurch: Towards a City Biography 1850–2000*. Christchurch: Canterbury University Press, 2000.

Cowie, Dean. 'The Treaty Settlement Process', in Nicola R. Wheen and Janine Hayward (eds), *Treaty of Waitangi Settlements*. Wellington: Bridget Williams Books, 2012.

Crocker, Therese. 'Introduction: Principles for Crown Action on the Treaty of Waitangi, 1989', Wellington: Treaty of Waitangi Research Unit, Historical Document Series 6, 2011.

————. 'Mandating Matters: Maori Representation and Crown Policy in the Early Treaty Settlements Processes, 1988–1998'. Wellington: Treaty Research Series, 2013.

Cunningham, Michael. 'Saying Sorry: The Politics of Apology', *The Political Quarterly* 70 (July 1999): 285–93.

————. 'Prisoners of the Japanese and the Politics of Apology:
A Battle Over History and Memory', *Journal of Contemporary History* 39,
no. 4 (2004): 561–74.

Dominy, Michele D. 'White Settler Assertions of Native Status',
American Ethnologist 22, no. 2 (May 1995): 358–74.

Durie, Mason. *Te Mana, Te Kawanatanga: The Politics of Māori Self-
determination.* Auckland: Oxford University Press, 1998.

Evans, Richard J. *In Defence of History.* London: Palgrave, 1997.

Evison, Harry C. *Ngāi Tahu Land Rights and the Crown Pastoral Lease Lands
in the South Island of New Zealand.* Christchurch: Ngai Tahu Maori Trust
Board, 1986–87 (3 vols).

————. *Ngāi Tahu Land Rights Supplements.* Christchurch: Ngai Tahu Maori
Trust Board, 1986.

————. (ed.). *The Treaty of Waitangi and the Ngāi Tahu Claim.* Christchurch:
Ngai Tahu Maori Trust Board, 1988.

————. *The Treaty of Waitangi and the Waitangi Tribunal: Fact and Fiction.*
Christchurch: Ngai Tahu Maori Trust Board, 1989–90 (2 vols).

————. *Te Wai Pounamu, The Greenstone Island: A History of the Southern
Māori During the European Colonization of New Zealand.* Christchurch:
Aoraki Press, 1993.

————. *The Long Dispute: Māori Land Rights and European Colonisation in
Southern New Zealand.* Christchurch: Canterbury University Press, 1997.

————. *The Ngāi Tahu Deeds: A Window on New Zealand History.*
Christchurch: Canterbury University Press, 2006.

————. *New Zealand Racism in the Making: The Life & Times of Walter
Mantell.* Lower Hutt: Panuitia Press, 2010.

Finlayson, Chris. 'Ngāi Tahu Negotiations', in Margaret Clark (ed.), *The Bolger
Years: 1990–1997.* Wellington: Dunmore Publishing, 2008.

Fisher, Martin. 'Balancing Rangatiratanga and Kawanatanga: Waikato-Tainui
and Ngāi Tahu's Treaty Settlement Negotiations with the Crown', PhD
thesis, Victoria University of Wellington, 2015.

————. 'Defenders of the Environment: Third-Party Interests and Crown-
Ngāi Tahu Treaty Settlement Negotiations,' *Stout Centre Treaty Research
Series* 13 (2015).

————. 'The Politics of History and Waikato-Tainui's Raupatu Treaty
Settlement', *New Zealand Journal of History* 50, no. 2 (2016): 68–89.

————. 'I riro whenua atu me hoki whenua mai: The Return of Land and
the Waikato-Tainui Raupatu Settlement', *Journal of New Zealand Studies*
23 (2016): 19–36.

————. 'Binding Remedies: The Ngāi Tahu Treaty Settlement Negotiations
in a Post-Haronga Context', *New Zealand Universities Law Review* 27,
no. 3 (2017): 505–27.

————. 'The Ngāi Tahu Treaty settlement negotiations with the Crown:
Key players and background,' *Te Karaka* 75 (2017): 20–21.

————. 'Quantification of loss – negotiations with the Crown,' *Te Karaka* 76
(2017): 38–39.

————. 'Battling it out in court: the litigation phase in the Ngāi Tahu
Treaty settlement negotiations,' *Te Karaka* 78 (2018): 36–37.

Frame, Alex. 'Raupatu Settlement – Legal Finality and Political Reality',
in Richard Hill and Richard Boast (eds), *Raupatu: The Confiscation of Māori
Land.* Wellington: Victoria University Press, 2009.

Furniss, Elisabeth. *Burden of History: Colonialism and the Frontier Myth in a Rural Community*. Vancouver: UBC Press, 1999.

Gardiner, Wira. *Return to Sender: What Really Happened at the Fiscal Envelope Hui*. Auckland: Reed Books, 1996.

Gibbs, Meredith. 'Are New Zealand Treaty of Waitangi Settlements Achieving Justice? The Ngāi Tahu Settlement and the Return of Pounamu (Greenstone)', PhD thesis, University of Otago, 2001.

Graham, Douglas. *Trick or Treaty?* Wellington: Institute for Policy Studies, 1997.

————. 'The Treaty and Treaty Negotiations', in Margaret Clark (ed.), *The Bolger Years: 1990–1997*. Wellington: Dunmore Publishing, 2008.

Hamer, Paul. 'A Quarter-century of the Waitangi Tribunal', in Janine Hayward and Nicola R. Wheen (eds), *The Waitangi Tribunal*. Wellington: Bridget Williams Books, 2004.

Hames, Martin. *Winston First: The Unauthorised Account of Winston Peters' Career*. Auckland: Random House, 1995.

Harris, Aroha. *Hīkoi: Forty Years of Māori Protest*. Wellington: Huia Publishers, 2004.

Hayward, Janine Alyth Deaker. 'In Search of a Treaty Partner: Who, or What, is the Crown?', PhD thesis, Victoria University of Wellington, 1995.

Hayward, Janine. 'Three's a Crowd?: The Treaty of Waitangi, the Waitangi Tribunal, and Third Parties', *New Zealand Universities Law Review* 20, no. 2 (2002): 239–51.

————. 'Flowing from the Treaty's Words', in *The Waitangi Tribunal*, Janine Hayward and Nicola R. Wheen (eds). Wellington: Bridget Williams Books, 2004.

Hayward, Janine and Nicola R. Wheen (eds). *The Waitangi Tribunal: Te Roopu Whakamana i te Tiriti o Waitangi*. Wellington: Bridget Williams Books, 2004.

Hickey, Maureen. 'Apologies in Settlements', in Nicola R. Wheen and Janine Hayward (eds), *Treaty of Waitangi Settlements*. Wellington: Bridget Williams Books, 2012.

Highman, Alexandra Emma-Jane. 'Te Iwi o Ngāi Tahu: An Examination of Ngāi Tahu's Approach to, and Internal Expression of, Tino Rangatiratanga', Masters thesis, University of Canterbury, 1997.

Hill, Richard. *Anti-Treatyism and Anti-scholarship: An Analysis of Anti-treatyist Writings*. Wellington: Stout Research Centre, Victoria University of Wellington, 2002.

————. *State Authority, Indigenous Autonomy in New Zealand/Aotearoa, 1900–1950*. Wellington: Victoria University Press, 2004.

————. *Māori and the State: Crown–Māori Relations in New Zealand/Aotearoa, 1950–2000*. Wellington: Victoria University Press, 2009.

Hill, Richard and Richard Boast (eds). *Raupatu: The Confiscation of Māori Land*. Wellington: Victoria University Press, 2009.

Hill, Richard, and Brigitte Bonisch-Brednich. 'Politicizing the Past: Indigenous Scholarship and Crown–Māori Reparations Processes in New Zealand', *Social and Legal Studies* 16, issue 2 (2007): 163–81.

Hill, Richard and Vincent O'Malley. *The Māori Quest for Rangatiratanga/ Autonomy, 1840–2000*. Wellington: Stout Research Centre, Victoria University of Wellington, 2000.

198 A LONG TIME COMING

Joseph, Robert. 'The Government of Themselves: Indigenous Peoples' Internal Self-Determination, Effective Self-Governance and Authentic Representation: Waikato-Tainui, Ngāi Tahu and Nisga'a', PhD thesis, University of Waikato, 2006.
————. 'Unsettling Treaty Settlements: Contemporary Māori Identity and Representation Challenge', in Nicola R. Wheen and Janine Hayward (eds), *Treaty of Waitangi Settlements*. Wellington: Bridget Williams Books, 2012.
Kawharu, I. H. (ed.). *Waitangi: Māori and Pākehā Perspectives of the Treaty of Waitangi*. Auckland: Oxford University Press, 1989.
Kelly, Stephanie. 'The Ngāi Tahu Māori Trust Board', Masters thesis, University of Canterbury, 1991.
Kelsey, Jane. *A Question of Honour? Labour and the Treaty, 1984–1989*. Wellington: Allen & Unwin, 1990.
————. 'From Lame Duck to Toothless Tiger'. *Mana Magazine* 3 (1993): 41.
King, Michael. *The Penguin History of New Zealand*. Auckland: Penguin, 2003.
Lawrence, David. 'Managing Parks/Managing "Country": Joint Management of Aboriginal Owned Protected Areas in Australia', Research Paper 2, 1996–97, Canberra: Parliament of Australia.
Locke, Cybele. *Workers in the Margins: Union Radicals in Post-War New Zealand*. Wellington: Bridget Williams Books, 2012.
Maier, Charles S. 'Overcoming the Past? Narrative and Negotiation, Remembering and Reparation: Issues at the Interface of History and the Law', in John Torpey (ed.), *Politics and the Past: On Repairing Historical Injustices*. Lanham, Maryland: Rowman & Littlefield, 2003.
Mason, Maika, and Russell Beck. *Pounamu Treasures: Ngā Taonga Pounamu*. Auckland: Penguin, 2012.
McAloon, Jim. 'By Which Standards? History and the Waitangi Tribunal', *New Zealand Journal of History* 40, no. 2 (2006): 194–213.
McCan, David. *Whatiwhatihoe: The Waikato Raupatu Claim*. Wellington: Huia, 2001.
McIntyre, Roberta. *Whose High Country? A History of the South Island High Country of New Zealand*. Auckland: Penguin, 2008.
McKinnon, Malcolm. *Treasury: The New Zealand Treasury, 1840–2000*. Auckland: Auckland University Press, 2003.
McLay, Geoff (ed.). *Treaty Settlements: The Unfinished Business*. Wellington: New Zealand Institute of Advanced Legal Studies and Victoria University of Wellington Law Review, 1995.
Mead, Hirini Moko and Neil Grove. *Ngā Pēpeha a ngā Tīpuna: The sayings of the Ancestors*. Wellington: Victoria University Press, 2001.
Mein Smith, Philippa. *A Concise History of New Zealand*. Cambridge: Cambridge University Press, 2005.
Melbourne, Hineani (ed.). *Māori Sovereignty: The Māori Perspective*. Auckland: Hodder Moa Beckett, 1995.
Metge, Joan, and Patricia Kinloch. *Talking Past Each Other*. Wellington: Victoria University Press, 1978.
Mikaere, Annie. 'Settlement of Treaty Claims: Full and Final, or Fatally Flawed?', *New Zealand Universities Review* 17, no. 2 (1997): 444–48.
Mills, Keri. 'The Changing Relationship between Māori and Environmentalists in 1970s and 1980s New Zealand', *History Compass* 7, no. 3 (2009): 678–700.
Minogue, Kenneth. 'Aborigines and Australian Apologetics', *Quadrant* (September 1998): 11–20.

————. *Waitangi: Morality and Reality*. Wellington: New Zealand Business Roundtable, 1998.

Moon, Paul. *The Occupation of Moutoa Gardens*. Auckland: Auckland Institute of Technology, 1996.

————. 'The Creation of the "Sealord Deal"', *Journal of the Polynesian Society* 107, no. 2 (1998): 145–74.

————. *The Sealord Deal*. Palmerston North: Campus Press, 1999.

————. *Fatal Frontiers: A New History of New Zealand in the Decade before the Treaty*. Auckland: Penguin, 2006.

Muirhead, Gavin. *Footprints to the Future: The Story of Landcorp's First 20 Years*. Wellington: Landcorp, 2009.

Mulholland, Malcolm (ed.). *State of the Māori Nation: Twenty-first Century Issues in Aotearoa*. Auckland: Reed, 2006.

Mutu, Margaret. 'The Role of History and Oral Traditions in Regaining Fagin's Ill-gotten Gains: Settling Ngati Kahu's Treaty of Waitangi Claims Against the Crown', *Te Pouhere Korero 3: Māori History, Māori People* (2010): 23–44.

————. *The State of Māori Rights*. Wellington: Huia, 2011.

Nobles, Melissa. *The Politics of Official Apologies*. New York: Cambridge University Press, 2008.

O'Malley, Vincent. *Beyond the Imperial Frontier: The Contest for Colonial New Zealand*. Wellington: Bridget Williams Books, 2014.

O'Malley, Vincent, Bruce Stirling and Wally Penetito (eds). *The Treaty of Waitangi Companion: Māori and Pākehā from Tasman to Today*. Auckland: Auckland University Press, 2010.

O'Regan, Tipene. 'The Ngāi Tahu Claim', in Hugh Kawharu (ed.), *Waitangi*. Auckland: Oxford University Press, 1989.

————. 'Old Myths and New Politics: Some Contemporary Uses of Traditional History', *New Zealand Journal of History* 26, no. 1 (April 1992): 5–27.

————. 'Negotiating with Politicians', in Margaret Clark (ed.), *The Bolger Years: 1990–1997*. Wellington: Dunmore Publishing, 2008.

Oliver, W. H. *Claims to the Waitangi Tribunal*. Wellington: Waitangi Tribunal Division, Department of Justice, 1991.

Orange, Claudia. *The Treaty of Waitangi*. Wellington: Allen & Unwin, 1987.

————. *An Illustrated History of the Treaty of Waitangi*. Wellington: Bridget Williams Books, 2004.

Palmer, Geoffrey. *Reform: A Memoir*. Wellington: Victoria University Press, 2013.

Parsonson, Ann. 'He Whenua Te Utu (The Payment will be Land)', PhD thesis, University of Canterbury, 1978.

————. 'Ngāi Tahu – The Whale That Awoke: From Claim to Settlement (1960–1998)', in John Cookson and Graeme Dunstall (eds), *Southern Capital, Christchurch: Towards a City Biography 1850–2000*. Christchurch: Canterbury University Press, 2000.

Pawson, Eric and Tom Brooking (eds). *Making a New Land: Environmental Histories of New Zealand*. Dunedin: Otago University Press, 2013.

Pihama, Leonie (ed.). *The Fiscal Envelope: Economics, Politics & Colonisation, Vol. 1*. Auckland: Moko Productions, RUME, 1995.

Poata-Smith, E. S. 'He pokeke uenuku i tu ai: The Evolution of Contemporary Māori Protest' in Paul Spoonley, David G. Pearson and Cluny MacPherson (eds), *Nga Patai: Racism and Ethnic Relations in Aotearoa New Zealand*. Palmerston North: Dunmore Publishing, 1996.

Price, Richard. *The Politics of Modern History-making: The 1990s Negotiations of the Ngāi Tahu Tribe with the Crown to Achieve a Treaty of Waitangi Claims Settlement*. Christchurch: Macmillan Brown Research Series, 1994.

Ratcliffe, Greg (ed.). *Compr(om)ising Postcolonialism(s): Challenging Narratives and Practices*. Portsmouth, New Hampshire: Dangaroo Press, 2002.

Reid, Joanna. 'The Grassland Debates: Conservationists, Ranchers, First Nations, and the Landscape of the Middle Fraser', *BC Studies* 160 (Winter 2008/09): 93–118.

Reid, John and Matthew Rout. 'Māori Tribal Economy: Rethinking the Original Economic Institutions' in Terry Anderson (ed.), *Unlocking the Wealth of Indian Nations*, 84–103. Lanham: Lexington Books, 2016.

Rose, Alex. *Spirit Dance at Meziadin: Chief Joseph Gosnell and the Nisga'a Treaty*. Vancouver: Harbour Publishing, 2000.

Ross, Ruth. 'Te Tiriti o Waitangi: Texts and Translations', *New Zealand Journal of History* 6, no. 2 (1972): 129–57.

Ruru, Jacinta (ed.). *'In Good Faith': Symposium Proceedings Marking the 20th Anniversary of the Lands Case*. Dunedin: University of Otago and the Law Foundation NZ, 2008.

Seuffert, Nan. 'Nation as Partnership: Law, "Race", and Gender in Aotearoa New Zealand's Treaty Settlements', *Law & Society Review* 39, no. 3 (2005): 485–526.

Sharp, Andrew. *Justice and the Māori: The Philosophy and Practice of Māori Claims in New Zealand since the 1970s*. Auckland: Oxford University Press, 1997.

————. 'Recent Juridical and Constitutional Histories of Māori', in Andrew Sharp and Paul McHugh (eds), *Histories, Power and Loss*. Wellington: Bridget Williams Books, 2001.

Sharp, Andrew and Paul McHugh (eds). *Histories, Power and Loss: Uses of the Past: A New Zealand Commentary*. Wellington: Bridget Williams Books, 2001.

Shortall, Stacey Anne. 'Aboriginal Self-government in Aotearoa-New Zealand: A View through the Canadian Lens', LLM thesis, University of Alberta, 1996.

Smith, Linda Tuhiwai. *Decolonizing Methodologies*. Dunedin: University of Otago Press, 1999.

Sorrenson, M. P. K. *Ko te Whenua te Utu/Land is the Price: Essays on Maori History, Land and Politics*. Auckland: Auckland University Press, 2014.

Spoonley, Paul. *Mata Toa: The Life and Times of Ranginui Walker*. Auckland: Penguin, 2009.

Spoonley, Paul, David G. Pearson and Cluny MacPherson (eds). *Nga Patai: Racism and Ethnic Relations in Aotearoa New Zealand*. Palmerston North: Dunmore Press, 1996.

Stevens, Michael. 'Muttonbirds and Modernity in Murihiku: Continuity and Change in Kai Tahu Knowledge', PhD thesis, University of Otago, 2009.

————. 'Ngāi Tahu and the "Nature" of Māori Modernity', in Eric Pawson and Tom Brooking (eds), *Making a New Land: Environmental Histories of New Zealand*. Dunedin: Otago University Press, 2013.

————. 'Settlements and "Taonga": A Ngāi Tahu Commentary', in Nicola R. Wheen and Janine Hayward (eds), *Treaty of Waitangi Settlement*. Wellington: Bridget Williams Books, 2012.

Stone, Damian. 'Financial and Commercial Dimensions of Settlement', in Nicola R. Wheen and Janine Hayward (eds), *Treaty of Waitangi Settlements*. Wellington: Bridget Williams Books, 2012.

Tau, Te Maire. 'Ngāi Tahu – From "Better Be Dead and Out of the Way" to "To Be Seen to Belong"', in John Cookson and Graeme Dunstall (eds), *Southern Capital, Christchurch: Towards a City Biography 1850–2000*. Christchurch: Canterbury University Press, 2000.

————. 'Matauranga Māori as an Epistemology', in Andrew Sharp and Paul McHugh (eds), *Histories, Power and Loss: Uses of the Past: A New Zealand Commentary*. Wellington: Bridget Williams Books, 2001.

Tavuchis, Nicholas. *Mea Culpa: A Sociology of Apology and Reconciliation*. Stanford: Stanford University Press, 1991.

Taylor, Louise Jane. 'The Fiscal Envelope: A Manifesto for Finality', LLB Hons thesis, Victoria University of Wellington, 1995.

Torpey, John (ed.). *Politics and the Past: On Repairing Historical Injustices*. Lanham, Maryland: Rowman & Littlefield Publishers, 2003.

Tuuta, Dion. *Māori Experiences of the Direct Negotiations Process*. Wellington: Crown Forestry Rental Trust, 2003.

Vincent, Eve and Timothy Neale (eds). *Unstable Relations: Indigenous People and Environmentalism in Contemporary Australia*. Perth: UWA Publishing, 2016.

Vowles, Jack and Peter Aimes (eds). *Voters' Vengeance: The 1990 Election in New Zealand and the Fate of the Fourth Labour Government*. Auckland: Auckland University Press, 1993.

————. *Voters' Victory? New Zealand's First Election under Proportional Representation*. Auckland: Auckland University Press, 1998.

Walker, Ranginui. *Nga tau tohetohe: Years of Anger*. Auckland: Penguin, 1987.

————. *Nga pepa a Ranginui: The Walker Papers*. Auckland: Penguin Books, 1996.

————. *Ka whawhai tonu matou: Struggle Without End*. Auckland: Penguin, 2004.

————. *Opotiki-Mai-Tawhiti: Capital of Whakatohea*. Auckland: Penguin, 2007.

Ward, Alan. *A Show of Justice: Racial 'Amalgamation' in Nineteenth Century New Zealand*. Auckland: Auckland University Press, 1974 (1st ed.), 1995.

————. *National Overview*. Wellington: Waitangi Tribunal, GP Publications, 1996.

————. *An Unsettled History: Treaty Claims in New Zealand Today*. Wellington: Bridget Williams Books, 1999.

Weyeneth, Robert R. 'The Power of Apology and the Process of Historical Reconciliation, *The Public Historian* 23, no. 3 (2001): 9–38.

Wheen, Nicola R. and Janine Hayward (eds). *Treaty of Waitangi Settlements*. Wellington: Bridget Williams Books, 2012.

White, Ben. 'Sites of Contestation: Perceptions of Wilderness in the Context of Treaty Claim Settlements', Masters thesis, 1994, Lincoln University.

Williams, David V. *Te Kooti Tango Whenua: The Native Land Court 1864–1909*. Wellington: Huia Books, 1999.

Wilson, Margaret and Anna Yeatman (eds). *Justice & Identity: Antipodean Practices*. Wellington: Bridget Williams Books, 1995.

Wishart, Ian. *Winston: The Story of a Political Phenomenon*. Auckland: Howling at the Moon Publishing, 2014.

Young, David. *Our Islands, Our Selves: A History of Conservation in New Zealand*. Dunedin: Otago University Press, 2004.

Waitangi Tribunal Reports and other unofficial documents

Daamen, Rose. *The Crown's Right of Pre-emption and Fitzroy's Waiver Purchases.* Wellington: Waitangi Tribunal Rangahaua Whānui Series, 1998.

Moore, D., B. Rigby and M. Russell. *Old Land Claims – Rangahaua Whānui National Theme A.* Wellington: Waitangi Tribunal, 1997.

O'Regan, Tipene. 'Ka korero o Kai Tahu Whanui', Waitangi Tribunal Wai-27, Document A-27, Macmillan Brown Library, University of Canterbury.

————. 'Te Kereme: The Claim, Lecture Two', Macmillan Brown Lecture Series, 1998.

Parsonson, Ann. 'Evidence of Dr Ann R. Parsonson on the Otakou Tenths', Report for Ngāi Tahu claimants in the Ngāi Tahu Waitangi Tribunal inquiry, C1, 1987.

Waitangi Tribunal. *Motonui-Waitara Report.* Wellington: Department of Justice, 1983.

————. *Kaituna River Report.* Wellington: Department of Justice, 1984.

————. *Report of the Waitangi Tribunal on the Manukau Claim (Wai-8).* Wellington: Waitangi Tribunal, 1985.

————. *Report of the Waitangi Tribunal on the Orakei Claim (Wai-9).* Wellington: Brooker & Friend, 1987.

————. *The Ngāi Tahu Claim: Supplementary Report on Legal Personality.* Wellington: Waitangi Tribunal, 1991.

————. *Ngai Tahu Land Report.* Wellington: Waitangi Tribunal, 1991, 3 vols.

————. *Ngāi Tahu Sea Fisheries Report.* Wellington: Waitangi Tribunal, 1992.

————. *Te Roroa Report.* Wellington: Department of Justice, 1992.

————. *Ngāi Tahu Ancillary Claims Report.* Wellington: Waitangi Tribunal, 1995.

————. *Report on the Te Tau Ihu Claims.* Wellington: Waitangi Tribunal, 1995.

————. *The Turangi Township Remedies Report.* Wellington: Waitangi Tribunal, 1995.

————. *Te Raupatu o Tauranga Moana: Report on the Tauranga Confiscation Claim.* Wellington: Waitangi Tribunal, 2004.

————. *Ngati Kahu Remedies Report.* Wellington: Waitangi Tribunal, 2012.

————. *Mangatu Remedies Report.* Wellington: Waitangi Tribunal, 2013.

Websites

Land Information New Zealand. 'Marginal Strips', https://www.linz.govt.nz/survey-titles/cadastral-surveying/publications/marginal-strips, accessed 11 January 2012.

Te Rūnanga o Ngāi Tahu, 'The Negotiators', https://ngaitahu.iwi.nz/ngai-tahu/the%20settlement/the-negotiators/ accessed 24 May 2020.

Te Rūnanga o Ngāi Tahu. 'The Settlement', https://www.ngaitahu.iwi.nz/ngai-tahu/the-settlement/, accessed 4 May 2013.

Tau, Te Maire. 'Ngāi Tahu – Spreading South and West', https://www.TeAra.govt.nz/en/Ngāi-tahu/page-3, accessed 30 July 2019.

IMAGE CREDITS

Sources for information for drawing maps: LINZ, Stats NZ, Eagle Technology, Esri, HERE, Garmin, FAO, METI/NASA, USGS.

i   The Arahura rivermouth. (2018-0304, Te Rūnanga o Ngāi Tahu Collection, Ngāi Tahu Archive)

       Bird's-eye view of southern Banks Peninsula. (2018-0311, Te Rūnanga o Ngāi Tahu Collection, Ngāi Tahu Archive)

ii   Rarotoka (Centre Island). (2019-0660, Te Rūnanga o Ngāi Tahu Collection, Ngāi Tahu Archive)

       Te Pou Hou, Te Pou Neherā and Te Pou Haumi, Waikoropūpū (Sealers Bay), Whenua Hou. (Courtesy of Atholl Anderson)

iii   Timore, Tītī Islands. (2018-0311, Te Rūnanga o Ngāi Tahu Collection, Ngāi Tahu Archive)

       Putauhinu, with Pohowaitai and Tamaitemioka in the background, Tītī Islands. (2018-0311, Te Rūnanga o Ngāi Tahu Collection, Ngāi Tahu Archive)

iv   Tūtaepatu Lagoon. (David Baird Collection)

       Pounamu hei tiki. (2019.0783.1, Te Rūnanga o Ngāi Tahu Collection, Ngāi Tahu Archive)

v   Sir Tipene O'Regan and Doug Graham at the initialling of the deed of settlement in Wellington, September 1997. (2013.P.1642, Te Rūnanga o Ngāi Tahu Collection, Ngāi Tahu Archive)

       Sir Tipene O'Regan, Anake Goodall, Jim Bolger and Doug Graham at the signing of the Ngāi Tahu deed of settlement at Takahanga Marae in Kaikōura on 21 November 1997. (2013.P.1543, Te Rūnanga o Ngāi Tahu Collection, Ngāi Tahu Archive)

vi   The Crown paepae for the signing of the Ngāi Tahu deed of settlement at Takahanga Marae. (2013.P.1857, Te Rūnanga o Ngāi Tahu Collection, Ngāi Tahu Archive)

       Sir Tipene O'Regan and Prime Minister Jim Bolger hongi at Takahanga Marae. (2013.P.1919, Te Rūnanga o Ngāi Tahu Collection, Ngāi Tahu Archive)

INDEX

Page numbers in **bold** refer to images.